The Time Bind

Also by Arlie Russell Hochschild

The Second Shift:
Working Parents and the Revolution at Home

The Managed Heart:
Commercialization of Human Feeling

The Unexpected Community:
Portrait of an Old Age Subculture

Colleen the Question Girl
(a children's story)

Arlie Russell Hochschild

The
TIME BIND

*When Work
Becomes Home and
Home Becomes Work*

METROPOLITAN BOOKS

Henry Holt and Company   New York

Metropolitan Books
Henry Holt and Company, Inc.
Publishers since 1866
115 West 18th Street
New York, New York 10011

Metropolitan Books™ is an imprint of
Henry Holt and Company, Inc.

Published in Canada by Fitzhenry and Whiteside Ltd.
195 Allstate Parkway, Markham, Ontario L3R 4T8

Library of Congress Cataloging-in-Publication Data

Hochschild, Arlie Russell, 1940–
    The time bind: when work becomes home and home becomes work /
Arlie Russell Hochschild — 1st American ed.
      p.   cm.
    Includes bibliographical references and index.
    1. Dual-career families—United States.   2. Work and family—United States.
3. Sex role—United States.   4. Working mothers—United States.   I. Title.
HQ536.H633   1997
306.3'6—dc21   97–3411
                                                            CIP

ISBN 0-8050-4470-1

Henry Holt books are available for special promotions and
premiums. For details contact: Director, Special Markets.

First Edition—1997

Designed by Kate Nichols

Printed in the United States of America
All first editions are printed on acid-free paper ∞

10   9   8   7   6   5   4   3   2   1

For

RUTH LIBBEY RUSSELL, *1908–1996*
PAUL LIBBEY RUSSELL, *1934–1996*

And for those in whom they live on,

DAVID, GABRIEL, JOHN AND BENJAMIN

CONTENTS

PART I

About Time

PART II

From Executive Suite to Factory Floor

PART III

Implications and Alternatives

ACKNOWLEDGMENTS

Many thanks, first of all, to Amerco's then CEO and his wife for their great civic spirit, their warmth, and their gracious invitation to study Amerco. To those at Amerco who guided my way—and you know who you are—many thanks and hugs. My special gratitude to the owners of The Blue Pine Bed and Breakfast (my home while doing research), who sent me off with a gift of homemade blackberry jam. For their gifts of time and faith, my thanks to those who generously opened up their busy lives in the hope that their experiences would help readers of this book understand their own.

I am grateful in a different way to the Alfred P. Sloan Foundation for funding my research, and especially to my program officer, Kathleen Christensen, for her unfailing support. Thanks, too, to the Ford Foundation for start-up funding, and to June Zeitlin and her coworker and pioneer in work-family research, Rhona Rapoport.

For insightful comments on early drafts, thanks to Michael Rogin and Todd Gitlin, and to Ann Swidler, who listened thoughtfully over weekly breakfasts to a series of shifting ideas in a continual blizzard of drafts.

For his editorial genius, my deep thanks to Tom Engelhardt.

Tom is in a class of editors by himself; he's the Editor King. Tom didn't simply read the manuscript, he inhaled it. He returned to me ten single-spaced pages of transformative commentary such as few writers are ever privileged to receive. It has been enormously rewarding and great fun to work with him.

And when I was already feeling blessed with extraordinary editing, Sara Bershtel, editorial director of Metropolitan Books, and Stephen Hubbell, senior editor, contributed yet another round of dozens of hours of work, pushing my logic to new end points I'd not imagined, ridding the text of remaining cobwebs, and otherwise sharing their brilliant minds and prodigious energy; many thanks, Sara and Stephen. Diana Gillooly did an excellent job of copy-editing the manuscript, and Riva Hocherman carefully combed through the notes and references and helped shepherd us all through a publishing time bind of our own. Thanks also to Jean Margolis for typing earlier drafts.

In the last few years, I've begun to wonder if there isn't something to the idea of fate. One day, out of the blue, Laurie Schaffner appeared at my office door, a Smith undergraduate wanting to find out about sociological research. Once a seventh-grade dropout, Laurie is now earning her Ph.D. in sociology at U.C. Berkeley and has for three years been a first-rate bibliographer and research assistant. She checked all the notes and references and drew up the tables in the Appendix; her scholarly work, comradely enthusiasm, and very fine mind are on every page of this book.

Bonnie Kwan typed and retyped this manuscript, kept an eagle eye out for errors, and maintained her good humor—and mine—as Federal Expressed revisions zinged crazily back and forth from her desk in San Francisco to mine in Maine to Tom Engelhardt's on Cape Cod to Laurie Schaffner's in Berkeley. Throughout, Bonnie combined first-rate work with acts of kindness and moments of great fun. Thanks, Laurie and Bonnie; I love you both.

Adam, my partner on the long journey, has been more important to my basic feeling about life than I can say. This has been especially true this last year, as we faced a series of terrible losses of people we love. Adam also brainstormed with me, read a draft, and accompanied me to Spotted Deer one summer, his own work in tow. On a morning days before she died, my mother remarked, "Men like Adam are very rare." A rare man, yes, and also a rare human being.

PART I

About Time

CHAPTER 1

The Waving Window

It is 6:45 A.M. on a fine June day in the midwestern town of Spotted Deer. At a childcare center in the basement of the Baptist church, Diane Caselli, a childcare worker in blue jeans and loose shirt, methodically turns over small upended chairs that rest on a Lilliputian breakfast table. She sets out small bowls, spoons, napkins, and a pitcher of milk around a commanding box of Cheerios. The room is cheerful, clean, half-asleep. Diane moves slowly past neatly shelved puzzles and toys, a hat rack hung with floppy, donated dress-up hats and droopy pocketbooks, a tub filled with bits of colored paper. Paintings of swerving trains and tipsy houses are taped to the wall.

At seven, a tall, awkward-looking man peers hesitantly into the room, then ventures a few steps forward looking for Diane. His son Timmy tromps in behind him. Diane walks over, takes Timmy's hand, and leads him to the breakfast table, where she seats him and helps him pour cereal and milk into his bowl. Timmy's dad, meanwhile, hurries toward the door.

One wall of the room has four large windows that overlook a sidewalk. In front of the second window is a set of small wooden steps children climb to wave good-bye to their departing parents. It's called "the waving window." Timmy dashes from the breakfast table, climbs up the wooden steps, and waits.

His dad, an engineer, briskly strides past the first window toward his red Volvo parked down the street. He stops for a moment in front of the waving window, tilts his head, eyebrows lifted clownishly, then walks on without a backward glance. Timmy returns to his cereal, sighs, and declares excitedly, "My Dad sawed me wave!" Diane and Marie Martin, the center's other childcare worker, exchange warm smiles over Timmy's head. As professionals they aren't supposed to have favorites, but sometimes it's hard not to.

A moment later, in a burst of excitement, Jarod and Tylor, four-year-old twins, bound in ahead of their mother, a quick-stepping, trim woman in a black and white business suit. A successful junior manager, she doesn't pause at the door, but with an air of pleasant authority, strides—clack, clack, clack—up to the breakfast table, as if in her kitchen at home. Car keys in hand, she pours out Cheerios and milk, consulting each twin about the amount. She watches them eat for a few minutes. Then, glancing at her watch, she bends down, offers long hugs, leaves the childcare room, and reappears outside. She feigns surprise at the first window, makes a funny face at the second, races to the third, and gives a big wave at the fourth. Finally, out of sight, she breaks into a run for her car.

At 7:40 A.M., four-year-old Cassie sidles in, her hair half-combed, a blanket in one hand, a fudge bar in the other. "I'm late," her mother explains to Diane. "Cassie wanted the fudge bar so bad, I gave it to her," she adds apologetically—though Diane has said nothing. Gwen Bell is a sturdy young woman, with short-cropped dark hair. Lightly made up and minimally adorned with gold stud earrings, she is neatly dressed in khaki slacks and jacket. Some Amerco mothers don business suits as soldiers don armor while a few wear floral dresses suggesting festivity and leisure. But Cassie's mother is dressed in a neutral way, as if she were just getting the job of self-presentation done.

"Pleeese, can't you take me with you?" Cassie pleads.

"You know I can't take you to work," Gwen replies in a tone

that suggests she's heard this request before. Cassie's shoulders droop in defeat. She's given it a try, but now she's resigned to her mother's imminent departure, and she's agreed, it seems, not to make too much fuss about it. Aware of her mother's unease about her long day at childcare, however, she's struck a hard bargain. Every so often she gets a morning fudge bar. This is their deal, and Cassie keeps her mother to it. As Gwen Bell later explained to me, she continually feels that she owes Cassie more time than she actually gives her. She has a time-debt to her daughter. If many busy parents settle such debts on evenings or weekends when their children eagerly "collect" promised time, Cassie insists on a morning down payment, a fudge bar that makes her mother uneasy but saves her the trouble and embarrassment of a tantrum. Like other parents at the center, Gwen sometimes finds herself indulging her child with treats or softened rules in exchange for missed time together. Diane speaks quietly to Cassie, trying to persuade her to stop sulking and join the others.

The center works on "child time." Its rhythms are child-paced, flexible, mainly slow. Teachers patiently oversee the laborious task of tying a shoelace, a prolonged sit on the potty, the scrambled telling of a tall tale. In this and other ways it is an excellent childcare center, one of a dozen islands of child time I was to discover in my three summers of field research at Amerco, a Fortune 500 company headquartered in Spotted Deer.* Scattered throughout the town, such islands—a playground, a pediatrician's waiting room, the back of a family van—stand out against the faster paced, more bureaucratically segmented blocks of adult work time.

Indeed, on that June morning, seated atop a tiny stool inside the center, I find myself musing impatiently, things *are* slow here. I watch Timmy pretend he is in an airplane for what seems like a very long time. Jarod and Tylor slowly sort out pieces of a puzzle an

---

*To protect the privacy of the people in this book, I have given the company a fictional name and declined to specify what its workers produce or where they live. I've also altered the names, occupations, and defining details of the personal lives of individuals. I have, however, tried to document as accurately as possible their experiences of life at home and at work and to capture the essence of the culture that infuses both worlds.

adult could arrange in a flash. I begin to feel slightly bored. I have, after all, left behind my own hectic university schedule—teaching classes, advising students, keeping up with a blizzard of faxes, phone calls, and e-mail messages—and I feel in a hurry to get busy with the task at hand.

I had come to Spotted Deer to explore a question I'd been left with after finishing my last book, *The Second Shift: Working Parents and the Revolution at Home.*[1] In that work I had examined the tensions that arise at home in two-job marriages when working women also do the lion's share of the childcare and housework. Such marriages were far less strained, I found, when men committed themselves to sharing what I came to call "the second shift," the care of children and home. But even with the work shared out, there seemed to be less and less time for the second shift, not to mention relaxed family life. Something was amiss, and whatever it was, I sensed that I would not find out simply by looking at home life by itself.

Everything I already knew or would soon learn pointed to the workplace as the arena that needed to be explored. As a start, I was well aware that, while in 1950 12.6 percent of married mothers with children under age seventeen worked for pay, by 1994, 69 percent did so; and 58.8 percent of wives with children age one or younger were in the workforce.[2] Many of these wives also had a hand in caring for elderly relatives. In addition, the hours both men and women put in at work had increased—either for college-educated workers or, depending on which scholars you read, for all workers. In her book *The Overworked American,* the economist Juliet Schor has claimed that over the last two decades the average worker has added an extra 164 hours—a month of work—to his or her work year. Workers now take fewer unpaid leaves, and even fewer paid ones.[3] In the 1980s alone, vacations shortened by 14 percent.[4] According to the economist Victor Fuchs, between 1960 and 1986 parental time available to children per week fell ten hours in white households and twelve hours in black households.[5] It was also evident, however you cut the figures, that life was coming to center more on work. More women were on board the work train, and the train was moving faster. It wasn't just that ever larger numbers of mothers of young children were taking paying jobs, but that fewer of those jobs were part time; and fewer of those mothers were taking time off even in the summer, as they might once have done, to care for school-aged children on vacation.[6] Women moving into the workforce—whether or not they were mothers—were less inclined than ever to move out of it. It was apparent, in fact, that working mothers were increasingly fitting the profile of working fathers. But those fathers, far from cutting back to help out at home, studies told us, were now working even longer hours. In fact, their hours were as long as those of childless men.[7]

All this could be read in the numbers—as well as in the tensions in many of the households I had visited. I was left with a nagging question: given longer workdays—and more of them—how could parents balance jobs with family life? Or, to put the matter another way, was life at work winning out over life at home? If so, was there not some way to organize work to avoid penalizing employees, male and female, for having lives outside of work and to ease the burden on their children?

I was thinking about these questions when a surprising event occurred. I was asked to give a talk at Amerco, a company about which I knew little except that it had been identified as one of the ten most "family-friendly" companies in America by the Families and Work Institute, by *Working Mother* magazine, and by the authors of *Companies That Care*.[8] At a dinner given after my talk, a company spokesman seated next to me asked if I had ever thought of studying family-friendly policies in the workplace itself. To tell the truth, I could not believe my luck. If there was ever a chance for families to balance home and work, I thought to myself, it would be at a place like this. Amerco's management clearly hoped my findings would help them answer a few questions of their own. In the late 1980s, the company had been distressed to discover a startling fact: they were losing professional women far faster than they were losing professional men. Each time such a worker was lost, it cost the company a great deal of money to recruit and train a replacement. The company had tried to eliminate this waste of money and talent by addressing one probable reason women were leaving: the absence of what was called "work-family balance." Amerco now offered a range of remedial programs including options for part-time work, job sharing, and flextime. Did these policies really help Amerco? Given current trends, it seemed crucial to top management to know the answer. Six months later I found myself lodged at a cozy bed-and-breakfast on a tree-lined street in Spotted Deer, ready to begin finding out.

The receptionist at company headquarters issued me a magnetized badge, a bit like one of those magic rings that children once found in cereal boxes, which opened company doors everywhere day and night. Over the course of three summers between 1990 and 1993, I "badged in" and "badged out" behind employees I was following around. I also checked in regularly with Amy Truett, the official in charge of the Work-Life Balance program in Amerco's Human Resources Division, which handled all matters having to do with personnel. A lively, dark-haired, plainspoken woman with a laconic sense of humor, Amy Truett was much beloved by those with whom she worked. Dressed in cheerful primary colors, she walked Amerco's corridors with deliberate strides, exuding an aura of friendly efficiency. It was Amy's job to make "balance" more than just a corporate buzzword. Perhaps to signal this goal, a psychologist hired in 1991 to help set up Work-Life Balance policies had hung on the wall of her office next to Amy's a series of photos of her daughter eating a drippy tomato, holding aloft a large fish, and making mud pies, each a still-life reminder that children are not icons to be safely worshipped from afar but messy, lovable, real people.

I interviewed top and middle managers, clerks and factory workers—a hundred and thirty people in all. Most were part of two-job couples, some were single parents, and a few were single without children. Sometimes we met in their offices or in a plant breakroom, sometimes in their homes, often in both places. Early mornings and evenings, weekends and holidays, I sat on the lawn by the edge of a series of parking lots that circled company headquarters, watching people walk to and from their vans, cars, or pick-up trucks to see when they came to work and when they left.

I talked with psychologists in and outside the company, child-care workers hired by Amerco, homemakers married to Amerco employees, and company consultants. Along with the Spotted Deer Childcare Center, I visited local YWCA after-school programs as well as a Parent Resource Center funded by the company. I attended company sessions of the Women's Quality Improvement Team and the Work Family Progress Committee, a Valuing Diversity workshop, and two High Performance Team meetings. A team in Amerco's Sales Division allowed me to sit in on its meetings. To their surprise—and mine—I also became the fifth wheel on a golfing expedition designed to build team spirit. During several night shifts at an Amerco factory, tired workers patiently talked with me over coffee in the breakroom. One even took me to a local bar to meet her friends and relatives.

The company gave me access to a series of its internal "climate surveys" of employee attitudes, and I combed through research reports on other companies, national opinion polls, and a burgeoning literature on work and family life. I also attended work-family conferences held in New York, San Francisco, Los Angeles, and Boston by The Conference Board, a respected organization that gathers and disseminates information of interest to the benefit of the business management community.

Six families—four two-parent families and two single-mother families—allowed me to follow them on typical workdays from dawn until dusk and beyond. I found myself watching a small child creep into her mother's bed at dawn for an extra cuddle and snooze. One day I sat for over an hour on a green plastic turtle watching two giggly girls slither down a small water slide into a pool. Many times children approached me to locate a missing button on a shirt or—more hopelessly for me—to play Super Mario Brothers on the Nintendo set, while a busy parent cooked dinner.[9]

It was thanks to this research project, then, that I had come to the Spotted Deer Childcare Center, where I was trying to adapt to the temporal rhythm of four-year-olds. The center had become part

of my on-the-job research because on-the-job parents were increasingly turning to nonrelatives to care for their children, and for
increasingly long periods of time. For children like Timmy, Jarod,
or Tylor, hours in daycare can now be remarkably long; and as one
national childcare study showed, the younger the child, the more
time he or she is likely to spend in daycare. Babies under one year of
age were found to stay on average forty-two hours a week.[10]

The director of Amerco's Spotted Deer Childcare Center, a
thoughtful woman of forty-four and a mother of two, observed,

> Most of our Amerco parents work from 8 A.M. to 5 P.M.
> They bring their children in half an hour ahead of time and
> pick them up a half hour after they leave work. It's longer if
> they have a late meeting, or try to fit in errands or exercise.
> It's a nine- or ten-hour day for most of the children.

When I asked her what kind of a day at the center she thought
would most benefit a child, she replied that on average most three-
and four-year-olds should have "an active morning, lunch, a nap
and go home after their nap—ideally six or seven hours." Though
she, like her colleagues at the Spotted Deer Childcare Center, felt
that most children did well under her care, nine hours, she remained
convinced, was generally "too long."

In her book *When the Bough Breaks: The Cost of Neglecting Our
Children*, the economist Sylvia Hewlett links the "time deficit"
caused by long parental workdays to a series of alarming trends in
child development. Compared to the previous generation, Hewlett
claims, young people today are more likely to "underperform at
school, commit suicide, need psychiatric help, suffer a severe eating
disorder, bear a child out of wedlock, take drugs, be the victim of a
violent crime."[11] or Studies have shown that long hours at home
alone increase the likelihood that a child will use alcohol or drugs.
In truth, scholars don't yet know what, if any, the exact links are
between these ominous trends and the lessening amounts of time
parents spend with children. But we needn't dwell on sledge-

hammer problems like child heroin use or suicide to realize that for children like those at the Spotted Deer Childcare Center, time is a problem. It's enough to observe that children say they want more time with their parents, and parents say they regret not spending more time with their children. In a 1990 *Los Angeles Times* survey of 1,000 families, for instance, 57 percent of fathers and 55 percent of mothers reported feeling guilty that they spent too little time with their children.[12]

At the Spotted Deer Childcare Center, the group of young break-fasters gradually expands, early arrivals watching the entertainment provided by yet more newcomers. Sally enters sucking her thumb. Billy's mother carries him in even though he's already five. Jonathan's mother forgets to wave, and soon after, Jonathan kicks the breakfast table from below, causing milk to spill and children to yell. Marie ushers him away to dictate a note to his mother explaining that it hurts his feelings when she doesn't wave.

Cassie still stands at the front door holding her fudge bar like a flag, the emblem of a truce in a battle over time. Every now and then, she licks one of its drippy sides while Diane, uncertain about what to do, looks on disapprovingly. The cereal eaters watch from their table, fascinated and envious. Gwen Bell turns to leave, waving goodbye to Cassie, car keys in hand. By our prior arrangement, I am her shadow for this day, and I follow her out the door and into the world of Amerco.

Arriving at her office, as always, exactly at 7:50 A.M., Gwen finds on her desk a cup of coffee in her personal mug, milk no sugar (exactly as she likes it), prepared by a coworker who has managed to get in ahead of her. The remaining half of a birthday cake has been left on a table in the hall outside her office by a dieting coworker who wants someone else to eat it before she does. Gwen prepares materials for her first meeting (having e-mailed messages to the other participants from home the previous night), which will inaugurate her official 8 A.M. to 5:45 P.M. workday. As she does so, she nibbles at a sliver of the cake while she proofreads a memo that must be xeroxed and handed out at a second meeting scheduled for 9 A.M.

As the assistant to the head of the Public Relations Office, Gwen has to handle Amerco's responses to any press reports that may appear about the company. This time the impending media attention is positive, and her first meeting has been called to discuss how to make the most of it. As the members of the publicity team straggle into her office and exchange friendly greetings, she sighs. She's ready.

Gwen loves her job at Amerco, and she is very good at it. Whatever the daily pressures, she also feels remarkably at home there. Her boss, a man who she says reminds her of the best aspects of her father, helps her deal with work problems and strongly supports her desire to rise in the company. In many ways, her "Amerco dad" has been better to her than her own father, who, when she was small, abruptly walked out on her mother and her. She feels lucky to have such a caring boss, and working for him has reinforced her desire to give her all to work—insofar as she can. She and her husband need her salary, she tells me, since his job, though more lucrative than hers, is less steady.

Gradually, over the last three years Gwen's workday has grown longer. She used to work a straight eight-hour day. Now it is regularly eight and a half to nine hours, not counting the work that often spills over into life at home. Gwen is not happy about this. She feels Cassie's ten-hour day at Spotted Deer is too long, but at the same time she is not putting energy into curbing her expanding workday. What she does do is complain about it, joke about it, compare stories with friends at work. Hers are not the boastful "war stories" of the older men at Amerco who proudly proclaim their ten-hour workdays and biweekly company travel schedules. Rather, Gwen's stories are more like situation comedies: stories about forgetting to shop and coming home to a refrigerator containing little more than wilted lettuce and a jar of olives, stories told in a spirit of hopeless amusement. Gwen is reasonably well informed about Amerco's flextime and reduced-hours policies, which are available to white-collar employees like her. But she has not talked with her boss about cutting back her hours, nor have her joking coworkers, and her boss hasn't raised the possibility himself. There is just so much to get done at the office.

At 5:45 P.M. on the dot, Gwen arrives back at Spotted Deer. Cassie is waiting eagerly by the door, her coat over her arm, a crumpled picture she has drawn in her hand. Gwen gives Cassie a long, affectionate hug. By the time Gwen and Cassie roll into the driveway of their two-story white frame house, surrounded by a border of unruly shrubs, it is 6:25 P.M. John Bell is already there, having shopped, taken the messages off the phone machine, set the table, and heated the oven. This is one of two days a week he leaves home and returns earlier than his wife. He has eaten an ample lunch, knowing that they usually have a late, light dinner, but this evening he's hungrier than he means to be. He plays with Cassie while Gwen makes dinner.

To protect the dinner "hour"—8:00 to 8:30—Gwen checks that the phone machine is on, and we hear a series of abbreviated rings several times during dinner. John says grace, and we all hold hands. It is time, it seems, to let go and relax. Right after dinner, though, it's Cassie's bath time. Cassie both loves and protests her nightly bath. Gwen has come to expect Cassie to dawdle as she undresses or searches for a favorite bath toy, trying to make a minivacation of it. Gwen lets Cassie linger, scans through her phone messages, and sets them aside.

At 9 P.M., the bath over, Gwen and Cassie have "quality time" or "QT," as John affectionately calls it. This they see as their small castle of time protected from the demands of the outside world. Half an hour later, at 9:30 P.M., Gwen tucks Cassie into bed.

Later, as Gwen and John show me around their home, John points out in passing an expensive electric saw and drill set he bought two years earlier with the thought of building a tree house for Cassie, a bigger hutch for her rabbit Max, and a guest room for visiting friends. "I have the tools," John confides. "I just don't have the time to use them." Once, those tools must have represented the promise of future projects. Now they seemed to be there in place of the projects. Along with the tools, perhaps John has tried to purchase the illusion of leisure they seemed to imply. Later, as I interviewed other working parents at Amerco, I discovered similar items banished to attics and garages. Timmy's father had bought a boat he hadn't sailed all year. Jarod and Tylor's parents had a camper truck they had hardly driven. Others had cameras, skis, guitars, encyclopedia sets, even the equipment to harvest maple syrup, all bought with wages that took time to earn.

John's tools seemed to hold out the promise of another self, a self he would be "if only I had time." His tools had become for him what Cassie's fudge bar was for her—a magical substitute for time, a talisman.

There were, in a sense, two Bell households: the rushed family they actually were and the relaxed family they imagined they could be if only they had time. Gwen and Bill complained that they were in a time bind: they wanted more time for life at home than they had. It wasn't that they wanted more small segments of "quality time" added into their over-busy days. They wanted a quality life, and Gwen, at least, worked for a family-friendly company whose policies seemed to hold out hope for just that. So what was preventing them from getting it?

CHAPTER 2

Managed Values and Long Days

From the Spotted Deer Childcare Center to Amerco corporate headquarters is a fifteen-minute drive past idyllic green fields of corn and alfalfa, and occasional herds of grazing Holsteins. The highway parallels a river that winds through a long, lush valley, and leads to a charming, small Midwest town built around a nineteenth-century Amerco smokestack, a reminder of its long history as a company town.

Ensconced in this sylvan valley, Amerco headquarters is an arresting new chrome and glass structure set pleasantly by the edge of the river. It forms the visual centerpiece of the village of Spotted Deer. Six thousand Amerco workers are employed in this valley; another twenty thousand are scattered in twenty-five plants across the United States and dozens more in other countries. Over a third of Amerco's employees and 25 percent of its managers are women.

An Amerco brochure distributed to visitors at corporate headquarters depicts a little boy gathering golden autumn leaves in his red wagon. The caption reads: "Maybe it's the fresh air, the wide, tree-lined streets, the kids and puppies and wagons on long, lazy summer afternoons. Whatever it is, this place feels just right to us."

As I walk around the community, I do indeed discover a Norman Rockwell–like world. Even though, here and there, tucked into the hills outside of town one can find run-down trailer courts, the brochure has the picture right—all except for those lazy afternoons.

Amerco's workers are clearly proud of its history as a successful, small-town company. Every Christmas they look forward to a century-old ritual in which the chief executive officer, a vigorous man of fifty-eight and a great-grandson of the founder, walks through the halls of every company building in the valley, including the company-sponsored childcare center, thanking workers for their contributions. Most employees seem to enjoy the traditional small-town life on the tree-lined streets that surround its headquarters. At the same time, they also seem to appreciate the company's willingness to innovate, as demonstrated by its worker participation and family-friendly policies.

The people I talked to felt Amerco was a desirable place to work. Because it is part of the thriving core of America's globalizing economy—from 1970 to 1996, Amerco has made consistently large profits—and because it has long enjoyed a reputation for respecting its employees, many more people apply for jobs at Amerco than get them. Like students admitted to top universities, most Amerco employees feel specially chosen and honored to be there.

The company's road to success has not always been an easy one. In the 1980s, Japanese competitors began selling to markets Amerco had assumed it controlled. At the same time, foreign capital investment flowed into Amerco, and Amerco, in turn, began to invest in foreign enterprises, diversifying its portfolio against possible hard times. Declining market share and fierce competition with a thriving Pacific Rim, a united Germany, and an emerging European Union all prompted Amerco to try harder to "delight the customer" (a company slogan).

To compete globally, most companies pursue some combination of three strategies. The first is to invest in workers by cross-training them in order to expand their range of skills, and by increasing their authority to decide how best to produce and deliver goods. Companies adopting this approach put more into the worker in the hope that they will get more out.

A second strategy is to invest less in workers—to lower wages, benefits, and job security—while trying to get the same amount of work out of them. Companies pursuing this strategy may fire or prematurely retire regular workers and replace them with cheaper temporary or contract workers. They may downsize or "outsize" various corporate functions and hire and fire workers as market demand rises and falls. These measures cut costs and presumably make the company more adaptable to fluctuating demand.

A third strategy, which is compatible with the first and helpful in handling the bad news attached to the second, is to create and manage a strong company culture. From the early 1980s on, Amerco's much-admired CEO put his heart into this third strategy. In the decade and a half since then, Amerco has proved to be a creative engineer of workplace culture, improving the motivation and commitment of its workers and assuring their consent to the company's mix of strategies for success in global competition. The centerpiece of the company's plan, set in place in 1983, was a work system known as Total Quality.[1] Instead of bureaucratic control, simplified jobs, and a many-tiered hierarchy, Amerco began to emphasize autonomous work teams, "enriched" jobs, and a less obviously hierarchical structure. The aim of this was to create more knowledgeable and company-identified workers who would be invited to share with their managers a "common vision" of company goals and to talk over ways to implement it. Sometimes workers were even encouraged to participate in designing the physical settings of their workplaces. In the Administration Center, where all of Amerco's accounting was centralized, teams chose office furniture and rugs, redesigned the work process, and helped hire new workers.

What progressive education did for schools, what Benjamin Spock did for childrearing, Total Quality is doing for work. It presumes a worker is a capable adult, not a wayward child. As with progressive education, top-down control does not disappear but reemerges in new forms. Under Total Quality, hourly workers organized into work teams are given much more responsibility for decisions from the beginning to the end of the production process. Total Quality heightens interdependence among workers on the factory floor who deal in different ways with the same goods or services. Each work team is given time lines, budgets, sales information, and the authority to manufacture and ship its product in the most efficient way. The only aspects of the process beyond the authority of the team are the customer's wishes, which are seen as sacrosanct—and the company's measurement of team performance.

The most important effect of Total Quality at Amerco was to create a shared culture made up of new values and practices.[2] To a company outsider, a culture is something that you live in, not something you engineer. But within the company people readily spoke of "engineering" culture. They spoke of "having" values and, in nearly the same breath, of "managing" them. Some even talked about company culture as if it could be bought and sold. Pat O'Mally, chief of the Division of Education and Training, remarked proudly, "It takes eight years for another company to imitate our changes in corporate culture. It's not something they can steal. It's good for eight years." To imagine that one "manages" values, one's own or those of other people, is itself a fundamental part of company culture.

Layer after layer of thin culture was thus poured on from the top. ("We believe in diversity. We believe in valuing the individual. We believe in delighting the customer.") The CEO would enunciate new shifts or reaffirm old themes in company culture in finely crafted speeches received with great seriousness. The higher up in the company (or the closer to headquarters) they were, the more attuned employees were to shifts in company culture. Employees at the upper levels took the ideas home with them, mulled them over, and decided if, and how much, they agreed or disagreed with them. Everyone was free to disagree with the CEO's speech. But the messages in the speech were bandied about. They were in the air. They felt like a good thing to believe in. Often a message such as "valuing the individual" or "honoring diversity" seemed moral, unifying, and agreeable. One day, reading the returns from a company survey on attitudes toward gender and ethnic diversity, I noticed a statement on the front cover of the questionnaire: "It is Amerco's policy to value diversity." The questionnaire asked people what they thought, but it also told people what the company would like them to think.

An Amerco handbook given out to new employees described a list of unwritten norms, and their corresponding career implications. For example: "Time spent on the job is an indication of commitment. Work more hours." Or "More hours indicates you are paying your dues." Or "Dress code is important. Be conservative, violate it and you won't fit in." This writing out of "unwritten" norms, this explicit articulation of Amerco culture, was what made it feel so different from the intuitive, uncodified cultures most of us inhabit. Amerco culture had been made explicit, but the very distinction between the explicitly stated corporate culture and the intuitive culture of private life was blurred, and this blurring between formal and informal understandings was itself a key part of company culture.

In deciding what kind of culture to create, the company looked outside itself for models. As airplane engineers borrow design from birds or mall designers borrow style from nineteenth-century village squares, so the company borrowed culture from family and community. For example, in a workshop for Human Resource managers that I observed, participants explored ways to make friendship work for the benefit of the company. As one manager told me, "The company can reduce mistakes by pooling problem-solving skills. You piggyback on ordinary friendships. Joe calls up Bill and talks about the family, the ballgame. Then at the end, Joe says, 'By the way, I'm also having problems with [some work-related dilemma]. . . . Do you know anyone who can help me with that?' We get them to call in some personal chips for work. 'If you owe me one back, you owe the company one back.' We need to educate our workers to do that." By linking the two, Amerco used naturally developing friendships to reinforce its own carefully planned business practices.

Furthermore, consciously or not, Total Quality piggybacked on the culture many women brought to Amerco—of bonding, encouragement, and nonhierarchical cooperation. In some ways Total Quality fostered a "motherly" work culture, and the feminization of Amerco's workforce fit right in. In some work teams, women celebrated one another's birthdays, shared stories of their children, helped with problems, and ran errands for each other. Total Quality directed this spirit toward the goals of work. A manager who helped organize a "recognition ceremony" in her Amerco division for some of her workers also commented, "I just got done organizing my mother's eightieth birthday party. Now I'm putting together this recognition ceremony. I want the participants to feel it really means something, like it did for my mother."

By officially espousing "values," Amerco had established itself as something other than a cold, economic machine.[3] In the nineteenth-century workplace, many owners created workplace rules without espousing a formal set of company values for their employees. Families, communities, and churches were supposed to do that. But like other leaders of transnational companies, the CEO of Amerco took it as an important part of his job to state company values through "mission" or "vision" statements. Amerco now said to its workers, in effect, "You don't have to check your values at the door. We have them here. Morally speaking, you are protected, safe, as if you were at home."

Whether employees spoke about this top-down corporate culture lovingly, critically, or, as was often the case, both lovingly and critically, they seldom escaped its influence for long. Every year employees received a questionnaire to fill out anonymously on a wide array of issues. These "climate surveys" did not just sample company culture, however; they were part of it. Return rates were high, and few people I talked with were cynical about filling them out. The ostensible purpose of these surveys was to find out how workers felt. Did an employee feel that his supervisor coached him enough? Built group support? Encouraged participation? Did a worker feel satisfied with her own on-the-job growth? Did a worker feel satisfied with the recognition he received for doing a good job? Did a worker feel she was given a real opportunity to improve her skills? Such questions did not simply elicit information. They established the idea that the company was trying to benefit the worker in these ways and genuinely wanted to know whether it was succeeding in doing so. The surveys gave people the feeling that someone was listening—as indeed someone was. They provided a way for workers to cast a moral vote on company matters. At the end of each questionnaire people were invited to write in extra comments, and thus the surveys came to serve as an anonymous way of expressing gripes, a "Democracy Wall" in the heartland of capitalism. Through these periodic surveys, employees were also reminded that Amerco was hoping to improve itself.

In fact, I came to realize Amerco *was* trying to improve, did want to know what was wrong, and did care. While Amerco's goal was production and profit, with its mission statements and surveys it wasn't simply trying to seem like a moral world; it was trying to be a moral world. It's not surprising, then, that employees would get upset if they thought a colleague or superior wasn't "walking the talk" on one or another of Amerco's missions. Whatever daily aggravations a worker faced, it was hard not to appreciate a company spirit like that. Perhaps that's why Amerco employees seemed so willing to embrace Amerco symbols. Honorees in various company competitions proudly wore pins and other items with the Amerco logo. As one employee put it, "In America, we don't have family coats of arms anymore, but we have the company logo."

It was in this climate of cooperation and accommodation that, in the early 1980s, a scattering of Amerco employees—working mothers and fathers, single people looking ahead to a future work-family crunch, and older people looking back at one—began to press for family-friendly reforms. Survey after survey indicated that working families at every level in the company hierarchy were strained to the limit. One survey presented employees with the statement "It is hard for me to manage my work and family/personal responsibilities." Three-quarters of the women and half the men agreed. Six out of ten women and half the men also agreed that "My health suffers as a result of meeting both my work and family/personal responsibilities." Half of hourly employees—factory and maintenance workers covered by union contracts—agreed that their marriages were suffering from the effects of time pressures. A third had a "great deal of difficulty" monitoring the activities of children home alone. One-quarter of them had "a great deal of difficulty" leaving work to take part in a child's school activity or a parent-teacher conference, or simply to care for a sick child.

The Amerco employees were soon joined by a new kind of social activist. Dressed in tailored suits, carrying leather briefcases, "human resources" advocates of family-friendly policies began to appear at yearly national conventions as early as the mid-1980s. Representing some two thousand American corporations these participants didn't look like disheveled 1960s activists. They didn't talk like them either, speaking instead of "buy-ins," "marketing ideas to internal customers," and "networking." They tossed around phrases like "piggybacking Work-Family onto Diversity" or "retrofitting Work-Family into Total Quality." Overwhelmingly female, white, and middle class, they acted as the social workers of the corporate world. Like many social workers, they were both part of the system and idealistically critical of it. They believed family policies were a key to company success; but how dehumanizing, one confided, to always "think of kids and old people as problems of child and elder care coverage."

In 1985, Amerco announced that it had a "mission" to help its workers balance work with home. The company unveiled a family-friendly policy with two distinct, and potentially contradictory, parts. The first part enabled a worker to spend more unworried time at work, while the second offered more unconflicted time at home. The first part consisted of policies and programs like high-quality childcare, childcare for sick children, emergency backup childcare, before- and after-school programs, and referral services for elder care, all of which enabled employees to focus better on their work for eight or more hours a day. Indeed, Amerco ultimately upgraded the modest childcare center where Timmy and Cassie ate breakfast in 1990, building a new five-million-dollar Community Child Development Center that offered places for 150 preschool-aged

Amerco children. The center's childcare workers, trained at the local Amerco Junior College, were subsidized by company grants and scholarships. Amerco also held childcare forums, elder care seminars, and parenting fairs, and sponsored a Parent Resource Center open to the local community.

The second type of family-friendly reforms allowed parents to work more flexible or shorter workdays, opening up more time for life outside of work. In this vein, Amerco offered paid maternity leave for up to four weeks before, and six weeks after, the birth or adoption of a child, and up to twenty weeks of unpaid family care leave for each child born or adopted. A company brochure touted the possibility of part-time work, job sharing, flexible hours, or work at home as employee options.

As time passed, however, it became clear to company activists that there were problems in bridging the gulf between the company brochure and daily life. Amy Truett was Amerco's troubadour of change, and she was an active advocate of both types of reform. It was her idea to develop a *Managing Smart* video to train managers to help employees implement alternative schedules of various sorts. At conference after conference, she would brainstorm ways to push for more support from top management, get around obstructionist middle managers, and encourage those workers who had checked the "yes" box to all those painful questions about work-family "balance." As Amy Truett explained in 1990,

> We're five years into our mission. We have another ten to go. The top managers believe family-friendly policies are the right thing to do. But none of them pack their own suitcases, so they don't *know* what mornings are like for most of us. Middle managers just want to make their budgets and minimize trouble, and we look like trouble to them.

Over time, employees began to judge managers on whether they "walked the talk" on work-family balance. Secretaries would gossip about top executives, noting whether so-and-so had "come around on work-life balance." Carefully, if casually, people watched one another—especially those in powerful positions—for signs of con-version. Potential converts to the new company values complained of being monitored, so they were careful to seem convinced, or just short of convinced, or were delicate in expressing their reservations. Their response to this scrutiny was also remarked on. "Why is he so guarded?" people would say. It was in this way that the actual values of daily work life trickled down from on high.

This, then, was the cultural atmosphere at Amerco when I arrived. In many ways, Amerco was better off than other companies. Its workforce was more stable than the norm, its union-management relations more cooperative (the last strike took place one hundred years ago), its profit margins greater, and the community in which it was set more rural, quiescent, and isolated. In one key way, though, Amerco was typical. Once a predominantly male institution, it was employing a steadily rising number of women. Whereas most of the men who worked for Amerco used to be married to women who stayed home, by 1990, 69 percent of Amerco men were married to wives in the workforce, and 84 percent of its employees with chil-dren under thirteen had no stay-at-home spouse. In addition, 12 percent of its employees cared for a disabled or elderly relative, and another 25 percent expected to assume such a responsibility in the near future.[4] Thus, the company's family-friendly policies, which originally were imagined as a magnet for women, not men, and for professionals, not production workers, would be relevant to many employees.

A company with a strong, managed culture, good intentions, and a rising number of two-job families with new needs—what more promising situation could there be, I asked myself, for the suc-cessful implementation of family-friendly reforms? Already, nearly half of Amerco's workers, like Cassie's mother Gwen, professed to need help balancing work with life. When I arrived at Spotted Deer in 1990, help seemed only a supervisor away.

CHAPTER 3

An Angel of an Idea

Almost from the beginning of my stay in Spotted Deer, I could tell that the family-friendly reforms introduced with so much fanfare in 1985 were finding a curious reception. Three things seemed true. First, Amerco's workers declared on survey after survey that they were strained to the limit. Second, the company offered them policies that would allow them to cut back. Third, almost no one cut back. Timmy's father, Jarod and Tylor's mother, Cassie's parents— they weren't cutting back. Amy Truett's "mission," barely born, had already split into two unequal parts. Programs that allowed parents to work undistracted by family concerns were endlessly in demand, while policies offering shorter hours that allowed workers more free or family time languished.

To try to make sense of this paradox I began, first of all, to scrutinize the text of the policy and the results of employee surveys. Amerco defines a part-time job as one that requires thirty-five hours or less, with full or prorated benefits.[1] A job share is a full-time position shared by two people with benefits and salary prorated. As with all attempts to change work schedules, I learned, the worker has to get the permission of a supervisor, a division head, or both. In addition, workers under union contract—a full half of Amerco's workforce including factory hands and maintenance crews—were not eligible for policies offering shorter or more flexible hours.

But I discovered that among eligible employees with children thirteen and under, only 3 percent worked part time. In fact, in 1990, only 53 out of Amerco's 21,070 employees in the United States, less than one-quarter of 1 percent of its workforce, were part-timers, and less than 1 percent of Amerco's employees shared a job.

Amerco also offered its employees a program called "flexplace," which allowed workers to do their work from home or some other place. One percent of employees used it. Likewise, under certain circumstances, an employee could take a temporary leave from full-time work. The standard paid parental leave for a new mother was six weeks (to be divided with the father as the couple wished). If permission was granted, a parent could then return to work part time with full benefits, to be arranged at his or her supervisor's discretion. Most new mothers took the paid weeks off, and sometimes several months more of unpaid leave, but then returned to their full-time schedules. Almost no Amerco fathers took advantage of parental leave, and no Amerco father has ever responded to the arrival of a new baby in the family by taking up a part-time work schedule.

By contrast, "flextime," a policy allowing workers to come and go early or late, or to be in other ways flexible about when they do their work, was quite popular. By 1993, a quarter of all workers—and a third of working parents—used it. In other words, of Amerco's family-friendly policies only flextime, which rearranged but did not cut back on hours of work, had any significant impact on the workplace. According to one survey, 99 percent of Amerco employees worked full time, and full-time employees averaged forty-seven hours a week. As I looked more closely at the figures I discovered some surprising things. Workers with young children actually put in more hours at work as those without children. Although a third of all parents had flexible schedules, 56 percent of employees with children regularly worked on weekends. Seventy-two percent of parents regularly worked overtime; unionized hourly workers were paid for this time (though much of their overtime was required), while salaried workers weren't. In fact, during the years I was studying Amerco, parents and nonparents alike began to work *longer* hours. By 1993, virtually everyone I spoke with told me they were working longer hours than they had only a few years earlier, and most agreed that Amerco was "a pretty workaholic place."

Amerco is not alone. A 1990 study of 188 Fortune 500 manufacturing firms found that while 88 percent of them informally offered part-time work, only 3 to 5 percent of their employees made use of it. Six percent of the companies surveyed formally offered job sharing, but only 1 percent or less of their employees took advantage of that. Forty-five percent of these companies officially offered flextime, but only 10 percent of their employees used it. Three percent of the companies offered flexplace—work at home—and less than 3 percent of their employees took advantage of it.[2] *

As Amerco's experience would suggest, American working parents seem to be putting in longer and longer hours. Of workers with children aged twelve and under, only 4 percent of men, and 13 percent of women, worked less than forty hours a week.[3] According to a study by Arthur Emlen of Portland State University, whether or not a worker has a child makes remarkably little difference to his or her attendance record at work. Excluding vacation and holidays, the average employee misses nine days of work a year. The average parent of a child who is left home alone on weekdays misses fourteen and a half days a year: only five and a half days more. Fathers with young children only miss half a day more a year than fathers without children.[4]

The idea of more time for family life seems to have died, gone to heaven, and become an angel of an idea. But why? Why don't working parents, and others too, take the opportunity available to them to reduce their hours at work?

*The 1993 Family and Medical Leave Act requires all companies employing fifty or more workers to offer three months of unpaid time off for medical or family emergencies. Although it is not yet clear what effect this law will have, research suggests few workers are likely to take advantage of it. Studies of earlier state family and medical leave laws show that less than 5 percent of employees actually use the leave.

The most widely accepted explanation is that working parents simply can't *afford* to work shorter hours. With the median income of U.S. households in 1996 at $32,264, it is true that many workers could not pay their rent and food bills on three-quarters or half of their salaries. But notwithstanding the financial and time pressures most parents face, why do the majority not even take all of the paid vacation days due to them? Even more puzzling, why are the best-paid employees—upper-level managers and professionals—among the least interested in part-time work or job sharing? In one Amerco survey, only one-third of top-level female employees (who belong to what is called the "A-payroll") thought part time was of "great value." The percentage of women favoring part time rose as pay levels went down: 45 percent of "B-payroll" (lower-level managers and professionals) and "administrative" women (who provide clerical support) thought part time was of "great value." Thus, those who earned more money were less interested in part-time work than those who earned less. Few men at any level expressed interest in part-time work.

Again, if income alone determined how often or how long mothers stayed home after the birth of their babies, we would expect poorer mothers to go back to work more quickly, and richer mothers to spend more time at home. But that's not what we find. Nationwide, well-to-do new mothers are not significantly more likely to stay home with a new baby than low-income new mothers. A quarter of poor new mothers in one study returned to work after three months, but so did a third of well-to-do new mothers. Twenty-three percent of new mothers with household incomes of $15,000 or under took long leaves (fifty-three weeks or more), and so did 22 percent of new mothers with household incomes of $50,000 or more.[5]

In a 1995 national study, 48 percent of American working women and 61 percent of men claimed they would still want to work even if they had enough money to live as "comfortably as you would like."[6] When asked what was "very important" to their decision to take their current job, only 35 percent of respondents in one national study said "salary/wage," whereas 55 percent mentioned "gaining new skills" as very important, and 60 percent mentioned "effect on personal/family life."[7] Money matters, of course, but other things do too.

According to a second commonly believed explanation, workers extend their hours, not because they need the money, but because they are afraid of being laid off. They're working scared. By fostering a climate of fear, the argument goes, many companies take away with one hand the helpful policies they lightly offer with the other.

Downsizing is a serious problem in American companies in the 1990s but there's scant evidence that employees at Amerco were working scared. During the late 1980s and early 1990s, there was very little talk of layoffs. When I asked employees whether they worked long hours because they were afraid of getting on a layoff list, virtually everyone said no. (Although there were, in fact, small-scale layoffs in certain divisions of the company, the process was handled delicately through "internal rehiring" and "encouraged" early retirement.) And when I compared hours of work in the few downsized Amerco divisions with those in non-downsized divisions, they were basically the same. Supervisors in the two kinds of divisions received just about the same number of requests for shorter hours.

Hourly workers were more anxious about layoffs than salaried workers, but fear of losing their jobs was not the main reason they gave for working long hours of overtime. For one thing, Amerco is a union shop, where layoffs are allocated by seniority, regardless of hours. In fact, even among a particularly vulnerable group— factory workers who had been laid off in the economic downturn of the early 1980s and were later rehired—most did not cite fear for their jobs as the only, or main, reason they sought overtime hours.

One possible explanation is that workers interested in and eligible for flexible or shorter hours don't know they can get them. After all, even at a place like Amerco, such policies are fairly new. Yet on closer inspection, this proved not to be the case. According to a 1990 survey, most Amerco workers were aware of company policies on flextime and leaves. Women were better informed than men, and higher-level workers more so than lower-level workers. The vast majority of people I talked with knew that the company offered "good" policies and were proud to be working for such a generous company. Employees who weren't clear about the details knew they could always ask someone who was. As one secretary remarked, "I don't know exactly how long the parental leave is, but I know how to find out." So why didn't they?

Perhaps the roadblock to getting shorter hours was not on the worker's side, but on the company's. Were family-friendly policies just for show? Perhaps companies like Amerco wanted to *look* good but not to *do* good. Perhaps they wanted to attract the best new workers and shine brightly before the corporate world by offering family-friendly policies but not to suffer the nuisance of implementing them. As this line of reasoning has it, the CEO winks at his middle managers and whispers, "We don't really mean this." He says this because he believes it's not in the company's basic interest to reduce employee time on the job.[8]

This may be true in many companies, but I concluded that it was probably not the case at Amerco. First of all, Amerco workers themselves generally believed that their CEO was sincere. When asked, 60 percent thought "senior management supported the family or personal needs of its workers." This reflects a high degree of confidence in top management's goodwill on this issue. Moreover, there is considerable evidence that flexible schedules benefit companies, not simply workers, and that many companies like Amerco know it.

Amerco saw strong business reasons to institute family-friendly programs. For one thing, "hiring the best" now often means hiring a woman. Women now make up half of the graduates of departments of business administration and receive a third of all bachelor degrees in computer and information sciences.[9] One way to gain an edge in what looked like an increasingly competitive hiring environment, the company figured, was to outshine its competitors in its work-family policies. A study of women engineers at the chemical company Du Pont found that it was the best performers, not the worst, who were leaving in search of jobs with better work-family balance. Skilled workers who leave voluntarily cost companies dearly. On average, for each skilled employee who quits, it costs a company $40,000 to hire and train a replacement. A study of Merck and Company found that losing an exempt employee costs the company one and a half times that employee's annual salary and losing a nonexempt employee costs the company .75 times the worker's salary. Also it takes a new worker at least one year to perform as well as the worker he or she replaces.

In a national study of fifty-eight employers, thirty-one claimed that family-friendly policies help attract desirable employees. Three-quarters claimed such policies lower absenteeism. Two-thirds felt they improve worker attitudes.[11] Companies may also enjoy reduced medical insurance costs as a result of lowered stress levels at work.

Beyond this, studies well known to Amerco management have demonstrated the costs of *not* instituting such policies—in increased absenteeism and tardiness, and lowered productivity. A 1987 study conducted by the National Council for Jewish Women found that women working for family-friendly companies were sick less often, worked more on their own time, worked later into their pregnancies, and were more likely to return to work after a birth.[12] Moreover, the study found that workers who took advantage of family-friendly policies were among the best performers, and the least likely to have disciplinary problems. All in all, there is no proof that flexible hours are not in a company's long-term interest, and substantial evidence that they are. It seems that Amerco would stand to benefit by having at least some workers use its family-friendly policies.

It might be argued, then, that such policies are in the interest of the company but not of the hapless middle manager who has to implement them. Amy Truett, the most forceful proponent of family-friendly reforms at Amerco, believed the real bottleneck was in the impermeable "clay layer" of middle management—and that there was no getting around it. The company brochure describing work-family policies notes in small print that any arrangement needs the approval of one's "immediate supervisor or division manager."

This, of course, leaves power in the hands of a middle manager who may see such policies as a matter of privilege, not rights.

We might call this the Balashev theory. In an episode in Leo Tolstoy's *War and Peace*, the Russian Tsar Alexander dispatches his trusted envoy Balashev to deliver an important warning to Napoleon, emperor of France, to withdraw his forces from Russia. Alexander gives Balashev exact instructions on what to say—that Russia will consider itself at war with France so long as French soldiers are on Russian soil. Balashev sets off. But along the way, he is detained by one person, then another, each with an urgent concern, each affecting Balashev's frame of mind. At last, he is brought, awestruck, before Napoleon. Swayed by more immediate influences, at the last moment Balashev softens the tsar's message. Napoleon need not withdraw his troops from Russian soil at all, only to the other side of a nearby river. Inadvertently, Balashev alters world history and war breaks out.

Perhaps expedient company managers in the outlying provinces of Amerco "do a Balashev." Although most employees felt that senior management supported family-friendly policies, they were convinced that fewer middle managers did; and indeed some middle managers did tell me that flexible schedules were "one more headache to manage." As the head of a large engineering division told me in a pleasant, matter-of-fact way, "My policy on flextime is that there is no flextime."

But if manager resistance were the main reason for the low usage of part time, job sharing, and leaves of various sorts, then friendly, progressive managers should receive more requests for flexible or shorter hours than recalcitrant managers. In fact, offices with progressive managers had only slightly more part-timers, job sharers, and flextimers than offices with resistant managers. Progressive managers received roughly the same number of requests as did resistant managers. For the most part, it was not that workers were applying and being turned away. It was that workers weren't applying.

For some women in male-dominated fields, one reason to work long hours, or at least to avoid shorter ones, may be the need to ward off "the evil eye" of male resentment. As an anonymous male respondent to a company survey declared, "Let's hope we're not starting another minority and women crisis [by introducing family-friendly policies]. White males can't stand another one like in the 1970s." A woman engineer (and mother) commented from the other side:

> Two of my coworkers, older men, won't say it to my face, but I know they think I got *their* promotion. Truth is I got *my* promotion. I earned it. But at work I feel I have to prove it. I don't know if that's behind my sixty-hour week or not.

In the formal company culture, white men are not supposed to resent white women and minorities, but some do. Many men have become good at disguising their disgruntlement, but women have become equally adept at detecting hidden expressions of it. The female newcomers I talked with "knew" just how resentful each man in each job classification was, or how recently he had "changed his tune." Still, the theory of the evil eye doesn't explain why women outside of "envy environments" do not try to claim more time at home; nor does it explain why these envious men themselves shy away from parental leave or shorter hours.

All of the explanations listed above have real merit. In certain circumstances, some of the obstacles were overwhelming. But by themselves, these road blocks are not formidable enough to account for such widespread acquiescence to long hours. In those cases where workers can afford to earn less money, are not afraid of being fired, have informed themselves of the new policies, lack envious coworkers, and work for a company that values balance and that has trained its "Balashevs" to do the same, the clues point to another underlying explanation for why workers are not trying to get more time for themselves.

A 1985 Bureau of Labor Statistics survey asked workers whether they preferred a shorter workweek, a longer one, or their present schedule. Sixty-five percent preferred their schedule to remain the way it is. Of the remainder, three-quarters wanted *longer* hours. Less than 10 percent said they wanted a cut in hours. In every age group, more women wanted a longer workweek than wanted a shorter one.[13] In a 1993 study by the Families and Work Institute in New York, researchers Ellen Galinsky, James T. Bond, and Dana Friedman asked a large random sample of workers how much time and energy they *actually* give to work, to family and friends, and to themselves. Then they asked how much time each respondent *would like* to devote to each of these. People responded that they actually give 43 percent of their time and energy to family and friends, 37 percent to the job, and 20 percent to themselves. But when asked what they would like, the answers were nearly the same: Forty-seven percent to family and friends, 30 percent to the job, and 23 percent to themselves.[14] Such studies imply that working families aren't using family-friendly policies in large part because they aren't *asking* to use them,[15] and they aren't asking for them because they haven't formulated in their minds a need urgent enough. Certainly, some parents have tried to shorten their hours. Twenty-one percent of the nation's women voluntarily work part time, as do 7 percent of men.[16] A number of others make informal arrangements that don't show up in survey results. Still, while hurried working parents report needing more time, the main story of their lives does not center on their struggle to get it.

Why aren't working parents forging a "culture of resistance" parallel to the social movement that professionals like Amy Truett are quietly creating on their behalf? Where is *their* mission statement, their vision? Even if parents don't dare knock on their managers' doors to ask for 85 percent work schedules, for instance, why aren't they privately questioning their own use of time? Parents like Timmy's father and Cassie's mother lament the fact that their lives are too crowded, their time with their children too limited. They claim they want extra time at home. But do they want something else even more?

CHAPTER 4

Family Values and Reversed Worlds

If working parents are "deciding" to work full time and longer, what experiences at home and work might be influencing them to do so? When I first began the research for this book, I assumed that home was "home" and work was "work"—that each was a stationary rock beneath the moving feet of working parents. I assumed as well that each stood in distinct opposition to the other. In a family, love and commitment loom large as ends in themselves and are not means to any further end. As an Amerco parent put it, "I work to live; I don't live to work." However difficult family life may be at times, we usually feel family ties offer an irreplaceable connection to generations past and future. Family is our personal embrace with history.

Jobs, on the other hand, earn money that, to most of us, serves as the means to other ends. To be sure, jobs can also allow us to develop skills or friendships, and to be part of a larger work community. But we seldom envision the workplace as somewhere workers would freely choose to spend their time. If in the American imagination the family has a touch of the sacred, the realm of work seems profane.

In addition, I assumed, as many of us do, that compared to the workplace, home is a more pleasant place to be. This is after all one reason why employers pay workers to work and don't pay them to stay home. The very word "work" suggests to most of us something unpleasant, involuntary, even coerced.

If the purpose and nature of family and work differ so drastically in our minds, it seemed reasonable to assume that people's emotional experiences of the two spheres would differ profoundly, too. In *Haven in a Heartless World*, the social historian Christopher Lasch drew a picture of family as a "haven" where workers sought refuge from the cruel world of work.[1] Painting in broad strokes, we might imagine a picture like this: At the end of a long day, a weary worker opens his front door and calls out, "Hi, Honey! I'm home!" He takes off his uniform, puts on a bathrobe, opens a beer, picks up the paper, and exhales. Whatever its strains, home is where he's relaxed, most himself. At home, he feels that people know him, understand him, appreciate him for who he really is. At home, he is safe.

At work, our worker is "on call," ready to report at a moment's notice, working flat out to get back to the customer right away. He feels "like a number." If he doesn't watch out, he can take the fall for somebody else's mistakes. This, then, is Lasch's "heartless world," an image best captured long ago in Charlie Chaplin's satirical *Modern Times*. In that film, Charlie acts the part of a hapless factory hand on an automated assembly line moving so fast that when he takes a moment to scratch his nose, he falls desperately behind. Dwarfed by the inhuman scale of the workplace, pressured by the line's relentless pace, Charlie quickly loses his humanity, goes mad, climbs into the giant machine that runs the conveyor belt, and becomes a machine part himself.

It was just such images of home and work that were challenged in one of my first interviews at Amerco. Linda Avery, a friendly thirty-eight-year-old mother of two daughters, is a shift supervisor at the Demco Plant, ten miles down the valley from Amerco headquarters. Her husband, Bill, is a technician in the same plant. Linda and Bill share the care of her sixteen-year-old daughter from a previous marriage and their two-year-old by working opposite shifts, as a full fifth of American working parents do. "Bill works the 7 A.M. to 3 P.M. shift while I watch the baby," Linda explained. "Then I work the 3 P.M. to 11 P.M. shift and he watches the baby. My older daughter works at Walgreens after school."

When we first met in the factory's breakroom over a couple of Cokes, Linda was in blue jeans and a pink jersey, her hair pulled back in a long blond ponytail. She wore no makeup, and her manner was purposeful and direct. She was working overtime, and so I began by asking whether Amerco required the overtime, or whether she volunteered for it. "Oh, I put in for it," she replied with a low chuckle. But, I wondered aloud, wouldn't she and her husband like to have more time at home together, finances and company policy permitting. Linda took off her safety glasses, rubbed her whole face, folded her arms, resting her elbows on the table, and approached the question by describing her life at home:

> I walk in the door and the minute I turn the key in the lock my older daughter is there. Granted, she needs somebody to talk to about her day. . . . The baby is still up. She should have been in bed two hours ago and that upsets me. The dishes are piled in the sink. My daughter comes right up to the door and complains about anything her stepfather said or did, and she wants to talk about her job. My husband is in the other room hollering to my daughter, "Tracy, I don't *ever* get any time to talk to your mother, because you're always monopolizing her time before I even get a chance!" They all come at me at once.

To Linda, her home was not a place to relax. It was another workplace. Her description of the urgency of demands and the unarbitrated quarrels that awaited her homecoming contrasted with her account of arriving at her job as a shift supervisor:

> I usually come to work early just to get away from the house. I get there at 2:30 P.M., and people are there waiting. We sit. We talk. We joke. I let them know what's going on, who has

to be where, what changes I've made for the shift that day. We sit there and chit-chat for five or ten minutes. There's laughing, joking, fun. My coworkers aren't putting me down for any reason. Everything is done with humor and fun from beginning to end, though it can get stressful when a machine malfunctions.

For Linda, home had become work and work had become home. Somehow, the two worlds had been reversed. Indeed, Linda felt she could only get relief from the "work" of being at home by going to the "home" of work. As she explained,

> My husband's a great help watching our baby. But as far as doing housework or even taking the baby when I'm at home, no. He figures he works five days a week; *he's* not going to come home and clean. But he doesn't stop to think that I work *seven* days a week. Why should I have to come home and do the housework without help from anybody else? My husband and I have been through this over and over again. Even if he would just pick up from the kitchen table and stack the dishes for me, that would make a big difference. He does nothing. On his weekends off, I have to provide a sitter for the baby so he can go fishing. When I have a day off, I have the baby all day long without a break. He'll help out if I'm not here, but the minute I am, all the work at home is mine.

With a light laugh, she continued, "So I take a lot of overtime. The more I get out of the house, the better I am. It's a terrible thing to say, but that's the way I feel." Linda said this not in the manner of a new discovery, a reluctant confession, or collusion between two working mothers—"Don't you just want to get away some-times?"—but in a matter-of-fact way. This was the way life was.

Bill, who was fifty-six when I first met him, had three grown children from a contentious first marriage. He told me he felt he had already "put in his time" to raise them and now was at a stage of life in which he wanted to enjoy himself. Yet when he came home afternoons he had to "babysit for Linda."

In a previous era, men regularly escaped the house for the bar, the fishing hole, the golf course, the pool hall, or, often enough, the sweet joy of work. Today, as one of the women who make up 45 percent of the American workforce, Linda Avery, overloaded and feeling unfairly treated at home, was escaping to work, too. Nowadays, men and women both may leave unwashed dishes, unresolved quarrels, crying tots, testy teenagers, and unresponsive mates behind to arrive at work early and call out, "Hi, fellas, I'm here!"

Linda would have loved a warm welcome from her family when she returned from work, a reward for her day of labors at the plant. At a minimum, she would have liked to relax, at least for a little while. But that was hard to do because Bill, on *his* second shift at home, would nap and watch television instead of engaging the children. The more Bill slacked off on his shift at home, the more Linda felt robbed of rest when she was there. The more anxious the children were, or the messier the house was when she walked in the door, the more Linda felt she was simply returning to the task of making up for being gone.

For his part, Bill recalled that Linda had wanted a new baby more than he had. So now that they were the parents of a small child, Bill reasoned, looking after the baby should also be more Linda's responsibility. Caring for a two-year-old after working a regular job was hard enough. Incredibly, Linda wanted him to do more. That was her problem though, not his. He had "earned his stripes" with his first set of children.

Early Saturday mornings, while Linda and the kids were rustling about the house, Bill would get up, put his fishing gear and a six-pack of beer into his old Ford truck, and climb into the driver's seat. "Man, I slam that truck door shut, frraaammm!, and I'm ready to go! I figure I *earned* that time."

Both Linda and Bill felt the need for time off, to relax, to have fun, to feel free, but they had not agreed that it was Bill who needed a break more than Linda. Bill simply climbed in his truck and took his free time. This irritated Linda because she felt he *took* it at her expense. Largely in response to her resentment, Linda grabbed what she also called "free time"—at work.

Neither Linda nor Bill Avery wanted more time at home, not as things were arranged. Whatever images they may have carried in their heads about what family and work should be like, the Averys did not feel their actual home was a haven or that work was a heartless world.

Where did Linda feel most relaxed? She laughed more, joked more, listened to more interesting stories while on break at the factory than at home. Working the 3 P.M. to 11 P.M. shift, her hours off didn't coincide with those of her mother or older sister who worked in town, nor with those of her close friends and neighbors. But even if they had, she would have felt that the true center of her social world was her plant, not her neighborhood. The social life that once might have surrounded her at home she now found at work. The sense of being part of a lively, larger, ongoing community—that, too, was at work. In an emergency, Linda told me, she would sacrifice everything for her family. But in the meantime, the everyday "emergencies" she most wanted to attend to, that challenged rather than exhausted her, were those she encountered at the factory. Frankly, life there was more fun.

How do Linda and Bill Avery fit into the broader picture of American family and work life? Psychologist Reed Larson and his colleagues studied the daily emotional experiences of mothers and fathers in fifty-five two-parent Chicago families with children in the fifth to eighth grades. Some of the mothers cared for children at home, some worked part time, others full time, while all the fathers in the study worked full time. Each participant wore a pager for a week, and whenever they were beeped by the research team, each wrote down how he or she felt: "happy, unhappy, cheerful-irritable, friendly-angry." The researchers found that men and women reported a similar range of emotional states across the week. But fathers reported more "positive emotional states" at home; mothers, more positive emotional states at work. This held true for every social class. Fathers like Bill Avery relaxed more at home; while mothers like Linda Avery did more housework there. Larson suggests that "because women are constantly on call to the needs of other family members, they are less able to relax at home in the way men do."[2] Wives were typically in better moods than their husbands at home only when they were eating or engaging in "family transport." They were in worse moods when they were doing "child-related activities" or "socializing" there.[3] Men and women each felt most at ease when involved in tasks they felt less obliged to do, Larson reports. For women, this meant first shift work; for men, second.

A recent study of working mothers made another significant discovery. Problems at home tend to upset women more deeply than problems at work. The study found that women were most deeply affected by family stress—and were more likely to be made depressed or physically ill by it—even when stress at the workplace was greater. For women, current research on stress does not support the common view of home as a sanctuary and work as a "jungle." However hectic their lives, women who do paid work, researchers have consistently found, feel less depressed, think better of themselves, and are more satisfied with life than women who don't do paid work.[4] One study reported that, paradoxically, women who work feel more valued at home than women who stay home.[5]

In sum, then, women who work outside the home have better physical and mental health than those who do not, and not simply because healthier women go to work. Paid work, the psychologist Grace Baruch argues, "offers such benefits as challenge, control, structure, positive feedback, self esteem . . . and social ties."[6] Reed Larson's study found, for example, that women were no more likely than men to see coworkers as friendly, but when women made friendly contact it was far more likely to lift their spirits.[7]

As a woman quoted by Baruch put it, "A job is to a woman as a wife is to a man."[8]

For Linda Avery self-satisfaction, well-being, high spirits, and work were inextricably linked. It was mainly at work, she commented, that she felt really good about herself. As a supervisor, she saw her job as helping people, and those she helped appreciated her. She mused,

I'm a good mom at home, but I'm a better mom at work. At
home, I get into fights with Tracy when she comes home
late. I want her to apply to a junior college; but she's not
interested, and I get frustrated with her, because I want so
much for her. At work, I think I'm better at seeing the other
person's point of view. People come to me a lot, because I'm
good at helping them.

Often relations at work seemed more manageable. The "children" Linda Avery helped at work were older and better able to
articulate their problems than her own children. The plant where
she worked was clean and pleasant. She knew everyone on the line
she supervised. Indeed, all the workers knew each other, and some
were even related by blood, marriage, or, odd as it may sound, by
divorce. One coworker complained bitterly that a friend of her husband's ex-wife was keeping track of how much overtime she
worked in order to help this ex-wife make a case for increasing the
amount of his child support. Workers sometimes carried such hos-
tilities generated at home into the workplace. Yet despite the
common assumption that relations at work are emotionally limited,
meaningful friendships often blossom. When Linda Avery joined
coworkers for a mug of beer at a nearby bar after work to gossip
about the "spy" who was tracking the deadbeat dad's new wife's
overtime, she was among real friends. Research shows that work
friends can be as important as family members in helping both men
and women cope with the blows of life. The gerontologist Andrew
Sharlach studied how middle-aged people in Los Angeles dealt with
the death of a parent. He found that 73 percent of the women in the
sample, and 64 percent of the men, responded that work was a
"helpful resource" in coping with a mother's death.[9]

Amerco regularly reinforced the family-like ties of coworkers by
holding recognition ceremonies honoring particular workers or
entire self-managed production teams. The company would decorate a section of the factory and serve food and drink. The production teams, too, had regular get-togethers. The halls of Amerco
were hung with plaques praising workers for recent accomplish-

ments. Such recognition luncheons, department gatherings, and, particularly in the ranks of clerical and factory workers, exchange of birthday gifts were fairly common workday events.

At its white-collar offices, Amerco was even more involved in shaping the emotional culture of the workplace and fostering an environment of trust and cooperation in order to bring out everyone's best. At the middle and top levels of the company, employees were invited to periodic "career development seminars" on personal relations at work. The centerpiece of Amerco's personal-relations culture was a "vision" speech that the CEO had given called "Valuing the Individual," a message repeated in speeches, memorialized in company brochures, and discussed with great seriousness throughout the upper reaches of the company. In essence, the message was a parental reminder to respect others. Similarly, in a new-age recasting of an old business slogan ("The customer is always right"), Amerco proposed that its workers "Value the internal customer." This meant: Be as polite and considerate to your coworkers as you would be to Amerco customers. "Value the internal customer" extended to coworkers the slogan "Delight the customer." Don't just work with your coworkers, delight them.

"Employee empowerment," "valuing diversity," and "work-family balance"—these catchphrases, too, spoke to a moral aspect of work life. Though ultimately tied to financial gain, such exhortations—and the policies that followed from them—made workers feel the company was concerned with people, not just money. In many ways, the workplace appeared to be a site of benign social engineering where workers came to feel appreciated, honored, and liked. On the other hand, how many recognition ceremonies for competent performance were going on at home? Who was valuing the internal customer there?

After thirty years with Amerco, Bill Avery felt, if anything, overqualified for his job, and he had a recognition plaque from the company to prove it. But when his toddler got into his fishing gear and he blew up at her and she started yelling, he felt impotent in the face of her rageful screams—and nobody was there to back him up. When his teenage stepdaughter reminded him that she saw him, not as an honorable patriarch, but as an infantile competitor for her mother's attention, he felt humiliated. At such moments, he says, he had to resist the impulse to reach for the whiskey he had given up five years earlier.

Other fathers with whom I talked were less open and self-critical about such feelings, but in one way or another many said that they felt more confident they could "get the job done" at work than at home. As one human resource specialist at Amerco reflected,

> We used to joke about the old "Mother of the Year Award." That doesn't exist anymore. Now, we don't know a meaningful way to reward a parent. At work, we get paid and promoted for doing well. At home, when you're doing the right thing, chances are your kids are giving you hell for it.

If a family gives its members anything, we assume it is surely a sense of belonging to an ongoing community. In its engineered corporate cultures, capitalism has rediscovered communal ties and is using them to build its new version of capitalism. Many Amerco employees spoke warmly, happily, and seriously of "belonging to the Amerco family," and everywhere there were visible symbols of this belonging. While some married people have dispensed with their wedding rings, people proudly wore their "Total Quality" pins or "High Performance Team" tee-shirts, symbols of their loyalty to the company and of its loyalty to them. In my interviews, I heard little about festive reunions of extended families, while throughout the year, employees flocked to the many company-sponsored ritual gatherings.

In this new model of family and work life, a tired parent flees a world of unresolved quarrels and unwashed laundry for the reliable orderliness, harmony, and managed cheer of work. The emotional magnets beneath home and workplace are in the process of being reversed. In truth, there are many versions of this reversal going on, some more far-reaching than others. Some people find in work a respite from the emotional tangles at home. Others virtually marry their work, investing it with an emotional significance once reserved for family, while hesitating to trust loved ones at home. If Linda and Bill Avery were not yet at that point, their situation was troubling enough, and by no means restricted to a small group. Overall, this "reversal" was a predominant pattern in about a fifth of Amerco families, and an important theme in over half of them.

We may be seeing here a trend in modern life destined to affect us all. To be sure, few people feel totally secure either at work or at home. In the last fifteen years, massive waves of downsizing have reduced the security workers feel even in the most apparently stable workplaces. At the same time, a rising divorce rate has reduced the security they feel at home. Although both Linda and Bill felt their marriage was strong, over the course of their lives, each had changed relationships more often than they had changed jobs. Bill had worked steadily for Amerco for thirty years, but he had been married twice; and in the years between marriages, he had lived with two women and dated several more. Nationwide, half the people who marry eventually divorce, most within the first seven years of marriage. Three-quarters of divorced men and two-thirds of divorced women remarry, but remarried couples are more likely than those in first marriages to divorce. Couples who only live together are even more likely to break up than couples who marry. Increasing numbers of people are getting their "pink slips" at home. Work may become their rock.

The Time Bind

The social world that draws a person's allegiance also imparts a pattern to time. The more attached we are to the world of work, the more its deadlines, its cycles, its pauses and interruptions shape our lives and the more family time is forced to accommodate to the pressures of work. In recent years at Amerco it has been possible to detect a change in the ways its workers view the proper use of their time: Family time, for them, has taken on an "industrial" tone.

As the social worlds of work and home reverse, working parents' experience of time in each sphere changes as well. Just how, and how much, depends on the nature of a person's job, company, and life at home. But at least for people like Timmy's parents, engineers at Amerco, it's clear that family time is succumbing to a cult of efficiency previously associated with the workplace. Meanwhile, work time, with its ever longer hours, becomes newly hospitable to sociability—periods of talking with friends on e-mail, patching up quarrels, gossiping. In this way, within the long workday of Timmy's father were great hidden pockets of inefficiency, while, in the far smaller number of waking weekday hours he spent at home, he was time conscious and efficient. Sometimes, Timmy's dad forgot the clock at work; despite himself, he kept a close eye on the clock at home.

The new rhythms of work are also linked to a new sense of self-supervision. Managers, professionals, and many workers in production teams describe feeling as if they are driving themselves ever harder at Amerco, while at home they feel themselves being driven by forces beyond their control. Under Total Quality's "just-in-time production" system, workers try to respond immediately to a customer's wishes. Goods are no longer supposed to lie around in warehouses; they cost too much to store. This means that an employee is always vulnerable to emergency calls to meet an order for which sufficient product inventory does not exist. Amerco work teams go from one collective emergency to another, producing goods "just in time." Periodic ship dates loom large, giving a hiccough-like rhythm to work time. In between demand-based emergencies, it is the worker who is, in effect, "warehoused" at work. (The rise of a contingency workforce in the American economy as a whole simply moves the warehousing from workplace to home.) The miracle of Amerco's engineered culture is that the company has managed to give employees, who labor according to a schedule imposed on them by others, the sense that they are still in control. This achievement has turned what might otherwise be a continual, heart-pounding, tension-provoking crisis at work into a kind of endless flow of communal problem-solving time. So Timmy's dad, for instance, lurched from one project deadline to the next at the office, but only when he came home did he feel truly pressed. He then tried to jam many necessary activities into his domestic life: a block of time for Timmy, another for Timmy's sister, another for his wife—all arranged like so many office hours, but without a secretary to control his flow of visitors and tasks.

Working parents' experience of time has changed, but relative to *what*? Let's return to Cassie's mother, Gwen Bell, and imagine two of her ancestors. Gwen's great, great, great, great-grandmother might well have tended a New England farmhouse in 1800. She probably lived a harder life than Gwen does, had many more children, and did tougher physical work, scrubbing laundry, tending cows, hoeing fields. But because her farm was both family and work in one, time with family overlapped and interwove with time at work.

Getting the hay in before a rain could be a matter of great urgency. But a typical day would rarely have had any of the exactly timed, carefully coordinated, closely calibrated arrivals and departures that Gwen experiences as she mixes business meetings, professional appointments, and Cassie's piano lessons with a trip to the hairdresser or auto repair shop. Events would have been more loosely arranged, more diffusely, informally related. Gwen's ancestor would have intuitively divided time into workweeks and Sundays, but not into a work year with a specific number of vacations days. She would have given birth many times, but not allocated time to the baby according to a company's six-week maternity-leave policy. She would have grieved for the dead but not in the three-day bereavement leave a company supervisor could authorize. Time was less geared to standardized, bureaucratic rules and more oriented to local custom. The hour on a neighboring town's clock tower might have differed from that on her town's, and it would not have mattered much, because the intricate coordination of a whole industrial order did not yet rest on the need for exactly synchronized time. Deadlines, opening and closing times, customer demands were all matters of informal agreement made according to community custom.

Little meaning would then have attached to the phrase "Time is money." Time was life. Much of life was work, but neither work nor time was so precisely measured in units of money. Without a meter to tick, time on a New England farm in 1800 was a little slower, and the cultures of work and home were not "reversed" for the simple reason that they had not yet been separated.

In the 1920s, Gwen's great-grandmother might well have been a housewife married to an urban factory worker. Historians tell us that people were, by then, becoming more self-conscious accountants of time. Gwen's city ancestor might have worked in a factory as a young woman but later quit to care for her children, a household, a garden, and perhaps a paying boarder. Though housework was arduous and unmechanized for a working-class homemaker, a woman could largely control the pace of her work. She lived according to what the historian Tamara Hareven has called "family time," while her husband in his factory geared himself to "industrial time."[10] It is this image of the domestic woman and the industrialized man that Christopher Lasch used as a model in *Haven in a Heartless World*.

During this time, the very nature of industrial work was transformed thanks to an engineering genius named Frederick W. Taylor. He introduced to factory life the principles of what he called "scientific management," imposing on the workplace and individual workers a rigorous standard of efficiency. Because time was now more exactly equated with production and therefore with money, time was also more precisely measured and bits of it more carefully saved.

The most notorious application of Taylor's idea of scientific management took place at the Bethlehem Steel Company in 1899. There, Taylor studied a Dutch-American employee named Schmidt as he shoveled twelve and a half tons of pig iron. He measured the exact speed of each move Schmidt made (Taylor's watch was calibrated in seconds) and quantified every detail of Schmidt's job— "the size of the shovel, the bite into the pile, the weight of the scoop, the distance to work, the arc of the swing, and the rest periods Schmidt should take."[11] Taylor taught Schmidt to shovel forty-seven tons of pig iron in the same amount of time he used to shovel twelve and a half. He went on to apply his principles to machinists, bricklayers, and other craftsmen.

Managers at Amerco today are not measuring the "bite into a pile" or the "weight of a scoop" of anything. Instead, under the Total Quality system, the worker is "empowered" to measure it all herself and be efficient in her own way. Meanwhile a low-grade Tayloresque cult of efficiency has "jumped the fence" and come home. Home has become the place where people carry out necessary tasks efficiently in the limited amount of time allotted. No efficiency experts stand by to calibrate Gwen and John Bell's work; the Bells have become their own efficiency experts, gearing all the moments and movements of their lives to the workplace. For Gwen's ancestor in 1920, the workplace was heartlessly Taylorized and home might indeed have seemed a haven from it. But for Gwen, her workplace has a large, socially engineered heart while her home has gained a newly Taylorized feel.

Even if they didn't intend to, Gwen and John regularly applied principles of efficiency to their family life. For them, as for so many other Amerco parents, saving time was becoming the sort of virtue at home it had long been at work. Gwen regularly squeezed one activity between two others, narrowing the "time frame" around each. Sometimes she brought the cellular phone into the bathroom while Cassie splashed in the tub. She checked the telephone answering machine messages and her e-mail while the dishwasher ran. Whenever she could get a lot done at home in less time, Gwen congratulated herself for solving a time problem. But except when she and John self-consciously applied the brakes, they found themselves "keeping the engine running all the time."

Numerous activities formerly done at home now go on outside the house as a result of domestic "outsourcing." Long ago, the basic functions of education, medical care, and economic production, once based in the home, moved out. Gradually, other realms of activity followed. For middle-class children, for instance, piano lessons, psychological counseling, tutoring, entertainment, and eating now often take place outside the home. Family time is chopped into pieces according to the amount of time each

outsourced service requires—fifty minutes for a psychiatric appointment, sixty minutes for a jazzercise class. Each service begins and
ends at an agreed-upon time somewhere else. This creates a certain
anxiety about being "on time," because it is uncomfortable (and
often costs money) when one is late, and precious time is squan-
dered if one is early. The domestic time that remains may come to
seem like filler between one appointment and another. Sometimes
television, which through advertising creates the need for further
services, fills in the temporal space.

Gwen and John Bell responded to their time bind at home by
trying to value and protect "quality time." A concept unknown to
Gwen's ancestors, quality time has become a powerful symbol of the
struggle against the growing pressures on time at home. It reflects
the extent to which modern parents feel the flow of time running
against them. Many Amerco families were fighting hard to preserve
outposts of quality time, lest their relationships be stripped of meaningful time altogether.

The premise behind quality time is that the time we devote
to relationships can somehow be separated from ordinary time.
Relationships go on during "quantity time," of course, but then we
are only passively, not actively, wholeheartedly, specializing in our
emotional ties. We aren't "on." Quality time at home becomes like
an office appointment. One wouldn't want to be caught "goofing
off around the water cooler" when one is engaged in serious quality
time. If childcare, summer camps, and psychiatry are kinds of
domestic outsourcing, then quality time falls into a new category we
might call domestic "in-sourcing."

Quality time holds out the hope that scheduling intense periods
of togetherness can compensate for an overall loss of time in such a
way that a relationship will suffer no loss of quality. But this, too, is
a way of transferring the cult of efficiency from office to home.
Instead of nine hours a day with a child, we declare ourselves
capable of getting the "same result" with one more intensely
focused total quality hour. As with Frederick Taylor and the hapless
Schmidt, our family bonds are being recalibrated to achieve greater
productivity in less time.

Feeling themselves in a time bind, most Amerco working parents *wanted* more time at home, protected time, time less intensely geared to the rhythms of the work world outside, time they simply did not have. They also yearned to feel different about the time they did have. But the lack of family time and the Taylorization of what little of it remained was forcing parents to do even more of a new kind of work: the emotional work necessary to repair the damage caused by time pressures at home. If Gwen considered her work at the office her first shift and her work at home her second, she also found herself engaged each day in an anguished third shift, coping with Cassie's resistance as well as her own exasperation and sadness at living such a Taylorized family life. When workers protest speed-up, industrialists can replace them. But when children react against a speedup at home, parents have to deal with it. Children dawdle. They sulk. They ask for gifts. They tell their parents by action or word, "I don't like this." They want to be having quality time when it's a quantity time of day; they don't want quality time in the time slot parents religiously set aside for it. Parents, for their part, displace struggles for time they might be having with managers at work onto children and spouses at home. As if she were Cassie's manager, Gwen would say early in the morning, "It's time to get ready for the Spotted Deer Center." "I don't want to get ready for the center," Cassie would whine. To which Gwen would respond in an anxious, coaxing way, "It's time. Hurry up. We're late." The emotional dirty work of adjusting children to the Taylorized home and making up to them for its stresses and strains is the most painful part of a growing third shift at home.

Parents now increasingly find themselves in the role of domestic "time and motion" experts, and so more commonly speak of time as if it were a threatened form of personal capital they have no choice but to manage and invest, capital whose value seems to rise and fall according to forces beyond their control.

What's new here is the spread into the home of a financial manager's attitude toward time. Few people feel that they simply "sell" their time to a workplace, which then manages it for them. More feel as if they manage a temporal portfolio there themselves. But this leads them to think of time with their partners, with their children, as a commodity to be invested or withdrawn, an "it" that they wish they could purchase or earn more of in order to live a more relaxed life.[12]

Many working parents strive mightily to counter this conception of time. They want not simply more time, but a less alienating sense of time. As one Amerco working mother put it, "I love my job, I love my family, and I don't want to move to the country. But I wish I could bring some of that ease of country living home, where relationships come first." In this alternative view, time is to relationships what shelters are to families, not capital to be invested, but a habitat in which to live. People are not time-capitalists but time-architects who structure time to protect their relationships. Looked at this way, a few Amerco families were still managing to build large time-houses, but many others were living in increasingly cramped time-quarters—and some were temporally homeless. Some time-shelters seemed solid and permanent—for instance, one family's inviolable Saturday breakfast; but too many others were like collapsible nomad's tents, pushed from one day to the next, from one week to the next. If many working parents wanted more time at home, most also yearned to approach time as home builders, even as they dealt with it like portfolio managers. Some were beginning to sense that they had invested in the wrong "stock"; others were feeling the strain of applying a time manager's perspective to those unbillable hours at home.

As I spoke with employees at every level of the Amerco community, I sought the factors in the company culture that militated against the use of the very family-friendly policies that it had advertised so proudly. But I was also curious about how events at home reinforced the values of the workplace. What was it in the lives of the families themselves, I asked, that made them complicit in the creation of their own time binds? To find answers, I knew I would have to explore work and family life from the top of the Amerco hierarchy to the bottom. I decided to start at the top.

PART II

*From Executive Suite
to Factory Floor*

CHAPTER 5

Giving at the Office

> *Career:* 1. Progress or general course of action of a
> person through life . . . 2. An occupation or
> profession, especially one requiring social training,
> followed as one's life work . . . 3. A course, especially
> a swift one . . . 4. Speed, especially full speed, "the
> horse stumbled in full career . . ."
>
> *Random House Dictionary*
> *of the English Language*

Entering the company cafeteria to pick up ham and cheese sand-
wiches for our noon interview, Bill Denton, a senior manager who
oversees all personnel issues at Amerco including the Work-Life
Balance program, banters with the cashier. "Is the pickle in my
sandwich free?" She smiles. On our way out, he nudges a young
man hunched over a spreadsheet who is munching on a sandwich,
"We'll expect that report in half an hour." They both laugh. In the
elevator, he chats amiably with a secretary as we rise to the ninth
floor and the offices of Amerco's most powerful executives. Inside
his office, he motions me to a chair, leans forward in his, and says,
"I've set aside an hour for you."

After thirty years with the company, Bill Denton, fifty-two,
exudes vigor, warmth, and a powerful sense of direction. He is a
sturdy man about five feet ten inches tall. He has neatly trimmed
brown hair and a rapid, confident way of speaking that leads one to
assume he is right about what he's saying. His four children, posed
in framed pictures behind his desk, look remarkably like him. How,

I ask, seeking a neutral place to begin, did he get started at Amerco? He answers as if I had asked him to describe the principle according to which he'd risen to the top, and this brings him immediately to the matter of time:

> Time has a way of sorting out people at this company. A lot of people that don't make it to the top work long hours. But all the people I know who *do* make it work long hours, some more than others. The members of the Management Committee of this company aren't the smartest people in this company, we're the hardest working. We work like dogs. We out-work the others. We out-practice them. We out-train them. By the time people get within three or four levels of the Management Committee, they're all very good, or else they wouldn't be there. So from that point on, what counts is work and commitment. People don't say, "He works like a dog." You just start to see performance differences created by a willingness to work all the time.

> Then there's a final elimination. Some people flame out, get weird because they work all the time, or they're no fun, so they don't get promoted. The people at the top are very smart, work like crazy, and don't flame out. They're still able to maintain a good mental set, and keep their family life together. *They* win the race.

Curiously unrushed, this sixty-hour-a-week manager of three hundred employees is a winner of that race—all those hours and he's still a nice guy. "We hire very good people with a strong work ethic to start with," he observes.

> People look around and see that. So then they work hard to try to keep up, and I don't think we can do anything about that. . . . It's going to be a long time before somebody becomes the CEO of a company saying, "I'm going to be a wonderfully balanced person"—because there are just too

many others who aren't. The environment here is very competitive.

Bill himself averaged ten hours a day, and given his handsome salary, his love of his work, and a willing wife, he was happy to do so. The twelve top managers I interviewed all worked between fifty- and seventy-hour weeks. One described himself as a "twelve-hour player," another as a "controlled workaholic." A third said, "They tell us to get the job done—but not to spend too much time on it. But the job takes time." Most executives came in weekends and all of them took work home. Interestingly, though, Bill estimated that only a third of the employees he considered workaholic "made a real difference" to the company while two-thirds of them did not. Managers often started or ended meetings with workaholic jokes. A colleague quipped at an 8 A.M. meeting, "How's the weather in Tokyo, Jim?" to a colleague who had arrived directly from the airport. "When I get home from a trip, I never know if I'm kissing my wife hello or goodbye," chimed in another to a round of rueful laughter.

Parking lots told a similar story about a workaholic company culture. The executive lot began filling around 7 A.M. and thinned out only slowly after 5 P.M. Even on the Fourth of July, the one day of the year other than Christmas when one might most expect Amerco employees to be off duty, there was a sprinkling of cars and vans in the parking lots around the central administration and engineering buildings, their windows rolled part-way down, as if their owners were saying, "I won't be long." A man in shorts, a row of pens in his shirt pocket, walked in rapid, long strides toward his office. Another was just leaving, briefcase in hand. A third had a child in tow.

To Bill, long hours did not seem imposed from on high. Instead, in his view, the corporation simply attracted people ready to attune themselves to company needs. "No one tells us to work long hours," Bill explained matter-of-factly. "You don't get the 'leaving *early* again?' We impose it on ourselves. We're our own worst enemy." Like the Protestants in Max Weber's classic study *The*

Protestant Ethic and the Spirit of Capitalism, they seemed to respond not to God's wagging finger, but to some internal urgency that pressed them to extend each workday. "You hear stories of managers who drag workers into conversation just as they're packing up to leave, or who make 5 P.M. bunker checks to see who's still there," one man told me, "but that's the exception." Of his three hundred employees, Bill noted,

> I don't decide how much work they do. *They* decide. If they could talk their coworkers into working less, then they could probably work less themselves.

If Bill's hours were long, they were also hours in a privileged zone, well protected from unwanted interruptions. At home, his wife screened his calls and greeted visitors at the door; his secretary did the same for him at work. Together, these two women took much of the uncertainty out of his workday. Like other top executives Bill told none of those stories so commonly heard from employees farther down the Amerco hierarchy—about disappearing cats, suddenly feverish children, emergency calls from elderly relatives, or missing babysitters. In a polite way, Bill's wife and secretary patrolled Bill's time, keeping a vigilant eye out for time-thieves or unauthorized time-squatters. Bill's secretary was his clock: she sorted out his schedule and his daily priorities for him, telling him when he had to do what. This allowed him to respond "spontaneously" to tasks as they presented themselves to him, and it generally left him available to concentrate on any one of those tasks until he got it done.[1] As he described it,

> I immerse myself. I love my job. I really enjoy it. If I don't like it, I don't do it at all. I have a bad habit that way. I'm *undisciplined*.[2]

Another manager commented: "I get in at 7:30 A.M., get myself a cup of coffee, and look over my schedule. Then I'm off and running. I don't look up till about 4 P.M."

In telling his story, Bill Denton frequently spoke of "players" on a "football team" or of winners on a "playing field." This image of work at Amerco as a football game came up regularly in conversations with those at the top but was absent from discussions with those at the bottom. When women in the boardroom, who seldom if ever watched professional football, spoke of their careers, they often relied on this vision of players on a football field. When men on the assembly line who did watch pro football described their jobs, they didn't use this image. Chess, poker, Monopoly, hunting—any of these might have been more apt—but football was the prevalent imagery in the executive offices of Amerco.

Metaphors guide how we feel. The image of football focuses attention on an engrossing, competitive enterprise that calls for exquisitely close coordination among all members of a team. One is doing something right if speed feels exciting instead of silly or frightening. If work is a football game, it imparts vitality, urgency, the potential thrill of victory to the often mundane tasks at hand. More important, to think in football terms is to set aside the parts of life that exist "off the field." The relationship between work and family life naturally disappears as an issue.

Bill could be a "player" because of a prior understanding with his wife, who lived entirely off the field. As he described their relationship,

> We made a bargain. If I was going to be as successful as we both wanted, I was going to have to spend tremendous amounts of time at it. Her end of the bargain was that she wouldn't go out to work. So I was able to take the good stuff and she did the hard work—the car pools, dinner, gymnastic lessons. In those days, it was easier to do. All her friends were in the same boat. Today, I don't know what somebody would do if they chose to do what Emily did. There might not be any other homemakers to share this life with.
>
> Emily left Oakmont College after two years when we got married. After we had our son, she decided she preferred to

manage the home. Later, she finished her degree at Lawrence College, but even then, she felt the best use of her time was managing me and the family.

I really had it made. I worked very long hours and Emily just managed things. I never had to worry about getting the laundry, figuring out how to get the kids here and there. Emily made that her life's work. The kids did eventually go away to boarding school, but before that I arranged to go to school plays in the middle of the afternoon and sporting events that started at 4 P.M. When the kids wanted me to be there, I was there.

It was the ultimate privilege, Bill felt, to live with a wife who wasn't counting the coin of sacrifice. Emily, too, was "in management." But these days, Emily's "business," the home, was being marginalized. Women more than a decade younger than his wife were becoming the junior executives Bill managed. But Bill presented Emily as the Good Sport Housewife. She didn't feel left behind or mind, he said, being dependent on him. She had enjoyed raising their four children before they set off for boarding school, and she still declared herself happy rooting for Bill from the stands. For his part, Bill made it clear that he felt lucky compared to men and women in two-career families. He had more time.

Given this situation, Bill wasn't escaping home for work, or work for home. He wasn't seeking a "haven" for he had two safe worlds, though one of them overwhelmingly dominated the other.

It was no accident that the top executives I interviewed loved their work—their work did a lot to make itself lovable. Take the travel, however burdensome, that was such an integral part of an Amerco executive's life. The job often called for staying at hotels in which one might find a chocolate carefully placed on the pillow of one's bed, hear the early morning "sssh" as a newspaper slid under the door, sip coffee brought by room service, and savor that rarest of all commodities, time free of responsibility. These were details the wives sometimes envied. ("After all, he's there enjoying a feast. I'm here eating my peanut butter sandwich with the kids," one executive's wife confided wistfully, as we sat by a sandbox in the tots' lot of a local park.)

The smooth efficiency of hotel life appealed to such executives. The Hilton, the Marriott, the Hyatt Regency, and their more modest imitators cater to them, advertising themselves as convenient adjuncts to the office with their conference rooms, fax machines, and message services. Each also promotes itself as a "home on the road," the sort of home Amerco executives most value, in which their time, however long the hours, is somehow their own.

Room decor tends to the bland, with curtains, rugs, and bedspreads in muted colors meant to be unobtrusively soothing. Hotel rooms are to shape and color what elevator music is to sound. Their purpose is not to capture attention or interest, but to seem familiar, comforting. Hilton hotel rooms in Madrid, Paris, and Mexico are guaranteed to look remarkably similar to Hilton hotel rooms in Atlanta and San Francisco. Wherever in the world one is, one comes "home" to the "same" room. It may not be surprising, then, that the interiors of the homes of some Amerco managers bore a strong resemblance to hotel decor, helping give them the sense that they lived a seamless life "at home" wherever they happened to be.

It was these top male executives, living protected lives, adequate husbands and fathers by their own lights, who were expected to implement Amerco's new family-friendly policies. They were to be the first line of defense for the harried, time-starved employees below them, desperately juggling commitments at home and at work. Some of these men were members of the Amerco Corrective Action Team, which dealt with the allotment of family-friendly benefits. They were to understand a mass of employees whose concerns were so different from theirs that they might have been living on another planet.

Half of Amerco workers cared for children thirteen or under, for elderly relatives, or for both, or said on a survey that they expected to provide such care in the near future;[3] and most workers who cared for the young and old had working spouses who were as pressed for time as they were. Was there a way to help such workers balance their lives and benefit Amerco too? This was the question the CEO had asked Bill Denton to answer. Bill was skilled at taking on missions that required him to understand circumstances different from his own. He was by no means a self-centered or inflexible man. He knew that his subordinates might feel different pressures and need work schedules different from his.

Bill Denton was unusual among managers in his willingness to throw out the old rules. If a woman was the best "man" for the job, so be it. Nor did Bill avoid the problem of family needs by shying away from female employees, who he felt were the ones most likely to press the issue. Bill believed that new talent was often to be found among women with families and among men with working wives. The company that took advantage of this workforce and adapted to its needs would have a leg up in the battle for a share of the global market. Bill also knew that the issue of work-family balance was coming to his company, his division, his workplace. He did not think, as some top managers did, that work-family balance was a problem for only "5 percent." He didn't minimize the need for such policies, at least not on the surface.

But two things kept Bill from acting on his understanding of the problem: his sympathy for the family circumstances of Amerco's workers had to compete with other urgent company concerns, such as meeting production goals; and he lived in a social bubble among men who also worked very long hours, had (house)wives at home, and assumed the normality of this arrangement. These two factors may have made him impatient with the issue of work-family balance. At one point he blurted out, "I'm *tired* of dealing with it. I wish we could just be done with it."

Daddy Is at Work

Bill faced a dilemma. He was supposed to help create a more family-friendly workplace. But circumstances undermined his motivation to act forcefully to do so. He did implement some changes, though, in line with the new emphasis on family friendliness: he became a "good daddy"—at work.

Like many of his peers, Bill Denton had practically grown up at Amerco. It was in his thirty years with the company that many of his most significant rites of passage had taken place. It was there that he felt most secure. So he naturally came to view the office as the proper place to express family feeling.

As Bill saw it, home was ideally a branch office of Amerco, but in addition, Amerco should now feel like a home. Part of a manager's job, Bill felt, was to make work an emotionally comfortable environment in which to be efficient. His job, as he and his colleagues intuitively understood it, was to give work a homelike feel by taking on the daddy role there.[4] Bill himself made an effort to be continuously available to those he managed and to "motivate" them to work well and hard. But for some employees the meaning of his concern was more personal.

Men who were curtailing their own roles as fathers at home spent long hours with "fathers" like Bill at work. Among both women and men who had lost fathers to workaholism or divorce, many were now rediscovering as working adults what it was like to have a dad who taught them to do something, a dad who scolded, who demanded, who coaxed, who cared. At last, after all these years, they could actually catch his attention.

Bill was a better father at work than he had been at home—first of all in the sense that he was nearly always there. At the office, Bill found he could handle his employees' mistakes with an equanimity he had rarely been able to maintain with his own children. At the office, his "sons"—and more recently "daughters"—were generally grateful and eager to learn. At home, his own son had no desire to learn Bill's trade and now was asking where his father had been all those years of childhood.

In truth, it was hard for most of these executive father figures to imagine pulling themselves away from work. It was simply more satisfying being Dad here than anywhere else. As one of them put it,

I know I shouldn't be seen here as many hours as I am, because this is creating an unwritten message about work hours. But I'm here because I like it, and I have a lot to do on top of that. That's a real dilemma for me. Sometimes I think I ought to work in my library at home. But then I wouldn't be here, and that diminishes the amount of time I'm available to people. A lot of my job is to be available to people, to give encouragement, and once in a while, a good word. People like to know I'm here.

After the company introduced the Total Quality philosophy of management, Bill found himself calling one meeting after another to "monitor the process." In these sessions, Bill led by encouraging one person, praising another, teasing a third; while employees from different divisions got to see each other, chat, joke, and develop camaraderie. Periodically, he would become exasperated with the time spent this way—up to a third of many workdays—and would urge managers in his division to reduce the number and length of meetings they held. In one such mood he noted with disgust but also a barely disguised hint of satisfaction,

> Partly, people come to meetings to get hugs. Partly, they come for blessings: "Yes, my child, it will be all right." Partly, they come to be seen. Partly, they come to share risks. Partly, they come to get information. But why are we group-solving our problems? That's what individuals are paid to do. I'm not sure a great idea has ever come out of a meeting. We can downsize meetings. It's madness.

But after blowing off steam, Bill called another meeting. Sure, they ate up time and extended the day, but people wanted to attend them and, well, why not?

As with the Spotted Deer Childcare Center, Bill's workplace often seemed to outshine the family for which it was supposed to be a poor substitute, offering satisfactions that its employees had been brought up to believe only the family should give. It was there, not home, that many of his office children felt themselves most appreciated.

Still, there were limits. "Office fathers" had to take orders from an office father yet higher up, and sometimes they were ordered to do things that were "bad for the children." They had to get more work out of people. They had to demote and occasionally fire people. This was a company, after all, and there was work to be done. When layoffs were to be made, Amerco typically turned to outside consultants to "wear the black hat," perhaps because to have done otherwise would have undermined the bond between workers and managers.

Being a good father at work came easily to Bill Denton, given his traditional idea of fatherhood and given his relationship to his own first boss at Amerco. As he explained,

> When I started with this company, my supervisor's first speech was this: "You've got young children at home. There are going to be plays, ballet recitals, soccer games. I expect you're going to need to go to those, and you should find the time to make that happen—but I'll still hold you accountable for the job getting done." I can't believe that these days managers don't say the same thing to their employees. I don't know what the problem is.

"Fatherhood" brought to Bill's mind an image of a child's performance—the part of childhood that comes closest to being a career. Like a business meeting, each concert or soccer game is a slot in time scheduled in advance by someone else. A concert recital might start at 2 P.M. and end at 3:30 P.M. A soccer game might go from 4 to 6 P.M., a play from 8 to 10 P.M. When Bill spoke of being a good father or of balancing work and family life, what came to mind were these well-bounded events in the "careers" of his children, extracurricular equivalents to the events of his day.

In addition to such performances, medical emergencies also seemed legitimate reasons for a good father to take time off from his job. A car accident, a football injury, a sudden illness might draw him out of even the most important meeting. Work demands

stopped at the hospital door. Focused on performances and emergencies—the best times and the worst, he said—he knew little about
those times when his children were offstage, unable to get started on
something, discouraged, or confused. True, Bill lived in a town
where work was near home. But something in Bill's ideas about
fatherhood and time made the everyday part of home life seem very
far away.

Sons and daughters now grown, many managers did look back
on their fathering years with a kind of mild regret that they had
spent so little time with their children. Perhaps this simply reflected
the influence of new ideas about fatherhood, even on these "ten-
hour players" in their fifties. "Did you have enough time with your
boys when they were growing up?" I asked one manager reputed to
have blocked a paternity leave for a gifted young engineer in his
plant. He replied,

> No. No. Well, the youngest one, yes. But I didn't bond well
> with my oldest child. Being the ambitious person I was, I
> worked incredibly long hours when I first started. We have a
> good relationship now, but I look back and I didn't get wise
> soon enough. I didn't take vacations for the first six years of
> my oldest child's life.

"If you had it to do over again," I asked, "would you do anything differently?" Here, he hesitated,

> I don't know. I can't answer that. Probably not. I'll tell you
> why. I was the youngest of six kids, the only one to go to
> college. My father was a machinist on the railroad in Peoria,
> Illinois. When I was in high school, he was laid off from
> work. It was a crushing experience for him, and for me. I
> wanted to do it differently.

His own success at work, his stilling of the memory of his father's
failure, these were more important to him than being a good father

at home, even in retrospect. As for Bill Denton, he avoided the question by putting it this way: "I'm pleased with how my kids came out."

It was not these top executives but their wives who spoke ruefully of their husbands' absences from family life. One whose husband had been fired from an unprofitable division came close to a breakdown in Amerco's Office of Career Transitions. Sitting next to her husband, she exploded at the young outplacement officer:

> My husband missed our children's *birthdays*! He missed their *games*! He missed the father-daughter *banquets*! Didn't the company get *enough* of his time? Because we saw *nothing* of him!

When top male managers themselves spoke of regrets for that lost time with children at home, it often took the form of a report on what their wives thought. One noted,

> My wife would tell you she missed me playing the role of father. She would tell you she was both mother and father. She's there to see firsthand what the costs are for our kids, so her insights would be better.

Another recalled,

> Only after twenty years did my wife tell me that she was hurt when I told her my job was my number one priority and my family was number two. I'm not sure I even remember having said it, but I'm sure I did.

Some of these executives were beginning to find the post–child-raising years unsettling at home, but this only reinforced their commitment to long hours at work. To be sure there were tantrums, rivalries, and strains at work, but for many of them, these were minor matters compared to the problems flaring up at home. Difficult as work could be, the exhausted executive's life there was more predictable and more protected from bad feelings than his life at home. It was in family life that the most troubling questions arose—Am I really worthy of love? Do I really love? These were not questions executives generally had to face straight on at Amerco. One's deepest motivations were more vulnerable to critical scrutiny at home than at the office, with its comforting, built-in limits. As one executive confided:

> I told my wife I work long hours at the office for her, but she doesn't believe it. She says I just work for myself, because I put in long hours when I know she doesn't want me to.

Some wives believed their husband used work as a mistress, and they often blamed the mistress, not the man. When one executive suddenly dropped dead of a heart attack, his grieving widow invited no one from the company to speak at the funeral. "Why should I?" she exclaimed to a friend. "It was the *company* that killed him!"

Widowed by their husband's long hours, if not by heart attacks, some women developed separate lives in the company of other executive wives. Involved in school or civic events, some of them came to feel that they no longer needed their husbands quite as much as they once had. At the same time, a number of the older homemakers, who had genuinely enjoyed their family lives, now found themselves feeling marginalized and slightly anxious at company cocktail parties where the main question people wanted to ask was "What do you *do*?"

Few of these wives seriously considered "leaving the bleachers" to join the "game." For the most part, they eschewed careers and disapproved of working wives who put in the hours their husbands did. Bill Denton often came home to his wife's dinner-table horror stories about negligent mothers with demanding careers, stories she'd heard from other homemakers who also had learned of them secondhand. Like Emily Denton, many of these mothers found themselves part of a dwindling band of volunteers at school, the Girl Scout troop, or the church Christmas pageant. "I think I'll scream if I hear one more time, '*I . . . can't . . . help . . . out,*' " a homemaker friend of Emily's declared, breaking into a singsong, " '*I* have to *work.*' " As community volunteers, it seemed harder these days to feel that they were doing desirable work for an appreciative community.

Given this work and family culture among top executives at Amerco, Bill took up the question of company family-friendly policies with a curiously split consciousness. Part of the time, he spoke as if there was hardly any problem at all. "In a small town like this," he explained, "you're a minute away from your house. Just get in the car and go. I did. I made my son's soccer games."

But when pressed, he slipped almost imperceptibly into a different line of reasoning. As all top managers did, Bill began talking about time as if it were hardwired not just to workers' skills but to their career aspirations. He refused to accept, he declared, the meritocratic principle suggested by some, "Judge the work, not the face time." His belief in flexibility stood in direct contradiction to one unbending principle: The time a worker works in and of itself, has to count as much as the results accomplished within that time. Time is a symbol of commitment.

Whether time mattered more than results was a key point of contention. But it became buried in the company's rhetoric. In an hour and a half meeting of the Corrective Action Team that I attended, Bill assembled a group of employees drawn from different sectors of the company to help implement and monitor Amerco's family-friendly policies. Bill sat with five other team members intently reviewing possible expressions of "Amerco's philosophy" with regard to work-family balance. Should it be:

Consistent with our valuing the individual, we believe it essential that our people lead balanced lives.

Or

> We recognize the legitimacy of the demands and pressures of
> our employees' lives outside work.

Or

> We believe that a solid work ethic is an important foundation
> block upon which a career can be built. However, hard work
> is not an end in itself, and alone, is not valued in and of itself.

Or

> Tired, overworked people, worried about their children,
> parents, and other nonwork issues do not give their best
> effort to the job, nor can they be expected to.

By the end of the meeting, the committee had settled on the first statement. But the basic question—Did the company evaluate employees based on their output or their work schedules?—remained only half-addressed. When Amy Truett asked Bill, "How would you define 'commitment'?" He answered immediately:

> I don't think we can get commitment with less than fifty or
> sixty hours a week. That's what other corporations are doing.
> To be competitive, that's what we need to do. In my gut, I
> can't believe we can do it very differently.

A chorus of voices arose in protest. But no one quite dared to ask the underlying questions. What is a "balanced life" then? With this kind of commitment, what room is left for family?

Top executives in another division of Amerco responded to Amerco's statement on work-family balance with less sympathy than Bill had when it appeared in an office memo a week later. Generally, they saw balance as strictly a woman manager's problem and so a limited one: a job share here, a part-time position there, and everything would be fine.

One thoughtful thirty-year-old male junior manager described to me a meeting of top executives who responded angrily, though confidentially, to the memo. His own childhood family had disintegrated as his parents spent less and less time at home, and finally divorced. "Now my mother lives in a small apartment in Orange County, California. My father married again and lives in Texas. I don't know where the crib I slept in as a baby is. I don't know where any of my old toys are. They must have given them away." Disguised in a seventy-hour-a-week company uniform, he spoke as a potential defector from an uncaring system:

> I was reporting on the results of a climate survey in my division. I said that the people I worked with wanted a better balance between work and family. I got it right between the eyes. Dave blew up at me: "Don't *ever* bring up 'balance' again! I don't want to hear about it! Period! Everyone in this company has to work hard. *We* work hard. *They* have to work hard. That's the way it is. Just because a few women are concerned about balance doesn't mean we change the rules. If they chose this career, they're going to have to pay for it in hours, just like the rest of us."

Another young male manager who had won the confidence of a group of top executives "leaked" this account of a conversation about family-friendly policies:

> The older guys had a meeting. They were asking themselves, "What's happening? Why are we being challenged?" They think that they're being criticized by the women. The way they managed their lives and the way they were brought up is being challenged. That is a major threat, and they won't tolerate it. They are starting to understand that this is serious stuff.

The anger and intensity of the response from managers in this division of Amerco signaled how fundamentally the new policies contradicted cherished notions of office life.

The increasingly acrimonious debate over the need for family-friendly flexibility set Bill Denton to thinking about a problem that was more relevant to his own life than he had originally believed. Toward the end of our interview, he talked about his three daughters and one son:

> Now that they're all in their twenties and they all work, their phone calls home are different. When my daughters were in boarding school, they would phone their mother and then talk to me at the end, to humor me. Now that they work, they want to talk to me: "Oh my God, you're not going to believe what my boss said," and "Should I try for this promotion?" Then, at the end, "Is Mom there?"

> Dawn, my oldest daughter, has worked for five years since graduating from college, but she wants to be a homemaker, like her mother. Her fiancé is a corporate lawyer. My second daughter, Jan, is a terrific student, superior athlete, driven, competitive, and has no desire to marry and have children. My youngest, Katie, just started graduate school and wants to have a career and a family. I think the road will be roughest for her. But it'll be hard for my son too. He's twenty-nine. His wife is an engineer, and they just had their first child. I don't know how they're going to work that out.

The issue of work-family balance had come home. After our interview ended, as Bill was walking me to his office door, he brought up the topic of women managers who race home after a grueling day to put dinner on the table and read to the children. His parting comment, one I was to hear again and again from top executives at just such closing moments, was "I don't know *how* they do it."

CHAPTER 6

The Administrative Mother

A day in the life of Vicky King revealed a paradox. She was known among managers as a strong advocate of flexible schedules. Her division had won awards for reducing errors and decreasing the time between orders and shipments over the previous three years, and this success gave her the confidence to go out on a limb on the question of time. Unlike Bill Denton, she judged most of her 150 workers by their work, not by the hours they put in. I asked her how many in her plant could work irregular or shorter schedules without a loss of efficiency. To my amazement, she answered, "85 percent." She explained,

> I need 15 percent core workers who work regular hours or longer. If benefits for part-timers were prorated, there would be no cost—in money or efficiency—to splitting one job into two, or two jobs into three, or instituting flex-time. It would probably increase the plant's efficiency. Workers would have to redesign their jobs, that's all. I'm all for it.[1]

Yet, paradoxically, Vicky herself lived the hard-driving, tightly scheduled, long-hours work life of Bill Denton. The only difference was that Bill Denton had his wife to care for children and home. Vicky had a son, a daughter, and an obliging husband who had no magical solutions to the problem of too much work and too little time at home. More than almost anyone at Amerco, she stood staunchly for the right to flexible, shorter hours. One afternoon she asked me,

> Did you ever see that film *Nine to Five*? Remember in the end how the women set up on-site daycare, they come and go on flextime? They job-share. And the business actually runs better because it's based on trust and flexibility. I loved that film. That's my vision.

But to be credible as an executive, Vicky worked inflexible, long hours. Her stand on time was family friendly; her life was centered on work.

People instinctively liked Vicky. A tall, lanky forty-five-year-old woman with graying blond hair, she walked the halls of Amerco with great long strides and laughed with gusto. She typically wore a linen skirt suit, a jacket with modest shoulder pads, and a pastel-colored blouse loose around the chest. This style reflected neither the latest fashions nor her personal taste but Amerco managerial norms in dress, which changed from time to time, informally and collectively.

As with many of Amerco's rising male stars, Vicky's career success held great personal meaning for her. She had grown up in a small midwestern family that was always on the financial edge. Her father ran a grocery store, and her mother was a housewife who was chronically anxious about the possibility of bad news, and usually unprepared when it actually arrived. After Vicky left home for college, her mother called at the end of each semester fretfully warning that the money would soon run dry and Vicky would have to drop out. With scholarships, jobs, and pluck, Vicky nonetheless put herself through engineering school. In the position she held at Amerco, she continually turned her mother's behavior inside out. If her mother waited for calamity to strike before acknowledging its existence, Vicky predicted problems with uncanny accuracy and made plans to avert them. Predict and avert, that's what she did for a living.

Happily married on a second try to Kevin, she had an eight-year-old son and a four-year-old daughter. Vicky and Kevin shared the "second shift," but under the increasing demands of two long-hour careers, that shift was becoming an ever smaller part of their life.

For Vicky, work was a well-ordered, high-pressure world in which she could blossom as a competent, helpful "mother." She created a homey atmosphere within a buzzing larger community, where all sorts of small dramas unfolded. Work was interesting to do, be in, and watch. Vicky was not exactly avoiding her home, but she worked hard to limit its pull on her life. She reported candidly on her return to work six weeks after the birth of her first child:

> People said to me, "You only took six weeks maternity leave?" I answered, "Gee, guys, that was six weeks I didn't have anybody to talk to. My friends are at work. The things that interest me are at work. My stimulation is at work. I am *delighted* to come back."

Vicky measured parenting, as Bill Denton did, by how well her children were doing, not how much time she spent with them. Unlike Bill, however, she did not define her involvement in terms of numbers of athletic events or school plays attended. Just as Vicky brought a maternal presence to the office, so she brought administrative skill to mothering Kevin Jr. and Janey. She was often calling to make arrangements with gym and piano teachers, a playground director, and two babysitters. During the week, she was an outsourcing mom; she only became a hands-on mom on sunny weekends at the family's mountain cottage. But despite her heroic efforts to be a mother-manager, she often felt she was coming up short. "I have never felt this out of control in my entire career," Vicky told me one day. "I came home from a business trip and looked at a note

I'd left for Cammy [the babysitter] to pick up Kevin Jr. at a different time on the weeks he's in camp. I had the wrong month *and* the wrong week. I said to myself, 'Oh my God, I'm slipping at work and home. There's no more left.' "

What was the solution to the Kings' time scarcity? Had they lived in China, grandparents might be raising their children while she and her husband did "productive labor." Had they lived in a Ghanaian village, her sister might have pitched in while she sold goods at the market. In the New England of the 1800s, Kevin Jr. might have been placed as a millwright's apprentice in a neighboring family short of boys. But in this town in the middle of America in the 1990s, no such options were available. Vicky's parents lived far away, and Kevin's were not disposed to help out much. The Kings' babysitter was a bright, ambitious college student who was planning to move on toward her own career soon. In the end, Vicky and Kevin were it, and they were hiring a great deal of help.

Vicky wore the same ten-hour time-uniform Bill Denton did, and added to such a schedule her role as domestic manager. However, she had no choice but to let go of the other jobs Bill's wife did—entertaining friends, cultivating a garden, doing needlepoint, looking in on elderly relatives, or volunteering to raise funds for the local school. The needlepoint Vicky could do without, but visiting her aged aunt—well, she wished she had the time to do that.

Bill Denton and Vicky King, male and female executives, fit a larger pattern. According to a 1990 Amerco survey, top-payroll men like Bill put in slightly longer hours at work than did their female counterparts, but adding together work at office and home, the "Bills" put in seventy-five hours a week while the "Vickys" put in ninety-six.[2]

Women who work also find that their efforts to balance job and family can place them in direct conflict with mothers who stay home. To arrange for Kevin Jr. to get to school, for example, Vicky called on a neighboring stay-at-home mom, Beverly, whose son, also eight, was one of Kevin Jr.'s playmates. Vicky suggested the boys set out at 8 A.M. each morning, as Vicky's job started at 8:15 A.M. and school at 8:30 A.M. Rolling her eyes, Vicky recalled,

Beverly told me, "Can't we just talk by phone at 8 A.M. each morning to figure out how to get the kids to school? Sometimes I like to let him sleep in. Sometimes he wants to go early." Then Beverly snapped and the truth came out: "*I decided to stop working so I could have flexibility.* I'm not giving that up now to accommodate *your* schedule!"

Beverly had reluctantly renounced her career in order to stay home with her child. Perhaps, like the hapless farmer's son in the LaFontaine fable, she secretly feared she had traded a fine cow for an old donkey, and the donkey for a hen. Now a stick was being offered for the hen, and she was determined to refuse that "stick"— that strict eight o'clock departure.

Beverly had adopted a homemaker's sense of child time. She was building spacious temporal castles around the early events of her child's life, starting with the moment he was to wake up. Holding down a career, to her, meant locking a child in a temporal prison, walled in by the rigid demands of work life. If a woman wanted to be a good mother, not a prison warden, she should give up her career, Beverly thought.

Vicky thought the problem was Beverly's. The 8 A.M. send-off was, as she saw it, the beginning of a happy day, not prison life, for Kevin Jr. Being a good mother meant knowing when her son's sailboat painting was coming home from after-school painting class, hearing about his playground friends and foes, not necessarily sitting home, awaiting his arrival. It was staying in touch with her son by phone, being responsible for having his needs met, even if she wasn't the one meeting them. Being a good mother meant choosing the right day camp and the right babysitter for her children. If Beverly's time with her child was less planned, more flexible, slower paced, more like time in a late-nineteenth-century haven from industrialism, such time for Vicky was a little more like time at work.

Vicky and Beverly had fallen on opposite sides of a strange temporal dividing line for women—ten-hour days on the one hand, no-hour days on the other. Until now, the two had been friends,

mother to mother. Vicky quickly smoothed over the small immediate crisis but, wary now, arranged for Kevin Jr. to walk to school
with the son of another working mom, an ally on her side of the
line. Now the two working mothers and their sons were friends,
while Beverly and Vicky seldom talked.

Vicky's husband, Kevin King, was a tall, lean, affable man with
an active dental practice in town. He wanted to be a full-fledged
father to his children, but he worried that he might be using parenting as an escape from a conflict he faced in his career. If, to
Vicky, work had been a way out of a childhood of emotional con-
striction and economic uncertainty, Kevin's work felt like an ill-
marked path through a series of booby traps. The son of a respected
orthodontist, Kevin carried on in the same profession, but his father
found fault with him at nearly every turn. Kevin took refuge from
this criticism in an avocation. A gifted artist, he began to paint
soulful, wind-torn landscapes that he exhibited in local art shows, to
which his father paid short, dutiful visits.

Meanwhile, his wife rose higher and higher at Amerco. For
Kevin, each of Vicky's steps up was a source of pride, but also of
unease. He enjoyed her energy and shared her joy, but one evening
at a Lion's Club dinner during which members were good-
naturedly "taxed" for some new piece of luck, Kevin was "taxed"
for Vicky's latest promotion. His fellow Lions ribbed him, "Now
you can retire, Kevin. Let Vicky bring in the money." He took it in
good humor, but that night as they were dropping off to sleep, he
asked Vicky with more anxiety than he meant to betray, "When do
you think all this talk will die down?"

Vicky's success created a dilemma for Kevin, but one so disguised by a happy marriage and two beautiful children that he felt
he had no right to complain. The children needed more parental
time, and frankly he, Kevin, *could* spend more time with them. But
it was still remarkably hard in a midwestern town in the 1990s for a
man like Kevin to get the public approbation he felt he deserved for
all he did at home. In the eyes of other people being a father
was very different from being a mother. Devoted as he was to his
children, spending more time with them only made it harder to

improve his public identity. Yet he knew that to expand his practice would lead to still more criticism from his father.

Faced with Vicky's rise and his own anxieties about public perception, Kevin began half-consciously to match Vicky, work commitment for work commitment. If Vicky had an unavoidable 5 to 6:30 P.M. meeting every Tuesday night for a month, Kevin would find that in his new position at the Lions he couldn't say no to any of their Wednesday evening discussions of finances. If Vicky had to travel in November, Kevin found reason to travel the following February. It wasn't exactly competition; it was matching. As Kevin saw it, this matching kept them even in the eyes of the world if he was home as much as Vicky, but not a second more. In this way, time spent at home came to signal weakness, not only to outsiders but within the marriage itself. And the family lost out.

By contrast, at work, Vicky put the force of her being behind the principle of flexible management and evaluation by results. If Bill Denton and others like him claimed that time, results, and credit were an indissoluble package, Vicky firmly disagreed whenever the chance arose. A fresh, rested dynamo, she insisted, "could cut through a pile of work like a sushi chef fan-chopping mushrooms." Why, she would ask, reward the guy who takes the longest time to do the job?

Vicky had learned about certain half-hidden practices at Amerco by listening to colleagues from other divisions discuss requests for time off. Two "high potential" men had asked their supervisor for a year off to travel around the world and do underwater photography of Australian coral reefs. "I want them back," their supervisor had explained sheepishly, "so we gave them an 'educational' leave."

If supervisors could make such large exceptions for "high potential men," Vicky pointed out, why couldn't they offer flexible schedules to parents who wanted to pick up their kids at 4:30 P.M. instead of 5:30 P.M.? So Vicky started collecting exceptions—"coral reefs," she called them. Dan Danforth was known to clear his calendar regularly between 11 A.M. and 1 P.M. to do real estate deals. He didn't *ask* his boss, but his boss knew and because Dan was a prodigious worker didn't complain. That qualified as a kind of coral reef. To enhance the cohesion of the Amerco sales teams, the various regional divisions went out for afternoon golf games from 1 to 5 P.M. about six times a year, always just before they took off on their road trips. Secretaries drove the golf carts, packed cold sodas in ice chests, cheered good shots. The trips were solemnly defended as an aid to cooperation and had become a custom, "almost work" but also another kind of coral reef.

If you looked hard enough, there were others as well. In 1975, Amerco had instituted a "40 percent system," whereby an employee could "retire" at age fifty, fifty-five, or sixty-five and then work 40 percent of his or her previous time. As one plant manager noted, "The 40 percent plan is very successful. We get their expertise. They get the balance they want." "Why," Vicky wondered, "couldn't Amerco implement a plan for young parents that it already successfully applied to older men?"

With her collection of coral reefs in mind, one day over lunch Vicky began to argue with Bill about the ways in which time and work were linked. Bill claimed that the sheer amount of time people were in their offices at Amerco did something for the workplace. Vicky lived according to that belief, but she didn't embrace it. After all, what was work? "Employees talked about it as if their jobs were clear, solid, defined," Vicky told me. But how much of a manager's job, she wondered, was simply being a good daddy to fatherless workers? And how necessary was this sort of work? Was it in fact work at all?

Without long expanses of time at the office, Bill claimed, the Amerco workplace wouldn't hum. To make it hum, inevitably one had to tend to human relationships. A well-functioning football team is basically a set of smoothly meshing relationships, Bill argued, and those relationships need nurturing, and this nurturing takes time. Bill staunchly defended his role as homemaker at work; while Vicky questioned the whole idea that there should be any equivalent at work to planting the garden, mowing the lawn, or playing with the kids—the very activities she was forced to curtail or eliminate at home. At home, of course, it was usually men who questioned the necessity of keeping the house tidy, the windows washed, the bathtub clean. It was men who promoted a strategy of "needs reduction." Now Vicky was intent on applying the same criteria to Bill Denton's "housekeeping" at work. By dessert, though far from a resolution, they had made a truce on this issue, and talk turned to children's impossibly difficult science projects, camping adventures, and other topics that affirmed their common ground.

The Unfinished Dance

At home, Vicky was locked in another struggle that refused to resolve itself—this time with her four-year-old daughter Janey. At work, Vicky was fighting to convince Bill that work and productivity were separate, that one could accomplish as much or more without being a ten- or eleven-hour player. At home, Janey was making her own case to Vicky that she needed the time for which Vicky was arguing.

The summer had seemed especially busy, and Janey-Vicky time had been unusually limited. During the week, Janey was enrolled in day camp. Her mornings began at 7 A.M., when Vicky woke her and helped her dress in preparation for her 7:30 A.M. day camp departure. Cammy, the babysitter, picked Janey and her brother up from camp at 5 P.M. and sometimes took them both out for dinner, not arriving home until 7 P.M. This had been fairly typical of Janey's Monday-through-Friday life. On Saturdays the family threw away the clock and drove off to their mountain vacation cottage for the weekend. At least that was the idea. But the previous weekend Janey had stayed with cousins while her parents had had a much needed, long awaited, night alone together. Vicky, whose job took her out of town from time to time, had also been away for a number of days in the last few weeks. This, as Vicky freely admitted, was pushing the idea of quality time to Janey's limit.

On this Thursday evening, when Cammy and the children came in, they found four adults—Mommy, Daddy, and two guests (I was one)—in the kitchen. Kevin Jr. skipped in to report on his day's activities. Janey hung back, clutching her blanket. "Mommy," she mumbled, clearly disgruntled to see us there. Only Mommy could greet her. Gradually, coaxed by both parents, Janey inched into the kitchen. Cammy smoothly and sympathetically filled in episodes from Janey's day that Janey refused to report. Addressing both children and adults, she gracefully bridged the gap. Later Vicky told me, "Cammy is real management material. I'm going to try to get her a job at Amerco."

During the adults' dinner, Janey was "invited" to take a toy out to the screen porch "where there's more room," and later still, she was urged to try out the swings in the backyard. After a short swing, however, Janey was back again, standing silently by her mother's chair.

Suddenly, as dinner was ending, to everyone's pleasant surprise, Janey announced that she wanted to do a dance. Her father rose from the table, went to the record player in the living room, and put on Janey's favorite dance music. Janey stood facing us, as from a stage. All eyes were on her—her hopeful parents, the polite guests, the helpful babysitter, and her "good" brother. She waited a few moments, then began. She danced a series of twirls to the right, then a series of twirls to the left. Then, looking directly at her mother, she collapsed on the floor in a heap of tangled limbs. "Go on," her mother urged gently. "Don't stop in the middle." The guests held their expectant half-smiles. It seemed the whole world waited and that somewhere a giant clock was ticking. Finally, Janey stood up. Again time stretched out while she remained motionless. "Okay," said her father reasonably, "if you don't want to finish the dance, then I'll have to turn off the music. You have one last chance to finish the dance." No, the dance was half-done but Janey *was* finished.

Cammy, who had positioned herself to protect the dinner party from the children, but also to allow for some check-in time with the parents suggested: "I think Janey is t-i-r-e-d." After reasoning with Janey, disregarding her, then reasoning again, Vicky put her napkin down with gentle deliberation, rose from the table, and drew Janey out of sight, though not fully out of earshot. Janey let go a mighty protest: *"Why? . . . Early . . . Want to. . . . Not fair!"*

We could hear Vicky replying in firm, soothing tones that sounded like well-worn steps up a ladder: *"If you . . . then I . . . We have to . . . We always . . ."* Taking the brunt of her daughter's ire, Vicky gently picked Janey up and carried her off to bed. Tomorrow, after all, was another busy day with another early start.

What was going on? Was Janey's unfinished dance simply the kind of thing kids do sometimes? Or was Janey perhaps saying, "I know you'd like me to perform well in front of your guests, but if you won't give *me* time, then I won't give *you* time, and I won't finish my dance." Maybe Janey was staging a kind of sit-down strike against a speedup on the domestic factory floor: "More quality time! More quality time!"

In the King household, both parents felt they were equally committed to doing the second shift. But Vicky spent more time coping with the children's resentment at having so little time with their parents. Vicky often tried to explain to Janey her view that love should not be measured by time spent together. She suggested that summer weekdays were mainly for work and day camp, while weekends were the appropriate time for them to relax as a family. The time for love, of course, was *all* the time, whether they were with each other or not. From Janey's point of view, though, weekdays, even at a day camp she liked, were too long. The result—for Vicky—was a lengthy first shift, an expeditious second shift, and an unacknowledged third shift, in which she desperately tried to make up emotionally for her child's unhappiness over a lack of family time.

Vicky was urging Janey to accept a promissory note against future parental payment. The bargain was this: If you're a good girl and "do your job" by being on your own from Monday through Friday, I promise to give you a great deal of attention on the weekend.

This bargain raised a new set of questions, though: How did Janey feel about this arrangement, and what could her mother do to influence her feelings? Given the fact that the situation was not likely to change, how should both mother and daughter deal with their feelings? A surprising amount of Vicky's scarce parenting time was spent working out answers to these abiding questions, or simply fending the questions off. In the meantime, Vicky was teaching Janey how to live on time credit. "If Mommy works now," Janey was learning, "she owes me play time later." But just how much time did Mommy owe Janey, and where was it to be and when? These issues remained to be negotiated. And Janey, young as she was, was mastering the art of bill collecting.

Vicky King was leading a work life that resembled Bill Denton's; but without a wife like his to call on, she was passing on the temporal costs of her career to her children, one of whom was fighting back. By the time Vicky rejoined the group at the dinner table, the storm was over. Everyone was quick to agree that Janey was t-i-r-e-d, her usual sort of crankiness at the end of a long day. Her brother had adapted himself better to his parents' long work hours. He did extremely well in school, which seemed proof in itself that all was well. His mother told me contentedly, "Kevin Jr.'s a good boy." His father agreed, and the babysitter, now retreating to the kitchen, left behind her vote, "Yes, he is. Janey was just tired." But did the unfinished dance tell a different story?

CHAPTER 7

"All My Friends Are Worker Bees":
Being a Part-Time Professional

The full-time people are just drowning. . . . You don't
want to go part time—you'll fall behind.

Two statements from the same interview
with a manager in the Finance Division

A family photo on an office wall is like a handshake: it introduces us
to a person. In a way, the difference in viewpoint between Vicky
King and Bill Denton was expressed in the family photos that ran
across the desks, down the halls, and through the buildings of
Amerco. The placement and content of these pictures varied
according to the position and gender of the person displaying them.
Men at the top like Bill Denton tended to have large individual
color photos showing the children in studio poses, or in shots taken
at important ceremonial moments (a graduation, a wedding, a chris-
tening), or at moments of familial adventure (rafting through white
water, pausing on a ski slope, lowering the jib on a sailboat). The
images seemed to say, I *do* make time for my children, and here they
are enjoying it. The more formal shots favored faces in close-up,
and their message seemed to be: Unlike some workaholic fathers, I
really know my children. Such photos, mounted like degrees, were
usually placed behind the executive ("Like football trophies," said
one junior manager tartly at a women's luncheon, a remark greeted
with an abrupt collective laugh of recognition). Seldom were family
photos found on the desks of male executives by their phones, or

next to their in-boxes. The pictures, it seemed, weren't for the executive himself to see, but for the seated visitor whom they faced over the man's shoulder. Photos of much older children, which might alert the visitor to the possibility of previous marriages, were displayed, as one observer noted, "on a case-by-case basis."

At the banks of desks in windowless inner spaces where women answered phones and typed reports for managers and professionals, one could see small, unframed photos discreetly placed beside word processors or telephones, or taped to walls where working mothers could see them. Photo displays in clerical offices often mixed formal school shots of individual children and informal shots of everybody in the kitchen at Christmas or in front of the house at a family reunion. These photos seemed like personal mementos, informal reminders of other lives, and they coexisted with children's drawings of beaming suns, lopsided cats, or, in one case, a zebra stepping confidently into a void.

Women managers—especially in male-dominated divisions—were caught between cultures. They tended to display neither large trophy photos, nor intimate snapshots of recent events. Instead, credentials—such as diplomas—and awards often hung on the walls behind them. Family photos were either missing or small and few in number.

Women managers and professionals seemed to find even the subject of family photographs a difficult one. Most said little about them, even when asked. However, one manager who worked very long hours in a predominantly male office declared with great feeling,

> When I first came to work here, there was a rule that you had to have a frame around anything you put on the wall. But the pictures of my children don't have frames on them, so I didn't feel free to put their pictures out at first. But these are my kids. I want to look at them. I don't have frames on them, and I never will!

Frameless they hung. But it was through their photo-less offices that most such women signaled that they were neither "one of the boys" nor quite "one of the girls." As a female manager who had tried without success to work 80 percent time explained, "Women on a career track make a conscious effort to tell the men they work with, 'I am not a mother and wife. I'm a colleague.' " At a day-long company seminar on "valuing diversity," a woman engineer and mother of four had explained sheepishly in front of a gathering of perplexed managers and uncomfortable female secretaries why the decision to "hang" or not to "hang" was a difficult one for a professional woman: "If I have my pictures on the desk, the men will think I'm a secretary." An offended secretary rose before the group to deliver a passionate oration in defense of her occupation, her photo display, and the way she balanced work and family life. For her, the three went together.

In factories, there were no office walls, no expanses of desk, and so no places for pictures of children. Occasionally, taped to the inside of a locker door, one could see a photo, not of a child, but of a smiling fisherman next to a dangling marlin or a triumphant hunter beside a glassy-eyed twelve-point buck. Family photos often emerged, however, midway through interviews with working mothers in the factory breakroom—from plastic holders in wallets, thick with small color photos of children, sisters, brothers, nieces, nephews, stepchildren, or sometimes ex-in-laws whom the bearer was "still close to."

In addition to such status variations in the type and display of photographs, there were also differences between one company division and another. The more rigidly hierarchical the division, the fewer family photos; the more informal and team-based, the more photos came out. The closer a worker's office was to Amerco central headquarters and the more formal the dress and office atmosphere, the more often pictures went behind, rather than in front of, the worker.

Photo displays symbolized an employee's willingness to say, "Here at work, please know that I have a family." For top managers like Bill Denton, having family photos meant I take an enormous amount of time from my family for my work, and since I do this despite the fact that I love my family, you can see how committed I am to work. For secretaries, having family photos often meant: I have another life. I may be subordinate here, but I express myself fully at home. For factory hands, and especially for the women among them, family photos sometimes meant: I may not be the boss here, but I have another life where I am.

Taken together, those hundreds of workers' photos represented a phantom world of the family—of people who believed in those workers, urged them forward, held them back, weighed them down, gave them a reason to be alive. Those photos were also an important reminder that however much work filled an emotional void left by real families and came to simulate family life, those real families, in all their complexity, were still there.

Inside a few of those photo-lined offices sat professionals who actually were trying to shorten their work hours. Shorter hours did sound to some Amerco employees like a real family-friendly solution to their pressed lives—if one could get them on the right terms. This was the thinking of Eileen Watson, a thirty-year-old ceramics engineer who worked in a predominantly male engineering division of Amerco and proudly set out photos of her one-year-old Hannah and husband Jim on her desk. The photos were small but there were five of them. "When men come into my office, most glance at the photos without commenting," Eileen told me. "When women come in, quite a few will say, 'How cute. How old is your baby?' "

The first time I met Eileen, she bounded into my borrowed office at Amerco with Hannah in a back carrier and Jim following her, toting a Santa Claus–sized canvas bag of paraphernalia. Eileen and Jim alternated telling their story as if weaving a braid. Eileen began. Little Hannah woke up; Jim lifted her out, continuing Eileen's tale while rocking the child. Eileen waited a bit, then took over again. Between them, they relayed the saga of Eileen's attempt to go part time:

> While Jim was going to engineering school, I was working sixty to seventy hours a week. I was Little Miss Career. I worked myself into being an expert on my product line and traveled to Germany and Japan. For eleven years I scratched

and clawed my way up to becoming a respected expert. I
wouldn't have *dreamed* of working part time. I worked up to
the day before I gave birth and was going to come back a few
weeks later.

I'm not a homemaker by temperament, I don't have any
friends in the neighborhood. All my friends are worker bees,
and I love my work too. I just don't get the same thrill at
home that I do from the data chase at work. So, it's because
of my child and only her that I want to be home.

I asked where she felt the most appreciated for her accomplishments.

I'm very good at what I do, and people at work appreciate
that. I don't get the same feelings of accomplishment at
home. I wish I did. I envy women who do. They have the
harder job, but I find home boring. I don't have anything to
do but wait until Hannah wakes up.

Nevertheless, shortly after Hannah was born, Eileen decided she
wanted to give up her exciting time at work and expand the more
"boring" time at home. Jim said he was considering making the
same sacrifice. They talked over who should take more time out and
jointly decided that Eileen should try to cut back to 60 percent for a
few years. As a recently hired worker at Amerco, Jim felt he was the
more vulnerable, and his supervisor was suspected of being a
"Neanderthal" on paternity leave. Eileen said, "Jim can't think of
asking for shorter hours."

So it fell to her to try to cut her hours. Sixty percent time
seemed right to her—not forever, but for now. She was at a level at
Amerco, she told me, below which assertiveness is considered abra-
sive in a woman and above which people wonder why women
don't push harder. So Eileen didn't know how aggressively to
pursue shorter hours. To make matters worse, she explained, "My
boss works ungodly amounts of time. I know there's friction

between him and his wife about it because he often buys her roses and almost never spends time at home."

Eileen approached her boss cautiously, and he greeted the news neutrally. "Sixty percent time? I haven't done this before. I don't know how to do this," he replied. Still, there was frequent discussion of the part-time option around Amerco, and Amy Truett was periodically sending him literature about "models" in other company divisions and elsewhere. In doubtful tones, her boss agreed to let Eileen try going to 60 percent time after she returned from a six-week paid parental leave.

> When I first came back, I discovered a lot of work had piled up. I had to fix mistakes people had made in my absence. There was new work. It was awful. But I got so I could breeze through it, and I thought things were going well. I hadn't heard any complaints or gotten any accolades. So I said, "Let's have a process check meeting." Boy, *then* the ceiling fell in. "This is a flop," my boss said.

As Eileen recalled it, when she asked her boss whether he wanted her to continue part time or preferred a full-time replacement, to her dismay, he said he'd rather hire someone else full time. Backing down, Eileen tried a different tack: "What do you need that you aren't getting from my 60 percent time?" she asked.

"We have more business this year than last," he said. "Work is harder. I don't see how you're going to do this job part time."

Eileen was not trying to do an eight-hour job in six hours or four, however, nor was she asking to be paid for it. A young, newly hired engineer had taken over three to four hours of her daily work, about 30 percent. Between herself, the new hire, and a veteran engineer in the division, 95 percent of the job was covered. The missing 5 percent could be put in other hands and paid for with the money Amerco was saving. In addition, Eileen pointed out, she regularly put in far more than 60 percent time. Although she got full benefits, she felt Amerco was making money out of the deal. The problem was convincing her boss. She explained,

I made them admit that they weren't unhappy with my work. They were scared about the *future*. So I said, "If it's working now, let's keep going. If it starts not to work, let's deal with that when it happens." I asked for a fax machine and a computer to take home. I traveled with my sales partner to present company equipment as usual. Everything was going fine.

Here Jim butted in, amused,

Well, with some glitches . . . Eileen was breast-feeding and took a breast pump to work with her. I was home with the baby feeding her with a bottle. One day as she was packing for her trip, she forgot to pack the manual, so she called me to ask, "Jim, did I leave a washer in the kitchen cupboard?" We tried to figure out how she could make the pump work without the washer.

Meanwhile, both her boss and her sales partner were quietly aghast at what they suspected she was doing—pumping breast milk on business trips. As Eileen explained,

Both of them are fifty-five, so it was different in their day. They didn't participate in the birth or rearing of their children. I'm not even sure if their wives breast-fed. So I handled it without mentioning anything. At lunch, and at 4 P.M., I took twenty minutes out and it wasn't any big deal.

On my last trip, I took Japanese visitors to the Mississippi Plant, and I had my little cooler with empty baby bottles that I filled with breast milk. Tony, my sales partner, asked me, "How are you going to get out of this one?" I told them, "Those are parts of a new product sample line."

Jim and Eileen were laughing, trading the baby back and forth and stumbling over each other to tell the story in proper order, correcting and urging each other on. Jim added,

The Japanese knew Eileen had a child. So they asked, "Where's your baby?" She told them that the baby was at home with his father. They were baffled that I could be alone taking care of our baby. When any calls came in, they were sure it was me calling Eileen ordering her to come home.

Eileen continued to excel in her job. But her boss was still skeptical about the 60 percent.

He thought that since I was part time, I must not be answering my phone, and the customer must not be satisfied. But I did my ten to three o'clock day. The secretary took all other calls with, "She's in a meeting and will get back to you." And I did. The customers didn't even know I was part time.

Finally, Eileen and her boss came down to the issue that, one level up, was dividing Bill Denton and Vicky King.

He said to me, "Eileen, I don't know how to do part time. My experience is that people who put in the hours are the ones who succeed." I said, "Measure me on my results." He replied, "No. It doesn't work that way. What matters is how much time you put into the job, the volume of work."

Eileen replied,

Say you and I mow your lawn. You got it done in three hours. I got it done in four hours. We do the same job but you get it done in less time. Should *I* be the better worker because it took me *longer*?

Her boss was quiet for a while, then replied,

I'm listening. I haven't said no. But this is a new one for me. It doesn't feel right yet. Everybody here has a large volume of work. That's all I know how to understand as a basis for getting ahead.

As Eileen's boss saw it, the work bargain was a given. "Part time," as its name implied, was only a part of a whole. To work part time was to renege on an agreement to do a whole, complete job. Formerly, he had had more of Eileen's effort, as he saw it. Now he had less. What seemed to carry little weight for him was the obvious financial benefit of the new arrangement. Eileen was now paid 40 percent less. Amerco also paid Laura, the new worker, less than they would have paid Eileen for the same hours and got a newly trained employee in the bargain. This was a plus for the company. It took some of Eileen's highly paid time to train Laura, but this was a temporary minus. Moreover, there was another factor benefiting Amerco: Eileen habitually worked *more* than her 60 percent time. For all of the appeal of a part-time schedule, she just couldn't bring herself to walk out of the office at 3 P.M. sharp, leaving behind unfinished business and toiling coworkers. On top of this, she was, by everyone's account, doing her usual first-rate job. Her boss saw all this but remained uncertain, and in this doubt-ridden, halting way, the arrangement lurched forward.

Then something happened that made Eileen realize the importance to her of the work she was trying to cut down on. She got fired. She was not fired by her boss in his office but by his boss, in a nearby hotel, as if to protect the social world at work from this befouling news. Eileen described the scene:

All forty-four of the engineering jobs in my division derived from government contracts. When the government cut back, the division and all forty-four people in it went under. My position got eliminated. My boss's boss, a man I'd never met, told me this in five minutes. He told me not to return to the office because I might upset the other employees. He told me to pick up my stuff on the weekend. I cried and cried for days. My work wasn't just a job to me, it was my life, my blood, my sweat and tears for the past eleven years. And they took all that away with the flick of a pen. It was like going through a divorce!

Time stopped for me. It was like somebody saying your mother died. I drove around and tried to reach Jim because I didn't want to go to the babysitter early and upset the kids.

My friends, the people I care about, were back at the office wondering what the hell was going on. They worried about me as much as I worried about myself. One woman who also got fired came back on the weekend, as she was told to do, and her badge [the magnetized card workers used to get into buildings] didn't work. The others just thought, "Screw it, I don't need my coffee cup."

Eileen's division chief told her that her new job was to look for a job inside or outside the company. If she didn't find a job inside Amerco within two months, the company would offer her severance pay.

The room was spinning. I was still a part of the "Amerco family." They wanted me to look within Amerco, but the placement counselor also said to look outside of Amerco. Was I *in* or was I *out*?

Eileen had ostensibly worked 60 percent time in her job, but it had felt to her like a "110 percent marriage." Since all the other members of her division lost their jobs too, it could not be said that she lost hers because she was part time. Still, it became important to her to discover whether there was the slightest link between her limited hours and her "divorce."

I asked the top guy, and he asked the really top guy, "Was Eileen fired because of being part time?" He said part time had nothing to do with it. Workaholics went down. Regular workers went down. Part-timers went down. The division went down.

Eileen found a job in another division of Amerco, as did nearly all the others. The second time I interviewed Eileen two years later she was working at this new full-time job. As she explained,

> The only job I could find was full time in Office Systems Design. Over here, there's nothing soft and fuzzy. It's just making money, money, money. I work through lunch hour until six o'clock. They'll eat you alive here. It's very aggressive, a marathon race.

Returning to work, she met a former coworker who greeted her, "Welcome back to the Amerco family." She remarked, "In his mind, *I* had left the Amerco family and was now returning. That stuck in my mind—'Welcome *back* to the Amerco family.'"

Did she still feel like Amerco *was* family? I asked. "In between a family and not a family," she answered.

> My job now is like a second marriage. They always say the first marriage is for love, the second for money. I wonder if that'll happen to my feelings about this job. Now it's like I'm dating. I'm keeping up the right front, but I'm not in love and I don't know if I ever will be.

Eileen was wary, but willing for another try at "love." She noticed that the other sixty people in Office Systems, who had not been fired, did not have her doubts.

During this period of time, Eileen and Jim had a second child, Danny. But the delivery was difficult. As Eileen recounted,

> We had real trouble with the second baby. He was in intensive care for ten days because his lungs hadn't developed properly. He couldn't breathe and he almost died three times in the first four days. The first time was when he was born.

He didn't move his fingers and he only stared to the right. The doctor was concerned about brain damage. Jim took off from work the first few days, but after our baby was out of the woods, he felt obligated to go back. Jim asked his boss for flextime. The boss denied it to him, but Jim began taking it anyway.

Of late, Danny had been experiencing some episodes that were possibly related to brain damage that could be seen on an MRI test. Twice he had lost all feeling in his leg and fallen down. So Eileen again forced herself to bring up the question of reduced time (and pay):

> My new supervisor practically whispered, "Maybe we can work it out, but don't breathe a word." I said, "Gee, over in Plastics they were proud of their family-friendly policies." He said, "Not over here. We don't have time."

Eileen felt as if she had done something shameful. She noted,

> I'm not supposed to get the office upset. Everybody else is putting in forty, fifty, sixty hours. People range from 120 percent to 150 percent time. They work 20 to 50 percent overtime on a regular basis.

Because of worry about Danny, and perhaps because of her recent "divorce" from work, Eileen added, "I'm never going to work that way. My family is what's going to last!"

For his part, Jim took a brief paternity leave, supported Eileen in her efforts to cut her hours, and praised the principle of shorter hours for men. But like nearly every working father I met at Amerco, he didn't seriously want to cut down on his own work hours. In his talk about time for home life, Jim spoke of himself as the kind of man who *could* see himself staying home. ("Sure, why not?") In talking with Eileen, he was the "new man." But when it came to really trying for shorter hours, and facing his male superior and coworkers, it just couldn't be done. The culture wasn't ready for it. In truth, Jim felt too anxious about losing his hard-won place at Amerco. In this cultural climate, part time for a male professional signaled lack of ambition—and that could damage one's long-term job security. If there was a taboo against working shorter hours, there was an even deeper one against the idea that a man's top priority might not be to rise in the world of work. Even Eileen wanted Jim to be "ambitious." She wasn't pressing him to ask for shorter hours. Both of them accepted a double standard. It was "normal" for Eileen to want shorter hours (though it was not normal for her to ask for or get them). It was not yet "normal" for Jim even to want them.

Oddly enough, the fear of seeming to lack ambition in the eyes of peers or supervisors was a powerful bond among men at Amerco, a fear that helped reinforce group identity. If work was offering previously homebound women a new professional identity, it offered men a distinctly male identity. In this sense, Jim was far more typical of men at Amerco than Vicky King's husband. His challenge was not to match his working wife hour for hour, as Kevin King was matching Vicky, but to match himself against the long hours of other men at work even as they strove to match him.

This competition struck Eileen as even more pernicious than the evil eye that men directed at her, because there was no way she could combat it directly. Eileen believed in equality, and it was this belief that led her to oppose the idea of a "mommy track" (which offered women flexibility but compelled them to surrender ambition).[1] Eileen was ambitious; she liked this about herself and so did Jim. What she wanted instead of a "mommy track" was an array of possible timetables that allowed women and men alike to combine ambition and the family. As she explained,

> To me, it seems like such a practical solution just to say, look, if you want to have children, that's going to take time. Take time off, treat that time like graduate school or like a sabbatical.

Come back refreshed, ready to go, with things organized.
Don't come back after six weeks. Or do come back after six
weeks but not full time. And change the time table on which
you rise to where you want to go. You may lose a little
ground. But you catch up later.

In fact, the real race could start later. We shouldn't think
about retiring at age fifty-five. We should work until age seventy. The real heavy-duty management commitment, time
commitment, should start in a major way in the mid-thirties.
We could still have twenty-five or thirty years to work. Our
most *productive* years would come *later*. When many fifty-
five-year-old Amerco men are burnt out and ready to head
for the golf course, we would be getting a second wind.

Eileen's vision of "part time with ambition" existed nowhere on
the Amerco landscape, and so part time was associated only with the
idea of permanently renounced ambition. Even for women, having
ambition was the only real entry card into the "Amerco family."

It was understandable, then, that few of the 20 percent of
women—and the less than 2 percent of men—who claimed on
Amerco's surveys to be interested in part time had acted on their
desires. In that sense, they had fared worse than Eileen in reducing
their hours.

On the other hand, a tiny number of midlevel professional
women had fared better than she had in getting their bosses to agree
to reduced schedules. One such woman was Jane Cadberry, a
thirty-three-year-old, highly successful manager of workers in the
Education and Training Division of Amerco. She told me,

I'm the only part-time manager in the company and I'm not
really part time. I no longer work thirty-two hours—not that
it ever really was thirty-two hours. I don't take Wednesdays
off like I used to, partly because I'm responsible for more and
partly because my kids are older. Typically, I'm able to take
my children to school every morning at 7:00 and pick them

up two afternoons a week at 1:30. The other days, I get
home at 6:15 or 7:00. I'm still the dinner maker in the house;
I don't want to let that go. But the fact is, I work forty or
forty-five hours a week.

Time spent at the office, however, was only part of it. Driving
me out to her home in the country for a swim and dinner, Jane
showed me how she regularly checked her voice messages on the
car phone. "I get an hour's work done going to and from work. My
secretary comes in at 7 A.M. on flextime, and I phone her from the
car as I commute to work and ask her to xerox a memo. By the
time I walk into the office at 7:45 for an 8 A.M. meeting, everything's ready."

Jane's situation differed from Eileen's in a number of ways: First,
Amerco had badly wanted Jane's skills when they hired her, so she
entered the company with a bargaining chip in hand. When the
company offered her a full-time job, she simply countered with an
offer of part time or nothing—and Amerco accepted. Second, she
had a sympathetic, innovative boss. Third, she was working in a
division with a fifty-fifty (not eighty-twenty) ratio of men to
women. Fourth, Jane herself was extremely time conscious and
superbly organized and a wizard at translating time-currencies. She
could tell from the look of a company project how many steps it
would require to implement, how much time it would cost her at
work, and what kinds of absences it might entail at home. Though
she disguised it gracefully, Jane kept a sharp eye out for every piece
of the "small change" of time that might be useful to her. Last, she
passed Bill Denton's final criterion for promotion: at the end of a
long week, Jane was still fun.

But for all the virtues Jane brought to her job, her experience
with part-time employment suggests a paradox: the only way to
keep a part-time schedule without violating the unspoken rules of
the workplace was, in effect, to work full time. Her intuitive understanding of this fact was apparent from the very beginning of her
employment at Amerco, when she agreed to consider *fifty* hours,
rather than the normal forty, to be the standard full-time schedule.

Almost immediately, she began to "add on" to her base of thirty-two hours, first by leaving the office later and later, and then by doing an ever greater share of her work at home. "Even on my days off," she told me, "I make phone calls at poolside."

Eileen and Jane approached the control of time differently—which showed up in how my interview with each ended. At 1:30 P.M., Eileen abruptly interrupted an animated story she and Jim were telling, suddenly remembering an obligation. As Jane's interview moved along, she glanced at her watch and, while graciously offering to meet again, warned, "I'll have to leave in ten minutes. Are there any questions we haven't gotten to?" In contrast, Bill Denton appeared not to manage his time at all. When my hour with him was up, his secretary knocked quietly, stuck her head in the office, and announced his next appointment.

Neither Bill Denton nor Vicky King wanted shorter hours. Both were deeply attracted to the lure of work. Eileen Watson understood that attraction, but she *did* want shorter hours. Why couldn't she get them? She was not inhibited by the loss of income or, even after being fired, by fear for her job security. She was not ignorant of the policies, nor did she work in an unusually envious environment. She did, however, encounter two Balashevs among her supervisors, one uninterested in her situation, the other kindly but intimidated—neither seeing how her shorter hours could be in the long-term interest of Amerco. She also collided with a company culture that viewed ambition and shorter hours as mutually exclusive. What, then, were her alternatives? Would she have to quit and leave town in search of an even more family-friendly company in order to have the kind of life she wanted?

In fact, she continued to tiptoe her way through a year of covert part-time work, a job that slowly but surely became, in effect, an eight-hour-a-day stint without overtime. Then Danny, their three-year-old, suddenly faced another medical crisis. Eileen described it this way:

It was awful. Danny lost feeling in his leg. We had been at the neurologist's office until 10 P.M. that evening. Both my husband and I had very important presentations to give at work in the morning. I had to present at 11 A.M. before a new group of engineers, and I still had some changes left to make. Jim's presentation was at 9 A.M. So I stayed home in the morning. I wanted to let Danny sleep in. If he woke up and was still wobbly on his feet, he would have to go to the hospital to get a brain scan to see if he was having an epileptic seizure. I got him up, and sure enough he was wobbly.

I called Jim's secretary, "Tell Jim I'll drop Danny off at the babysitter, and he's to pick him up and take him to the hospital by noon." I got to the sitter by ten o'clock. When Jim finished his talk he called me at 10:30 A.M. and said, "I've got him. Don't worry!" I went to the office, changed my presentation, and gave it. The session in which I spoke ran from eleven to one o'clock. I asked my boss if I could give my presentation first and leave. It upset me that I had to tell my boss my personal problem. Now I know that in his mind I'm a "mom," not an engineer.

I dashed to the hospital. Danny was screaming. He'd pulled all the tubing and wires out of his hair. Then they gave him so much medication he fell asleep. Jim and I sat by his bedside. We didn't say much. We just sat waiting for him to wake up so we could take him home.

One of us could have gone back to the office at that point, but neither of us did. Though we felt we should. I hate it that we felt that way when our baby was lying in a hospital bed with something so wrong.

I said to Jim, "I have to get out of here just for a second. Let me walk. I'll walk to Woolworth's to buy a little toy for

Danny for when he wakes up." So I left the hospital and walked along the road. I just walked and walked. I just wanted to keep walking, to wave down a truck and get in, and keep on going.

But the next week, Eileen was back at her desk at Amerco.

CHAPTER 8

"I'm Still Married":
Work as an Escape Valve

Denise Hampton reported with pride that her five-year-old son, Cliff, another regular at the Spotted Deer Childcare Center, had recently shown a burst of interest in fitting together twenty-four-piece puzzles—or so the caregivers at the center had been telling her. Now, at 1 P.M. as I began to talk with Denise in her office at Amerco, Cliff was probably settling down for quiet time. Too old for a real nap, he usually capitulated to the center's metabolic slow-down by looking at a book about airplanes he brought with him every day. His eight-year-old sister, Dorothy, was in third grade.

Assistant marketing director for one of Amerco's most popular new product lines, Denise got forty to fifty phone calls or e-mail messages a day. A vivacious, petite woman with a pixie haircut, Denise sprinted through a volume of work that a slower, more methodical coworker might barely have finished in twice the time. Racing to the end of her workday, Denise wanted nothing more than to collapse at home with a glass of chardonnay, cuddle with her husband, read to her kids, and maybe even unplug her answering machine.

When I asked her what had changed at home and work over

the two years since we had last talked, she declared with a laugh,
"I'm still married, to the same *guy* even!" Denise had broken out
of an alcoholic family, partly by adopting a kindly neighbor as
her mentor when she was a teenager, discovering another mentor
in a college professor, and recently finding yet another in a
highly successful, older female manager at Amerco. A brilliant
student at school, she was now consolidating a string of successes
at work. The private side of life had always proved harder for
her, but even there she had actively sought help and felt she had
benefited from therapy.

Denise had married, borne a son, divorced, and married again.
Her second marriage, to Daniel, though now a decade old, had
never been quite as enjoyable as she had hoped. From the beginning
there were difficulties. Denise's son Dillon, then in his early twen-
ties, had so fiercely resisted her remarriage and so bitterly criticized
her new husband that she felt she had no choice but to cut off all
contact with her son. Dillon had finally apologized, but the pain of
that decision lingered still. Her two children by her second marriage
(whose small photos faced her on her office desk) seemed to be
thriving. She said she gave her best energy to them. She proudly
noted that in their evening readings they were already up to the fifth
volume in C. S. Lewis's *Chronicles of Narnia*. But often the children
had to remind her to read more slowly. Even at home Denise felt
speedy, and, if her career and her motherhood were going well, she
was puzzled by her lifeless marriage. Despite her natural gaiety,
there was palpable sadness in her voice when she spoke of it.

The Hampton's log house was a half-hour's drive from town on
a hundred acres of land next to a small man-made lake. The sheer
size of the house and land suggested that someone had time to keep
it up. The Hamptons planted their own garden and made their own
maple syrup (thanks mainly to Daniel). The head of an eight-point
buck Daniel had shot hung on their living room wall (Denise rolled
her eyes insisting, "That wasn't *my* idea"). The activities husband
and wife fondly talked about—maple syruping, gardening, hunting—suggested leisure, but their schedules indicated rush. In fact,
Denise often steered clear of most of the family's leisure activities.

After all, what choice did she have, she thought, but to catch up on her relentless phone messages and e-mail.

A supervisor of twenty workers at an Amerco plant down the valley, Daniel did not aspire to become another Bill Denton. He arrived at 8 A.M. and left punctually at 5 P.M., and in the eyes of his boss this made Dan a time-dissident. "Quitting for lunch on the dot of twelve again?" his boss would gibe. For his part, Daniel observed wryly that his boss was engrossed in a book called *Outperformers: Super Achievers, Breakthrough Strategies, and High-Profit Results*, about how managers can learn to perform at their peak all the time. "The work-family balance idea is having a short walk-through in my plant," Daniel said.

Highly articulate, intelligent, radiating a deep, sweet sadness, Daniel had hoped to find in his marriage, his fatherhood, and his life at home some healing from a difficult boyhood. His parents in their treatment of him had evidently fluctuated arbitrarily between careless indulgence and harsh discipline. It was an experience that left him feeling unsafe whenever he felt called upon to assert how *he* wanted things to be. He had struggled with this inhibition all his life. In his marriage it meant that he found himself asking how Denise wanted to organize the evening, what she wanted him to do for dinner, and inwardly criticizing himself for having to ask. His passivity, in turn, reminded Denise of the helplessness of her "evening parents," who, dazed by whiskey, couldn't make decisions either. Such behavior sent her into a flurry of frantic I-can-take-care-of-it activity at the end of long, demanding days at work and left her feeling resentful and isolated.

Of the two of them, it was Denise who was running the home, but it was also Denise who was running away from home. When I asked her about her average day she said,

The alarm goes off a little before six. My goal is to have showered and washed my hair by six-thirty. Then I go downstairs and get things organized and get the kids up by quarter to seven. Cliff and Dorothy need to be at school by eight, so it works out just right.

I can't get out of work by five. I accept that now. It's always six o'clock, at least. And then I have to pick up the kids, grocery shop, race home, and cook.

The day is usually jam-packed, and Daniel and I inevitably have some confusion about who's supposed to do what. I try to sort out the plans. Did I leave anything out? Did I forget anything? Is anything going to happen tonight? In the evening, when I walk in the door, Daniel and the kids are all grumbling. I try to make sure Dorothy has her homework done for school, and we need to eat something. If they would just give me some space. . . . If only I could take fifteen minutes to change my clothes and have a glass of wine and maybe look at the news.

Denise worked in an "old boys" office at Amerco that, over the years, had been grudgingly hiring more women. When she was pregnant, Denise recalled,

Men in my office were putting money on the table that I would never show up at work again when the baby was born. I had to prove that when I came back, I was as good as I was when I left. Men were waiting to say, "I *told* you so."

Partly, Denise thought, the older men were offended to see someone choose not to replicate their own way of life.

They took no time off for paternity leave, and they feel they've paid their dues to Amerco. So when I took time off, they used that as an excuse to say I wasn't paying my dues like they had or that I wasn't as good a manager as they were.

In fact, Denise's coworkers seemed uncomfortable with the choices she'd made in both parts of her life, questioning her commitment as a mother as well. She recalled the snide remarks: "One man commented pointedly to another man in my presence, 'It takes a lot more than paying the *mortgage* to make a house a home.' "

In such a climate, ostensibly neutral questions from her male colleagues about how she might balance work with family felt to her like attacks. "They *corner* you with questions. When I was pregnant, they asked me, 'What are you going to do when both you and Daniel have emergencies at work?' " In this atmosphere, Denise wanted absolutely nothing to do with flexible or shorter hours. With a gender war on, shorter hours meant surrender.

In *The Evil Eye: A Folklore Casebook*, anthropologist Alan Dundes argues that whenever some people seem luckier than others in situations of "limited good" (when there is a scarcity, for example, of status, wealth, or health), the have-nots are presumed to envy the haves. In so-called primitive and ancient societies, the have-nots are also thought to possess the magical power to cause harm.[1] The envious have-not is thought to cast an "evil eye" on the object of envy—a healthy baby, a beautiful wife, a bumper crop of corn. The lucky person tries to avert harm by wearing an amulet, repeating verbal incantations, or symbolically disguising or misrepresenting his or her good fortune.

To the outsider, it may seem absurd that men at Amerco would think of themselves as have-nots, since they almost completely dominated the upper ranks of management and prevailed at most other levels of the company as well. But the modest introduction of women into Amerco's professional ranks has produced a powerful backlash. Thus, men and women triggered different responses to good luck. When a man got a promotion in a situation of "limited good"—a budget freeze, a downsizing—he experienced a glance from the evil eye. But when a woman was promoted, she received a drawn-out stare. When Denise Hampton was promoted, for example, a male colleague congratulated her, then added, "It sure is a good time to be a woman."

Denise had always been a hard worker, a "Type A" she would say, "but not a workaholic." Soon enough, though, she began to wear the workaholic amulet of long hours. By working long hours, she symbolically subtracted from the "luck" of her promotion. "Yes, I was lucky to be promoted," she seemed to say, "but I'm suffering for it." By rushing through her long day, like a rich man in rags, she was asking, "If I'm so poverty-stricken in time, how could anyone envy me?"

If one were to draw an evil-eye map of Amerco showing who gave it and who got it, Denise would be located in the danger zone. Male resentment of women tended to run highest in the formerly all-male preserves of the company. Men in upper-middle management and high-paid unionized production jobs—jobs in which men had always been an overwhelming majority—felt more resentment than did those men in the "administrative middle," where males were outnumbered and rewards were less. A 1993 company climate survey, inviting anonymous write-in comments from managers in the "high-envy" ranks, received replies like the following:

White men should have access to the same career planning that women and minorities do.

I have noticed more and more women in upper-level management. My only concern is that when we promote a woman or minority, it's because that person is the best one for the job.

I received a long-awaited, well-deserved Division Cash Award. I was told that one reason I got it was that I had been good at suppressing my frustration and disappointment when I was passed over for a promotion in favor of a woman.

But Amerco women didn't need survey results to know what men were thinking. Among their colleagues they tended to see four types of men. The first type, they felt, judged a woman as he would a man and saw both as full human beings. These were the men with whom it was wonderful to work. The second type judged a woman as he would a man, but applied to her the same harsh, competitive frame of mind he applied to his fellow men. A third type, often polite, helpful, and unthreatened, saw women as exotic foreigners. A fourth type saw women as alien rivals who were out to get *his* promotion. It was this fourth type of aggrieved and "displaced" male colleague who truly cast the evil eye.

Though generally quiet about the matter, men of this fourth type often resented women's "luck" in supposedly being able to take advantage of Amerco's family-friendly policies, which they saw as inapplicable to men. Occasionally such prejudices would seep out during required group training sessions for professionals and managers called "Men and Women as Colleagues." One engineer in Research and Development, for instance, suddenly exclaimed, while searching faces in his group for support, "All the working *mothers* get to use these policies while *we* don't. Why should the company make it easy to blend work and family? That's prejudice against those of us with traditional families. And we have to do without the extra money of two incomes."

Rising to the challenge of warding off the evil eye at work, Denise gave her all without regret. At home, however, she gave only part of herself and with mixed feelings. For she felt within herself an intensifying conflict between her need to plan dinner, for example, and her desire not to. She couldn't understand why this was so, but every night became a bizarre kind of agony:

I would come home, pour a glass of wine, open the refrigerator, and try to figure out what to cook. As I did I would begin to cry. I couldn't break the cycle of crying between six and seven o'clock. That got to be a daily habit. I was feeling sorry for myself. Why couldn't Daniel see that I needed help? He's supposed to take care of me. I count on him for that. Of course, his response was to just put more distance between us. This has gone on for a couple of years, and it's going on still.

Denise suspected that her problem had something to do with the fact that, as a child of alcoholics, she'd grown up never daring to

depend on anyone, a state of mind that had come to include Daniel.
So each night she took charge and edged him out of decision
making. At the same time, she desperately wanted him to decide
what to cook for dinner, to cook it, and in general to take responsibility at home. She wanted a husband at work on the second shift,
two children, not three. For his part, Daniel dreaded making decisions without her for fear of being slapped down. Yet he, too, had
deeply conflicting desires, for he wanted an open, communicative,
nurturant wife, even as he treated Denise like an executive dele-
gating tasks to him as she saw fit.

Each was suffering in silence—Denise crying by herself at the
refrigerator, Daniel brooding during his commutes to and from
work. Looking back over the past few years Denise reflected,

> I feel guilty that Daniel had the short end of the stick. I didn't
> realize until quite recently how upset he was, and how left
> out he felt. I had no clue about that. Of course, he never said
> anything. That makes me feel very guilty. About my kids
> too. It seems like such a long stretch of time I haven't been
> there for them. All they see is the stress and anxiousness of
> my trying to get through the chores. They should remember
> laughter and not Mom crying because she can't figure out
> what's for dinner.

To some extent, Denise dealt with her domestic problems by
bringing work home, only half-heartedly limiting its demands on
her. In fact, she also brought her frantic work pace home:

> The marketing phone calls are still coming in at home. I
> leave work, and before I can get home, take a breath, and
> relax, the phone rings and I have to be "on" again.

Given their impasse, Denise frankly felt more relaxed when
Daniel wasn't there. Then no decisions had to be made—and standards could be guiltlessly relaxed:

It's entirely different when Daniel's traveling. I'll pick up a pizza, or I'll say let's jump in the car and go to McDonald's, or the kids will eat cereal and I'll eat a salad. I let them watch cartoons. I mean it's just much more relaxed.

With Daniel, life had become tense; while at work, for all the tensions, Denise also enjoyed enriching friendships. As Denise recounted,

I was in New York last week with five colleagues. We sat down for lunch in this nice restaurant, nothing extravagant, and when the meal was put before me I sighed and said, "It is so *nice* to be here." The guys all looked at me like "what does this mean from this woman?"

Two of the men have always had stay-at-home wives. One man is a bachelor, and one is married to a homemaker who used to have a career, so he's been in both situations. The one woman is a professional whose children are grown. The bachelor is the most caring of them all. We've developed a very good friendship.

Meanwhile, Denise's in-laws began rising to Daniel's defense. As Denise put it,

Daniel told his sister that I was about to divorce him, and, of course, their behavior toward me changed instantly. They decided I had a drinking problem. To them, two glasses of wine is a drinking problem.

So Denise struggled on with her disappointed husband, her watchful in-laws, and her growing children, while her mentor, her friends, her fear of the evil eye, and her sense of success pulled her deeper into Amerco's world. I asked her if she felt that, all in all, she got as much time at home as she'd like. "No," she responded automatically; but when I asked her if it was possible to get more time, she replied,

> No. In fact, I see less need for time at home because now the kids are getting involved with activities. They tend to have more commitments. My daughter has baseball games at night sometimes. Those days I come home from work at 8 or 8:30 P.M.

"What's their bedtime?" I asked. "Nine o'clock," she answered. "We might get into bed at eight-thirty to start reading. But then it'll be nine-thirty before you know it. One more drink of water or one more hug or, oops, I forgot to go to the bathroom."

Denise had answered my question about needing time at home by telling me that her children needed her less now than before. In effect, she was orienting herself more toward work. Part of the reason for this might be found in the kinds of support she could expect at work and at home. Katherine, her mentor at Amerco, for example, "made all the difference in the world for me personally. I used to be a little scared when I came to work every day. She broke me in on the job so that it was no longer scary." Denise proudly described a difficult but successful confrontation she had had with Janet, an intimidating twenty-seven-year veteran secretary, who she felt abused flextime and then defied all criticism. "If Janet's son had an 11 A.M. dental or eye appointment, she stayed out the rest of the day. Katherine helped me confront her." At work, Denise had a role model, a coach, and a series of triumphs to report to her. At home, she got less help with matters of greater consequence, matters she felt less and less competent to deal with. Denise had one childhood friend in Seattle she called often, but otherwise, her close friends were at work.

Although Denise didn't often allow herself to "get lost" in her work like Bill Denton, her sense of free time was work oriented. She felt most relaxed, she said, in those hours after 5 P.M. when she was at work, her daughter was at her baseball game, and Cliff was with his dad at home. But the freest, most carefree times of all were when she traveled to conferences in other cities, relaxed and commiserated with coworkers about life at home.

Although Denise Hampton counted herself a hundred percent behind family-friendly reforms, she wasn't the least bit interested in shorter hours herself. The family's "vote" on whether Denise should take more time at home was: six "yes" (the two children, Daniel, his mother, and his two sisters) to one "no" (Denise). No one had thought to vote on whether Daniel should devote more time to home. That issue had never even made an appearance in their marital conversation despite the fact that Daniel felt more emotionally centered at home than his wife.

Denise wanted more time than she had. But she didn't want more time at home. Her life there was too laced with strain and her life at work too filled with promise and—with the evil eye. The more often Denise came home late, the more Daniel tensed up and did nothing; the more she had those crying spells at the refrigerator, the more she found herself waiting eagerly to return to the office the next morning. The marriage remained in place— more or less—but without work as her escape valve Denise could not imagine it lasting harmoniously. Things seemed strangely upside down to her—but who had the time or the opportunity to sort it all out?

Driving me back to my bed-and-breakfast in the family van, Daniel shared his thoughts about how to escape the cycle in which his family seemed hopelessly trapped:

> There are no easy fixes to the balance between home and work. It's a deep problem. Family teamwork is crucial. We need to transfer the idea of teams we have in sports and production to the family.

But where, I wondered, did sports teams and companies originally borrow the idea of cooperation from if not the family? Surely, the family was the original "team." Now the idea of the team, embraced by top managers like Bill Denton, had been adopted by Vicky King and others as a bridge between the traditional workplace and a new workplace that could accommodate two-job families like the Hamptons. A family model of cooperation had become a company model. But what model was left for the family? Daniel Hampton opened the door of his van, shook my hand warmly and concluded, "I'm still hoping we can make our family a good production team."

CHAPTER 9

"Catching Up on the Soaps":
Male Pioneers in the Culture of Time

"I've just talked to two men who took paternity leave."

Arlie Hochschild

"Oh? Who's the other one?"

Amy Truett

Sam Hyatt was a gifted engineer, seven years with the company, and the father of a three-month-old baby boy. In 1990 he was one of two men in the company who requested and received formal parental leave. Amerco, like many companies nationwide, offers six weeks of paid leave to the mother. Beyond that, it allows twenty weeks of unpaid leave that can be split in any fashion between husband and wife. Sam and Latesha Hyatt decided that Latesha should take eighteen weeks and Sam two.

After the birth of a child, many men at Amerco arranged informally with their bosses to take a few unpaid days off using accumulated sick leave because the forms for parental leave were said to be "a hassle." To his astonishment and dismay, Sam discovered that he was the first man in the company to apply formally for paternity leave. I asked Sam, a gentle thirty-three-year-old African American man with an easy laugh, to tell me how he ended up being a trailblazer at Amerco.

"I come from a family of six children in Cleveland," he replied. "My mother was a single parent and worked several jobs to support

115

us. I'm the third oldest and I had some responsibilities for my younger brother and sisters. We went through tough times, not just financially but emotionally." He described how he took college preparatory courses in a public school, was accepted by California Polytechnic Institute, and graduated in three years with a degree in mechanical engineering. While in college, he learned of an Amerco summer scholarship/intern program. The company offered him an internship and, pleased with his summer work, offered him a job upon his graduation. Along the way, he met and married Latesha, a chemical engineer who also worked for Amerco.

Amerco was a predominantly white company as was the town of Spotted Deer and its surrounding valley communities. But in pursuit of its mission to increase diversity, Amerco began in the late 1980s actively recruiting gifted minority students at technical colleges and universities, hiring them as summer interns, and, if all went well, offering them jobs when they graduated.

This pathway to Amerco placed Sam Hyatt in a curious mix of circumstances. The company was eager to draw the best from every racial and ethnic talent pool and was busy trying to make minority newcomers feel welcome. So, for example, Amerco made sure that one local radio station played music likely to appeal to many African Americans. The company also hired the only local barber skilled in black hairstyles. Yet it was also true that blacks, Chicanos, and Asians together still made up a very small percentage of Amerco's workforce. And the community lacked the sort of racial mix that might have reduced Sam's occasional sense that people expected him to represent the "black position" on whatever came up.

In fact, what the working-class whites who lived in the sur-rounding countryside knew about African Americans they seemed to have learned mainly from television shows about violent crime. When Sam first came to Spotted Deer, he got lost driving on a mountain road and stopped at a bar-restaurant to ask for change to make a call. The steely-eyed faces that greeted him made him think of some sheriff's posse in a small Mississippi town in the 1950s. He froze and backed out. That only had to happen once to impress him with a sense of his vulnerability as a black man in this white valley.

Still, at Amerco and at home, life was good. With a flourishing career, a loving wife, and a new house Sam happily prepared for the birth of their first child. Latesha planned to take four and a half months of maternity leave, and Sam's first official act as a father-to-be was to ask the company for time off.

Two months before Latesha was due, I approached my supervisor, somewhat unsure about how he would respond. Amerco had just published a paternity-leave policy in 1988. When I got my hands on it, I didn't realize that I was the first to use it. I'm not sure if I'm still the only one. I filled out the form and took it to my supervisor. We get along really well. I'm not uptight with him generally, but for some reason I was this time. He sensed my nervousness and said, "Don't worry about it, this is great." In a matter of days or a week, it was signed by my manager. The form acted as an agreement that I could take leave without pay for two weeks.

Sam was doing well at work. His supervisor's professional development report noted that he "continuously met and usually exceeded his customers' requirements, and that he was doing a superior job as a department supervisor after a very short time in the position." When his wife was just about to have the baby, Sam noted,

I was working on a big project to design, fabricate, and test equipment, and it was time to install it—a difficult time to be away from work. But my father had missed my birth and then my boyhood, and maybe that's why I wanted to be there for my own child from the beginning.

After eight hours at the hospital, Sam greeted a squalling, eight-pound baby boy, wrapped him in a blue blanket, and laid him in his bassinet. As he nursed his wife back to health, he cared for the house and spent hours attuning himself to this new small being, whom they named Adam.

When, two weeks later, he returned to his nine-hour days, he encountered a wide variety of reactions:

> To the women at the office, I was a great hero. Sam *cooks*! Sam does *laundry*! Sam takes *paternity leave*! But most of the guys I'm not close to ignored it. They all knew, but they acted as if they weren't supposed to know. They were thinking, "Where were you? On vacation?" My close friends teased me, "It must have been fun, what did you do? Did you change diapers? Come on, it must have been a *great* time. You sat around and watched TV." They thought I was using this time as an excuse to get away.

They saw Sam's paternity leave as time when he was not working, but relaxing, goofing off. They didn't link paternity leave to paternity.

Sam faced a choice. He could let the playful jabs about "catching up on the soaps" go and accept the obvious implications: that because women give birth to babies, babies are a women's thing; that men have no role at or around birth, so paternity leave is unnecessary or silly. Or he could respond. But he would have to be careful, he felt. He couldn't be too "politically correct" because, for many of his colleagues, the issue of paternity leave was fraught with unacknowledged tension. Many of them were feeling pressure from working wives who had sacrificed time from their own budding careers and yearned for appreciation as well as some parallel gesture of commitment, no matter how small.

Sam stood his ground but parried the jabs lightly:

> I let them know what I really did. And I told them what it meant to me. They responded, "Well, it's not for me, but great, if that's what you want," that type of thing. I tried to convey the idea that this is a great opportunity for men. If I had it to do all over again, I told them, I'd take *more* time off.

A few younger men who perhaps dreamed of taking paternity leave themselves someday applauded Sam, as did a few older men who imagined that they might have taken one, had they been given the chance.

At home, Sam's leave, however brief, established a pattern:

> I comb Adam's hair every morning and dress him. I hear guys say, "I'm going home to babysit." Or they say, "I have to play Mr. Mom," as if there's no such thing as Daddy or Father. I don't say anything, but I despise these statements.

> I correct them when they say, "Do you have to babysit?" When they ask me, "What are you doing?" I say, "I'm going home to be a dad." Or, "I'm going home to be with my family." I don't honestly know if they sense the difference between "babysitter" and "dad."

After four and a half months, when Latesha returned to her regular schedule, they both began waking up at 5:30 A.M. to spend more time with Adam. At 7:30 A.M., they dropped Adam at his sitter's. "We rarely get a chance to see him at lunch," Sam continued. "We just can't manage the time. We pick him up at 5:30 P.M. and go home." After a year, Latesha decided to take part time, cutting her working day back to six hours. As Sam explained,

> We've named Latesha as the primary caregiver. Still, my role is not to help, it's to act. All the time we're talking about who does what. We're still working it out. Latesha would like an equal partnership. But I wouldn't be comfortable being the one going part time. First, because of my work, and second, because she's more organized than I am.

As it was, Sam had begun to feel that he was pressing the limits of acceptability at Amerco. Because he rarely took work home and rarely worked weekends, he felt his superiors were watching him with an eagle eye. As he put it,

> My use of time doesn't come close to that of my superiors. I don't know if I'm going to change or if, eventually, they are. I love the work. I just don't like the workaholism. Higher-level managers all tell you that family is "number one." Every moment they get, they talk about how their child just won the fifty-yard dash and show you pictures. It's number one to them, but you look at how they live and you have to wonder. To me, family life really is number one.

Still, Sam often found it hard to get out the office door anywhere near 5 P.M.:

> Often, I have a four to five o'clock meeting. Then I have to clean off my desk, return a few calls. If it's my turn to pick up Adam, I may call the babysitter and ask if she can hold out another twenty minutes or so. To leave at five o'clock, I need a good excuse. Adam's not a good excuse.

Sam and Latesha were still resisting the press of work, but without many allies. Their home life was not anchored to a circle of kin who called, visited, meddled, and supported. Both had moved far from their hometowns. Latesha missed her mother and sisters in particular. Even though she found most people at Amerco friendly and outgoing, a semiconscious vigilance against unwanted looks or remarks proved a strain for her, and so she found their time alone together a particular relief. She was as unwilling to give up their family time as Sam was to give up his idea of being a "real dad."

Upon learning that there were only two men in the company who had formally applied for paternity leave, a white manager asked me who the other one was. When I mentioned Sam Hyatt, he mused, "Maybe he got to take it because he's black." That made me wonder: Did the men who ribbed Sam for "catching up on the soaps" think that an exception had been made for him? Were they not asking for their paternity leaves because they were *white* and so had little chance of getting them? It was hard to know how Sam could win.

Certainly, if a boss wanted to resist setting a paternity-leave precedent in his division, he could always behave disagreeably when prospective fathers requested leaves. One worker found himself locked in a fierce struggle with his boss over his request for a single week of paternity leave.

"Call it vacation," his boss suggested.

"I'd like it in addition to vacation," the worker said. "Can you deduct it from my pay?"

"Take it for free, then," his boss replied, irritated.

"I'm not asking for something free," came the response.

"Well, I can't give you paternity leave. It's too much paper-work. Why don't you just take it unofficially?" The following summer, the worker discovered to his dismay that his boss had deducted his paternity leave from his vacation time. When that boss left for another job, the worker had to struggle with his new boss to restore his lost week of vacation time. Such were the isolated trials of male time-pioneers.

Had this worker and Sam Hyatt become fathers in Sweden, however, they would have been among the half of Swedish fathers who take six weeks *paid* paternity leave.[1] In middle-class Swedish families, it would have been very much the thing to do, and even in working-class circles they would have encountered few objections. But at Amerco, the few pioneers of paternity leave were largely invisible and knew little of one another.

Sam Hyatt had, for instance, never heard of John West, who, like him, was consciously attempting to atone for an absent father (as well as an absent mother) by being there for his child. John was a shy, thin, thirty-two-year-old man with blond hair, who initially seemed more eager to tell the story of his wife's family than his own. "My wife's father was a workaholic veterinarian who put in ten- to sixteen-hour days. She didn't want me to be like her father." It was his wife's strong desire for him to take paternity leave that led him to request it.

As for his own story, he quickly filled in the details of his family's slow-motion collapse in Southern California—a childhood without Christmases, Thanksgivings, or any other symbols of family time or connection. By age sixteen, he found himself in a "no-parent" family:

> My brother and I were left unsupervised for days at a time when we were in elementary school, really for ten years of our lives. It made us less trusting but more self-reliant. My brother cooked and I cleaned. Both of us still do that in our marriages today.

While John at first saw himself as merely his wife's proxy on the issue of paternity leave ("This was *really* important to her!"), his own eagerness for it soon showed through as well:

> As soon as Tamara was pregnant, I approached my supervisor. So I gave him six to seven months' notice. My supervisor is new at Amerco and he said, "Oh? Okay." I brought him the book, pointed to the page, and he said, "We'll see as time gets closer if it really fits into our work schedule." I hounded him and I got two weeks.

I asked John how it was being home on paternity leave.

> I cleaned and cooked and did all that good stuff while Tamara recuperated from her delivery. I tried to keep her in bed as much as possible, and I took care of the baby. It worked out really well.

His male coworkers were surprised to learn of the paternity-leave program and quick to evaluate it in financial terms:

> At first, they envied me a bit until I pointed out that it was unpaid. So then the envy went away, and they said, "Oh

gosh, I'd never do that, I'd go broke." Well, *I* don't think they'd go broke.

For John, far more than money was at stake:

In my family, there's nothing left. My mom lives in an apartment. My dad lives in a condo. I have no idea where all the toys and clothes and mementos I had when I was growing up are. I can't find the crib I was born in.

When we go to visit my in-laws, I realize what a close family is. Tamara goes home to see her room with all her furniture and pictures just as it was. She can pass on to our daughter the toys she herself played with as a baby. Christy is wearing dresses Tamara used to wear. I can't tell you how much I enjoy that.

John also gave some tentative thought to trying to cut back his work hours:

Tamara goes back to full time in January. I brought it up: "Hey, maybe I could go part time." We could split days so that I'm home when she's not, and she's home when I'm not.

In the Research and Development Division where I work, there are some young couples who are breaking the ice with part time. So I think if I was ever to ask to work twenty to thirty hours a week, it might be possible.

But in the end John could not bring himself to ask for fewer hours, a decision he rationalized in this way:

I'm a closet workaholic. There are times my wife has to jolt me back into family life. The last hour at work I get nervous that I've stayed at work too long. Going home in the car, I worry she'll be in a bad mood. My family comes first, but sometimes I ask myself, do I really *need* to be home? Or is this a passing thing? If I don't get home for an hour, is Tamara going to die? No, probably not. But if I don't meet this deadline at work, maybe the consequence will be severe.

When Tamara was home on maternity leave, John happily left it to her to be the watchdog of family time. She then declared that 6:30 P.M. would be their official dinnertime.

Tamara keeps telling me that if I really work hard for eight hours, I can get everything done. I can come home and forget about work. So I try to gear myself to that. But sometimes I also want to linger and talk to colleagues and not dash right home.

John nevertheless wanted Tamara to keep him on what he called "the straight and narrow." He liked the idea of being called home by a waiting wife.

Interestingly enough, when Tamara returned to work after her maternity leave, John found himself taking on the same role, helping Tamara to limit her work time:

My wife is very conscientious about work. She says, "I have to make this deadline," and, "Oh my God, I'm never going to make it, I'm so far behind." I ask her, "What happens if you postpone your deadine? Is there a problem with that?" She thinks it's dangerous not to meet her deadlines. But work isn't school. Nobody's grading you. Even project schedules aren't written in stone. You can talk to all the people who establish your deadline and see if you can get it moved.

Though both John and Tamara talked seriously of their need for more time at home—and each actually made moves to recapture small amounts of work time for their family life, for their child—their efforts to rein in each other's schedule told a somewhat different story. Whatever they believed their deepest time-desires to be, both of them were voting with their feet. For each of them, the pull of work was stronger than the pull of home, and only the constant application of self-control (or the control the other could apply) could right the balance. As for so many other two-job couples like them, there was no one in the company, at home, or in the neighborhood capable of weighing in on the side of the family.

John's workplace response to his situation at home was a curious one. He began putting a certain amount of effort into helping colleagues get up the nerve to ask for flextime schedules. He recounted one such story:

> My coworker Betty told me her daughter was doing badly in school, but she couldn't get home from work early to help her. Betty told me, "I'm working so hard; there's no way I can go half time." So we talked about her coming in early, leaving at three o'clock, and taking a computer home. She said, "What if my boss says no?" I said, "So what?" "He's going to think badly of me," she said. I answered, "For two days. Then he's going to forget it." Eventually, Betty went to her supervisor and cut a deal. She leaves at three o'clock and works two hours at home on the computer.

John also went out of his way to encourage men to get on the paternity-leave bandwagon:

> I was talking to a guy on the company softball team I play on. His wife is expecting, and the guy was saying, "Oh, I could never ask for paternity leave. My boss wouldn't let me." I said, "How do you know? Did you ask him?" "No, no, but he just wouldn't let me." So I told him, "Asking is the hardest part. *Ask* him!"

John became an informal chronicler of people's efforts to get shorter hours. He told this story of a woman who wanted to come back part time after she'd had a child:

> Her boss hated the idea but didn't think he had the right to hate it. So he sabotaged it by killing her with kindness. He eliminated all her responsibilities and arranged for her to still get paid. She was devastated. She was a very hard-driving person who wanted to do the work, not just get paid. In the end, her boss left the company, and now she's back full time.

By acting like a self-taught prison "lawyer" whom other inmates consult, John seemed almost to have convinced himself that he had actually altered his own schedule. But, in truth, he was an armchair revolutionary, part of an invisible army of working fathers who dream up hypothetical selves who share the second shift, play with their kids, and seldom postpone family time; while they themselves work like mad.

The Men Who Didn't Ask

Five years after the birth of his son, Jimmy Wayland felt he had completely missed the boat. A handsome, dark-haired, consultant specializing in overseas sales, Jimmy had not even thought of paternity leave when his child was born. In fact, he had felt that his wife wanted the entire experience of a new infant for herself, and yet, to his puzzlement, she seemed to resent being left alone. "I had no idea what was stewing in her mind," Jimmy remarked. Both his mother and his mother-in-law pampered and fretted over the baby. Jimmy felt excluded and responded by immersing himself in his work.

As Jimmy described his domestic story,

> My wife was in a hurry for us to reach what she felt was success. She's a good person, she just wanted to move more

quickly than I did. She saw me as too "laid back." She was always dreaming about the next house, the next job, the next stage of life. My philosophy was to enjoy the one we had. She'd come home from work and start cleaning. If I had a sandwich in my hand, she'd be cleaning up the mayonnaise before I'd finished. Maybe she was just nervous, but she expressed it by trying to make everything "perfect," the kitchen, the house, me.

With the pressure of a small baby and both of our jobs, my wife felt she was doing it all. And she felt it was too much to handle. I didn't have a clue she was as mad as she was. It was actually the day she was supposed to go part time that she left me and the baby.

She'd been so good all her life. At home, she was good. At community college, she had a 4.0 average. Then, when she got unhappy with me, she ran off with a rambling man and left me and Joshua when he was a year and a half. We had a big custody battle. Everyone sided with me and I won.

For a long time, Jimmy, who was thirty-two when I first met him, had felt his personal life was "in a shambles" while his work life flourished. But after the custody battle, he miraculously reestablished a friendship with his wife and in time gave her back half the custody he had legally won. Soon, they were "discussing everything" and splitting holiday care of their son. Each took care of Joshua when the other had to travel.

Jimmy's parents would pick up Joshua from the sitter if Jimmy had to work late or go back into work after dinner, and this helped. But even with the new, more collaborative arrangement, Jimmy felt there was a problem. "Joshua works an eight-to-five job just like I do," Jimmy remarked, "which is tough because he loves being home with me. Life has been hard enough for him, so I feel like he needs all the time I can give."

Jimmy elaborated,

> Joshua is never going to know what a summer is like without
> having to get up and be shuffled off somewhere. He's never
> going to experience free time with me around. So I spoil
> him. I give him some leeway at home. If he doesn't want to
> eat supper right away, I don't force him, and sometimes he
> goes to bed later at night than he should. Maybe he's stalling
> for time, but he says the most hilarious things at nine-thirty at
> night. We have our best conversations then.

At work, Jimmy described himself as "not a sixty-hour man":

> Here in the plant, we have a macho thing about hours. Guys
> say, "I'm an eighty-hour man!" as if describing their hairy
> chests. I personally work about forty-four to forty-eight
> hours. My boss is a nice guy. I can't tell you that my boss or
> my boss's boss refuses me permission to take time off. I
> almost wish they *would*. Then I'd *really* give them a piece of
> my mind.

Jimmy thought he spent too much time at Amerco not doing
"real work," and this meant that he needed to add time at the end of
the workday to get it all done:

> Work begins at 7 A.M. since we start getting calls from over-
> seas then. Between nine and nine-thirty, three people might
> grab me to talk about a sale. Then I have a meeting from ten-
> thirty to eleven, and probably between eleven-thirty and
> twelve noon someone will ask me to go out to lunch. I go
> around in a caffeine high from one meeting to another to
> another. Meetings are a whirlwind job within the job. It's
> like a tornado.

> I really like my coworkers, but I now spend so much time
> saying, "No, I can't" take on more work or do more favors

that those relations are getting strained. There are so many things to do on a given day. I'm gone for a couple of hours, and I have twenty electronic messages on my computer when I get back. People are working weekends; you can see by the dates. They send things Friday at 10 P.M., Saturday mornings at 9 A.M., Sundays at 9 P.M. Of the twenty messages on my machine, I have to do something about twelve of them. My head spins. At the end of the day, finally, I'll think out a memo. That's my real work, and that edges out an early pick-up for Joshua.

In his heart of hearts, Jimmy wanted to rise up the Amerco ladder. But he also wanted Amerco to understand, if not honor, men like himself who were caught between the demands of work and home. As he explained,

> You have the high-risers grabbing all they can. Then you have the discontent of the lower-downs. Then you have confused people in the middle like me. A day doesn't go by where I don't talk about overload. It's an underground conversation here. You don't want to say it too loud. We're in this whirlwind; we work ourselves to death. Then when we die: What purpose did we serve? Is it worth it? But we're afraid to get off the roller coaster for fear we won't be able to get back on.

What made it hard on working parents like himself, Jimmy mused, was the absence of an "honorable middle rank." He continued,

> Amerco isn't doing a good enough job matching people's opportunities for money or job titles to their family values. What if you don't want to go for the top, but you don't want to level out? We need to be assured that it's okay if we make that middle choice. We need to be told, "You may lose out on some money or a promotion down the road, but we still

value you." A lot of us feel we can grow and should be rewarded—without becoming top managers. I don't worry about seeming like a loser, a goof-off, deadwood. I worry about not seeming like a serious player. We need to change the definition of serious player. A serious player now means someone who has aspirations to go as high as he can, someone who puts in an incredible amount of time, often at the expense of the family. Amerco needs to recognize serious players with serious families.

Three years later, when I visited Jimmy again, he seemed to be turning into the very man his ex-wife had wanted him to be—a rushed, rising executive who had left the "honorable middle" behind. Just as in 1990 he had thought managers in general "couldn't have a life," now he was a manager without much of a life. He had, he claimed, simply moved the "ambition bar" one notch upward. He had also found a steady girlfriend who had quit work to be a "wonderful stepmom" to Joshua. The result was that he and Joshua did fewer things together. "Joshua can play with his little sports figures on the floor for hours, then go outside and shoot baskets by himself," Jimmy commented wistfully. "Now, I have to invite myself to do things with him."

If, in 1990, Jimmy had agonized more openly about his situation than most of the other middle-level male professionals I interviewed, others found themselves, however silently, trapped in the same dilemma. These men ranged from middle managers to technicians, data entry workers to administrative support personnel. Those in the "middle," like Jimmy, often secretly dreamed of a more moderate work pace and way of life. Men in such jobs tended to be neither fully absorbed into a cult of professional workaholism nor pressed by desperate economic need. They worked hard. They wanted to be, as Jimmy put it, serious players. But half of Amerco's male middle managers had working wives; two-thirds had children under thirteen. In the absence of help from housekeepers or kin, they faced the need and often a fair amount of pressure to pitch in at home. So, many of them seemed inclined to resist very long hours.

Such men in the middle might seem poised to resist the process by which the worlds of home and work were being reversed; but they felt torn between the pressure to do more at home and a company-supported image of the serious player as a long-hours man. Even the smallest actual exchange of work time for home time became a monumental decision in their minds. Sam Hyatt took two weeks off for his child's birth, then tried to hold the line on extra hours, but when he was promoted and sent to another state, even that minimal level of resistance to the pull of work crumbled. John West and Jimmy Wayland both talked a good line about the need for more time at home, but neither of them could bring themselves to "walk the talk," and both ended up as long-hours men.

The sociologist William Goode has observed that upper-middle-class fathers advocated a greater role for men at home, though the pressures of career often prevented them from living out what they claimed to believe. Working-class men, on the other hand, often actually did more at home than they thought they should.[2] Today, a confused group of men may be emerging between the other two, men who feel even more strongly than the upper-middle-class fathers that they *should* be doing more, and are even less able to live up to their ideals.

As Amerco's surveys showed, Amerco women were far more interested than Amerco men in expanding time at home, more informed about Amerco's family-friendly policies, and more likely to say they valued these policies. More surprising was the gap between men at the top and men in the middle. Larger percentages of men in the middle with children in childcare, for instance, supported paternity leave than did men above them in the corporate hierarchy. In one 1990 Amerco survey, 13 percent of top male employees thought childcare leave for new fathers was a policy of "great value," while 26 percent of men one level down and 43 percent of administrative and technical men did.[3] (Hourly workers were not surveyed.) Among women, 43 percent of top employees supported childcare leave for new fathers, while 38 percent of workers one level down and only 27 percent of administrative and technical workers agreed.

I can think of two possible explanations for these differences. Men in lower management were younger than men in upper management and perhaps more sympathetic to the idea of participating at home. In the administrative ranks, men were also more likely to work among women. In fact, over half of all administrative workers were women, which meant that these men talked with women every day. Maybe as a result they came to see the world a bit more from a woman's point of view. But no matter why they wanted more time for family life, the vast majority of them still weren't pressing for it. The reasons they gave for their inaction did not have to do mainly with money or job security, nor did they generally lack information about policies such as paternity leave or job sharing, nor were they avoiding the evil eye. Many of them simply could not imagine bucking Amerco and the kind of recognition it promised in return for a full-scale dedication of their time to the company. Both Amerco's official managed culture and the informal male culture of the workplace proved so overwhelmingly powerful that there seemed to be a silent pact to acquiesce to long hours. Did men submit to these hours because they "had" to, because the other guys were doing it, because they liked being at work, or because the pull of family life was too weak?

Jimmy Wayland spoke for many when he said, "I don't define my success as career success, but I'm living as if I do." In the end, for these men—and for increasing numbers of women as well— work was winning out. What had transpired both at Amerco and in society at large was a subtle but complete recasting of the notion of the "family man." Traditionally, "family man" meant a good provider, one who demonstrated his love of wife and children by toiling hard at the office or factory. In the modern workplace, however, "family man" has taken on negative overtones, designating a worker who isn't a serious player. The term now tacitly but powerfully calls into question a worker's masculinity. It was precisely to avoid being classified as a "family man" that the majority of men at Amerco, including Jimmy Wayland and John West, stayed clear of the policies that one might have expected a "family man" to embrace.

CHAPTER 10

What If the Boss Says No?

I can't imagine going through that again. It was just too hard on them. I would have to wake Kenny up out of a sound sleep to get him ready, feed him, throw him in the car on those cold winter mornings. Get him someplace by twenty minutes after seven, so I could get to work by eight. I could never do that again. I *would* never do that again.

Connie Parker, secretary and mother
of children now ten and sixteen

When Connie Parker had a showdown with her boss, Arney Stoltz, a hard-driving ex-marine with a "hair-trigger temper," about taking time off, she stomped out to tell a coworker what happened. That coworker then told Amy Truett's secretary, and soon Amy heard the story, which had gained drama in the retelling. The tale was transformed in ways sympathetic to Connie as it made its way through the Human Resources Division, and in ways sympathetic to Arney as gossip traveled over the golf links, into the e-mail chatter of the line managers in the Product Accessories Division, and even onto the walls of the men's bathroom.

Secretaries like Connie, who fight for the right to trade time for money, usually lack the clout to force the issue. Typists, customer service agents, telephone operators, receptionists, file clerks, and billing agents can hardly say to the company, "We're expensive to train and hard to replace, so give us time off when we need it." Many of these "administrative workers" or "support staff," as they are called at Amerco, answer the phone, type, xerox, or deal with customers each day. For them, availability—or "face time"—is a major aspect of their jobs.

Connie, a spunky, straight-talking, thirty-six-year-old mother of two and wife of a refrigerator repairman, was the secretary supporting a salesperson in the Accessories Division. She had once crusaded against having her job include the washing of coffeepots for the office, so she had a "rep" with management as a troublemaker and she skirmished from time to time with her boss. She began her interview with me by recalling the sacrifices she'd had to make to keep her job:

> I've worked for Amerco for fourteen years. Financially, I've always had to work. I've had no choice. But I just can't imagine going through what I went through again, working full time and raising two kids. It's just been too hard. There were so many things Dolores and Kenny couldn't do or have. Dolores doesn't get ballet lessons unless I find another mother to drive—and they expect you to take your turn, but you never can because you work. Kenny can't go to Boy Scouts. He was in Boy Scouts two years ago, when they had meetings at five at night. But this year, Boy Scouts begins at three and ends at four-thirty, so he doesn't get to go. Those are the things you feel bad about. I'm just glad they're grown up now.

But at ages ten and sixteen, they weren't quite grown up, and Connie was still looking for solutions:

> In the summer, they're both home all day, bored to death. They fight with each other, then call me at work. Kenny goes to a park program down the street from 10 A.M. till 2 P.M., and we belong to the country club nearby, so we sometimes pick him up at noon and take him to the pool, where he can get lunch. Then I pick him up on my way home. Dolores is getting her license and that will help. Then

they can run to the mall. There's not a lot to do in this town for kids, but the mall gives them something besides sitting and watching TV all day.

I asked Connie, a salaried worker, to describe her ideal work schedule, and she replied,

If you can afford the cut in pay for the hours, the ideal situation would be to get home when they get home from school, 3 P.M., so you can take them to ballet and Boy Scouts. Or I could work four days a week so at least there's one day I'm home, and it would free up my Saturday, which I spend cleaning.

Connie didn't want to hire someone to pick up the children, as Vicky King and other top women managers did. She wanted to *be* that person. This was not because she couldn't find anyone to help with the children. She described her babysitter as "like a mother" and "more patient than me" and her husband as "great, thank goodness." But that was not enough for Connie. "I consider myself a good mother," she said. "But my kids aren't having a good childhood."

Employees higher up the Amerco ladder happily delegated aspects of their parental role to others—a wife, a babysitter, a day-care center. Connie Parker had less money and less desire to outsource parts of her motherhood. She did not even have the urge to do less housekeeping. "My husband Alan suggested we hire a cleaning service, but I didn't want to. I'm a fanatic about my cleaning. I'd redo what they did. I'm a hyperactive person, I make up a list and go down it."

Connie did not hire an afternoon sitter partly because the children did not want her to. But keeping them home alone was also a way of holding down her own place as a traditional mother, even when she wasn't filling it. Other working mothers compressed their motherly activities into shorter amounts of time, or postponed favored activities to weekends or the summer. Connie remained at the family switchboard at all times. When the kids had a problem, they called her at the office, not her husband or the babysitter.

Connie wanted control over parenting, but over a curiously limited version of it. She did not aspire to building a dog house with Kenny, or helping Dolores write a column for the school newspaper, or starting a family photography project, or organizing a neighborhood vegetable garden. She had worked from eight to five for so long that she found it hard even to imagine what she would do if she had more time. She did not see herself as a recreational, educational, or civic-spirited mom. She wanted to be able to drive Dolores to ballet lessons and Kenny to Boy Scouts. Her dream was modest: to be a suburban mom–chauffeur.

But that was no trivial matter to her. Kenny had severe asthma that kept him up many nights and in and out of the hospital; so, for now, Connie wanted time off from work to drive him to the doctor's for a series of asthma shots that frightened him. As she spoke, she took a sip of coffee; then she folded her arms and launched into the story of her attempt to get that time:

> Two years ago, I began picking up my son at twenty minutes to four every Wednesday for his weekly shots. After the shot, we'd have to wait to make sure he'd have no reaction, and by the time we'd get done, it would be a quarter to five, so I'd just go on home rather than back to work. I did that every Wednesday for six weeks.

Connie's boss Arney was an energetic supervisor who believed that maintaining a clear, strong hierarchy in the office was the best way to fight the company's battle for market share. He'd had run-ins before with clerical workers under him, Connie included, when they seemed to challenge his rules. At the time Connie first approached him, Arney might have been worrying about how his sense of discipline and command fit into the new order, which was based on persuasion, loyalty, and "valuing the internal customer." At home, Arney was raising two rambunctious daughters and coping with a restless wife who reportedly talked more and more these days of getting a part-time job herself. The secretaries working under him surmised that he felt besieged on all sides. The secretaries and Arney shared the familiarity of small-town adversaries. Each knew a lot about the other's personal life, but the secretaries knew more.

This may have been why Arney looked with special skepticism at a request for weekly afternoons off from the most outspoken of the typists in his division. Before she left the office for the first time to take Kenny to the doctor's, Connie had hurriedly said something to Arney; but Arney had been on the phone, hadn't caught her message, and certainly hadn't OK'd it. He was out of the office when she left the second time, but heard about it from a coworker who wanted credit for covering for Connie. The day after her third departure, Connie recalled, the first confrontation occurred:

> Arney called me into his office, shut the door, and said, "I know you take Kenny to get his shots. . . ." Right then I froze, because I knew what he was going to say next. He said, "I'd like you to make some other arrangements for that." I tensed up. I told him, "I can't make any other arrangements." He said, "Are you *sure* you can't make any other arrangements?" I told him, "I don't know what you expect me to do. Kenny has to have these shots."

Connie focused singlemindedly on the *medical* nature of her trips to the doctor. An earache, a case of appendicitis, asthma—these were "real" human needs. She had a much harder time admitting that Kenny was *afraid* of his shots and that she couldn't imagine anyone else comforting him quite as well as she could.

Arney pressed her to call on her "backup system." Wasn't there a sitter, a grandmother, a husband who could take Kenny? Arney appealed to her to understand that a working mother's job was to devise and maintain a well-functioning stable of substitutes for herself. Connie stuck to her point: "I don't know what other arrangements I can make."

And that's when Arney exploded. As Connie recounted the
episode,

> He yelled, "*I* don't know either, but I'm sure *you* can find
> someone! First of all, I don't understand why you're leaving
> so early and what takes so long to get a shot." So I said,
> "Listen, Arney, I'm taking my son to get his shots. If you
> don't want to pay me for the time I'm gone, that's fine, but
> *I'm* taking him." And I got up and walked out.[1]

The next day, Connie called her doctor's office.

> I was so mad! I told the nurse what happened and I said, "I'd
> like the doctor to write a note explaining to this joker why
> my son needs shots, why I have to stay there for the reaction,
> and why it takes me an hour to do this." I wrote Arney a
> note with my doctor's name and telephone number. "Dr.
> Moore said he'd be more than happy to discuss Kenny's
> allergy shots with you if you want to call him, or he'll write
> you a note explaining the need for them." I stuck it on his
> desk and walked back to my office.

> A while later, Arney came into my office and said, "I got
> your note. I didn't say Kenny didn't *need* shots. And I don't
> need an explanation of why he needs shots. I asked if you
> could make *other arrangements*."

> I looked up and I said, "Arney, there *are* no other arrange-
> ments." I will never forgive him for that. When it comes to
> my son's health, I say, go ahead and fire me.

The truth was Connie could have made other arrangements.
Her mother and husband had both offered to take Kenny for his
shots. But Connie wanted to do it herself, and she wanted credit as
well for all the other times when she had made "other arrangements" in order to stay at work:

I bet I miss only three days a year. Arney isn't looking at all the days Kenny was sick when I took him to my mother's, or when Alan stayed home. I make a lot of other arrangements. If I took off all the time I really should take off for the kids, Arney would flip out. If I could get part time, I'd schedule the shots on Fridays. A lot of people in sales leave at 3 P.M. to play golf. They're getting paid to play golf. I'm not saying they shouldn't play golf. But, then, don't tell me I can't take my son to get his asthma shots!

When Vicky King stepped out of the office, people assumed she was off to an important meeting. When Connie, a secretary, left her desk to make photocopies, Arney suspected her of getting her hair cut. This double standard of trust made it even harder for a secretary to go part time. "The only people I ever hear of getting part-time jobs are the women managers," Connie observed.

They go on maternity leave and come back to part time if they want to. I know of very few A&Ts [administrative and technical staff people] who do this. But I have heard of a list of at least thirty-five A&T employees that were interested in part-time work. About 50 to 60 percent would like it.

The double standard was part of a larger class system Connie keenly resented:

We're invisible. We used to joke that we ought to stamp "A&T" on our foreheads; then they'd know right off the bat that they wouldn't have to speak to us. Some women managers who have lunch with us are told to cool it: "Too much socializing with the A&Ts."

Most of us A&Ts don't have four-year degrees. So I guess they think we're not as intelligent. Yet, in the next breath, they say they want to "empower" us. That's the new buzzword. Well, great, these people don't even trust us for half an hour but they want to empower us to make big decisions? Well, either empower me or don't. At home, I'm an adult with my children, but as soon as I come to work, I'm a little kid back in school.

As Arney Stoltz saw the Connie Parker situation, it was "a perception problem." Arney began our interview by patiently laying out the issues as he saw them: "If I let Connie take Wednesday afternoons, I'll have Laura asking me for time off next. She's got three-year-old twins. Rena has the desk on the other side of Connie, and her dad just had a stroke. We have a *business* to run."

Arney was right about the women in his office. One secretary, Kim Lombardo, wanted to teach piano at her son's school on her lunch break. Rena Socci did need to visit her stroke-stricken father, who spent his days nearly helpless in his wheelchair. The list of family responsibilities was at least as long as Arney feared.

Fundamental to this tug-of-war was an understanding about time. Arney thought Connie, like "all the secretaries," was "a clock-watcher." The less you pay people for their time, he reasoned, the less they like their work. And the less important work time seems to them, the more likely they are to want time off the job. In fact, people greatly exaggerated their hours, he told me. "I can pick up the phone at 4:30 or 5 P.M.," he declared pointedly, "and get voice mail. I go into some of our plants, and you can fire a shotgun at five and you're not going to hit anyone." Arney himself was a serious player. Serious players, he believed, had a higher status than clock-watchers. So it made sense that they should watch the clock for the clock-watchers.

But there was an additional reason Arney opposed part time. Arney's greatest fear was that if he were forced to accept part time or flextime as operating principles, "the girls" might use these policies as vehicles of revenge for the small indignities they had suffered at his hands. I asked Arney what he'd said when Connie offered to take a pay cut. "Nothing," he replied. Money was not the decisive issue. "An asthma shot here, a dentist appointment there, a frantic call from a child home alone. Amerco can't deal with all that."

Indeed, the pressure of family needs was, to Arney's mind, a large part of what a manager was supposed to manage. For Arney, time on the job was the basis for a moral accounting. It was his job to defend Amerco against the enemies of company time, as he had in the past defended his country against the enemies of its territory. A manager needs to defend work time especially in a period filled with business crises, and the previous year, 1991, had seemed to him like nothing but a long series of crises.

As Arney saw himself, he was exactly the sort of guy you would want to have around when there was trouble. He told me a story to illustrate the point. Once, he said, he found himself behind a hit-and-run driver, so he followed the car, ran it off the road, and made a citizen's arrest. The law is the law, and sometimes a person has to act heroically to enforce it. The marines had fostered in him an honest respect for the capacity of emergencies to make men into heroes. No high-speed chases were going to come out of Connie's Wednesday disappearances, but Arney nevertheless saw her as a kind of hit-and-run time-thief and himself as the hero of the situation. It was no fun being the "bad guy" of the office, but sometimes a man had to do his job, had to uphold the company's law, whether he liked it or not. It was all well and good for the CEO to give a moving speech about a family–friendly Amerco, Arney thought, but what happened after that? How was the guy who manages, the man in the middle, to get the necessary work out of those below him in order to meet his departmental budget?

It only made matters more difficult that Connie and the other women in his department were countering his military style of authority with a democratizing streak of office satire. They whispered about Arney's hot temper and called him "*Ar*-nold" in a certain exaggerated tone, as if he were a silly little boy. They also armed themselves against him by being hyperefficient, establishing a moral zone within which they were free to lampoon him with open expressions of their disdain. "You've heard of the 'new man'?" Connie once said in a low voice to coworkers. "Well, Arney's the 'old man.' "

If the CEO's mission statements formed the building blocks of company culture, it was in mandated workshops and smaller group meetings that these slogans were translated into practical guidelines for behavior. In Amerco culture, rule number one for any manager was to be aware of doctrinal shifts, and to be able to gauge how deep they went. No sooner had a new idea like "flexible management" or "empowerment" been announced than managers had to decide whether or how much to "manage" it. Such cultural changes came in quick pulses, followed by waves of one- or two-day workshops and smaller meetings. So a manager's conversion became the object of intense scrutiny by those who stood to win or lose depending upon the sincerity of his change of heart. If Arney Stoltz walked into a Valuing Diversity workshop, did he come out of it a new man or the same old *Ar*-nold spouting a new line?

So it was that Arney Stoltz, former marine, attended a training session one afternoon to watch a video called *Managing Smart*. The video dealt with family-friendly planning in the department, and Arney was expected the next week to begin implementing the principle of flexible management and "participatory solution seeking." He was under pressure to convince those he supervised that he had really come to believe that family-friendly policies were crucial to Amerco culture.

Anticipating scrutiny from his employees, Arney tried to assume the necessary look, but he wasn't good at posing. The women in the typing pool soon concluded that Arney wasn't even trying to be sincere. He was dissenting. He didn't *believe* that Amerco should be family friendly. However, as a forty-seven-hour man—rather than a sixty-hour man—he wasn't expecting to rise much higher in company ranks. There were limits to how much he worried about being caught dissenting on an issue about which he thought the company president was, with all due respect, wrongheaded. Nonetheless, rather than rock the boat too much, Arney finally signed off on Connie's Wednesday absences and warned her to watch it next time.

But Connie was left wanting still more time for life at home, and three years later, in 1993, a second time-skirmish took place—over a proposal she made to work thirty hours a week. A company brochure had announced that such a work schedule was available, with a pay cut but full medical benefits, as long as a supervisor or division head approved. When their children were younger, Connie and her husband could not have afforded such a loss of income, but now time seemed more valuable to Connie than money; so she called Human Resources, and Amy Truett set up a meeting with Arney. As Connie told the story,

> We had the meeting—Amy, Arney, and me. Amy and I suggested that I leave at 3 P.M. every day, or take Fridays off on a trial basis for six months. If it didn't work, we'd go back to the way it was before, or another woman would work the other ten hours. Arney seemed surprised. He doesn't smile a lot, so it's hard to read him.

From Arney's point of view, Connie had lived up to his worst fears. Those ten hours would simply disappear. What "other woman" did she imagine would fill in? It was obvious that Connie didn't feel responsible, but far worse, now other secretaries in his division would want part time, too.

Continuing, Connie described in a near whisper what someone had told her:

> Arney said he had never come so close to hitting a woman as he had that day. It was Amy he wanted to hit for interfering in a manager's job. Those were his exact words. He said it in front of someone and that person told me.

> Arney's boss, Jack Clark, was upset, and Jack's boss, Paul, was upset, too. But he made light of Arney's comment: "It was just an expression." He told me we had surprised Arney. With all that preparation, can you imagine?

Among administrative workers in Amerco as a whole, only 26 percent of women and men said they would be "willing to work fewer hours with less pay in order to spend more time with the family." Among those who provided elder care, 29 percent responded the same way; among those who used childcare, 39 percent. Connie was in the minority in two ways. First, she wanted time more than money. Second, she acted on that feeling. In doing so, she revealed the enormous obstacles that can exist even in a family-friendly company. To make time for family, one first had to make arrangements at work, and this was not necessarily as easy as company brochures implied. Managers higher up were showing their commitment in the currency of time, while production workers lower in the hierarchy more often needed the money. It was in the middle of the company hierarchy—above the factory floor but below corporate management—where relatively more workers wanted family time that the war over time was clearest. It was there that the Amerco time-police walked the beat more than they "walked the talk."

Connie lost the struggle for part time, but she went down in style. As she concluded with a sly smile,

> I arranged to spend my vacation time a day a week all summer. So, I'm working four days a week, except I get paid for it. I'm doing the same thing they said I couldn't do, and they're paying me. I was willing to do it without pay. No one is coming in to back me up Fridays, and Amerco didn't fold.

Despite Connie's triumphal tone, her "arrangement" was no victory. Instead of forcing the company to be more flexible, she ended up redistributing her own free time in a slightly different way. In stealing from herself, Connie was fairly typical of Amerco employees, who would dip into sick days and personal days to handle family emergencies. Then, well before the year was out, they would find that they had overdrawn their reserve of free days, leaving them with no alternative but to steal from vacation days, holidays, and sleep when circumstances required. So time-thievery *was* rife at Amerco, just as managers like Arney Stoltz feared, but the victims tended to be the "thieves" themselves.

CHAPTER 11

"I Want Them to Grow Up to Be Good Single Moms"

> I haven't ripped up the wedding photos. I keep my wedding album on the coffee table for Esther to look through. She'll ask, "Were you happy then?" I'll say, "Yes." I want them to know that there's some good in marriage.
>
> *Becky Winters, factory worker on a rotating shift*

From her workstation on the night shift of a rotating seven-day schedule, Becky Winters motioned with her head for me to join her. An attractive woman of thirty-one, she wore her long blond hair flipped in the back but high-standing in front, a style popular among the "girls" at work. Beneath the crown of hair, her eyes were shielded by large, plastic safety glasses. She had small, tasteful stud earrings in her ears. A pink cotton jersey and white jeans revealed a trim figure. Her job was to take parts off a conveyor belt, place them on a scale, read a gauge that weighed them and tested their size, and either return them to the belt or discard them. Beside the scale was a copy of *Cosmopolitan*, its cover featuring an elegant blond woman. Becky took it with her on breaks.

"The money's good but I feel brain dead," Becky told me. This surprised me a little because she had the opportunity to participate in an innovative twenty-step process called the Matrix Program, in which she could cross-train on a variety of machines in the plant. At the end of twenty months, a worker could read dozens of types of gauges and assess the quirks and foibles of numerous kinds of machines. While interviewing the manager of her plant, I noticed a stack of framed Matrix graduation certificates on a table near his desk, but Becky didn't covet one. She wasn't on the job, she told me, to expand her horizons but to collect pay, meet friends, and, to some extent, escape family life.

She earned $11.20 an hour for forty hours a week, more for four hours of required overtime, and she wanted all the overtime she could get. According to the Bureau of Labor Statistics, factory workers now average four hours, forty-two minutes of overtime a week, the most hours registered in the thirty-eight years during which the agency has kept track.[1] For Becky, Amerco was hardly the exciting, expansive place that it is for the ten-hour players at the top; but it held little of the pain of life at home.

Half of Amerco workers are paid by the hour, and about a third of these hourly workers are women. Of hourly women, 23 percent are, like Becky, single mothers; nine percent of hourly men are single fathers. In this respect, both groups are close to the national average.[2] Like most other hourly single mothers, Becky was a relatively new worker, so she was low on the seniority totem pole and couldn't get the most desirable work shift—steady days. The less desirable alternatives were, in descending order, steady evenings, steady nights, or a rotating shift that changed every week. Thirteen percent of all Amerco employees and 36 percent of all hourlies work rotating shifts, including over half of the single mothers in the company's plants. As Becky put it, "In all this talk about family-friendly policies, we are the forgotten people."

For the past five years, Becky had worked a rotating seven-day shift. This meant that every week she had a different schedule. She worked five days from 7 A.M. to 3 P.M., followed by a day off; then five days from 3 P.M. to 11 P.M., followed by two days off. Then came five nights, 11 P.M. to 7 A.M., followed by five days off—her "long weekend." For Sundays, she was paid time and a half. I visited her at the plant toward the end of the third "week" of the cycle, when she was looking forward to the long weekend.

While we talked, her two daughters were snuggled into bed with her seventy-year-old mother, Mary, who slept over on nights when Becky worked. Becky took the girls for two of her shifts; her ex-husband Derek filled in for the third (and had the girls every other weekend as well).[3] Mary helped out during the fourth "vacation" week, and many afternoons. A tireless worker, Becky's mother was the most important person in Becky's life. Her father had worked two jobs to support her mother, who had kept an immaculate house and raised Becky and her two brothers. Becky remembered her dad sleeping most of the time he was home and drinking more and more heavily as the week went on. By Saturday afternoon, she would often find him snoring on the living room floor in front of a flickering television. Those Saturdays Becky remembered playing on their porch with her Barbie doll. ("Barbie got married every other day.") The family had no common meals and enjoyed few vacations together. Mysterious phone calls from women and missing vacation money eventually led Becky's mother to suspect that her husband's "long hours" at work included other activities. The day Becky graduated from high school, Mary filed for divorce."[4] After thirty-four years of marriage, Becky's dad took his pension for himself, which was why—at age seventy, having raised three children—Mary was now working full time at near minimum wage pay at a childcare center.

"It's been difficult," Becky told me, "raising two girls from the age of two and three alone."

I have no family except my mother here to help. My older brother passed away in January. I have a younger brother in Oklahoma. My father lives right down the road, but he's nothing to me. My biggest support is my mother.

When I later interviewed Mary in her tidy three-bedroom home, she explained, "I try my best to help Becky out, but I'm seventy and I don't know how long I can last." In the United States as a whole, a quarter of the children of single mothers (and 14 percent

of married mothers' children) are cared for by grandparents.⁵ But
the supply of grandmotherly help is beginning to dry up as more
grandmothers take on paid jobs or move elsewhere to retire.

In fact, the supply of *all* family help—the reserve pool of childcare that previous generations relied on—is rapidly disappearing as
more and more Americans join the workforce.⁶ According to the
Census Bureau, in 1977, 13 percent of all children under the age of
five with employed mothers were cared for by grandparents or
other relatives in the child's home. By 1991, the figure had dropped
to 10 percent.⁷ For instance, while Becky and I were drinking
coffee in the breakroom at two o'clock one morning, Sara-Jo, her
coworker, joined us. "Everyone works," Sara-Jo commented
matter-of-factly.

> My mom works in the Marriott Hotel, day and night shifts.
> My brother works at Safeway, mostly days, some evenings. My
> sister Carol works at the Food Mart, mainly days but once a
> week the night shift. My mother's sister mostly works evenings
> and some afternoons. That's why my husband and I work
> opposite shifts, so we can cover the twins between us.

In addition, as the elderly live longer, they are more likely to need
care themselves. In this respect Becky was lucky that her mother
was still in good health and willing to lend a hand. Her father was
another matter, however. Although Joe lived "right down the
road," he had been estranged from Becky since she was a teenager.
"He has no relationship with the girls," she told me, barely repressed anger in her voice.

> He's glad to see them if I bring them by, and he tries more
> now. He came to Esther's dance recital. We see him on
> Christmas and Easter. I go out with him and his new wife on
> his birthday.

Her father, now sixty-seven, had also refused to share the care of his
older son, Becky's brother, while he was dying of a brain tumor,

something to which Becky and her mother reacted with outrage and disbelief. Mary was forced to pay all her son's funeral expenses out of her childcare worker's salary, while Joe spent his pension, the family suspected, on extended trips with his new wife. Worse yet, in their eyes, with his second family Joe showed evidence of being the kindly husband and father they themselves had long yearned for. "My dad's wallet is full of photos of his second wife's four children and fourteen grandchildren," Becky said in a strained voice. "He goes to all her children's and grandchildren's ball games and functions. You don't even see our family pictures in his house."

Becky's ex-husband, Derek, seemed to be undergoing a similar metamorphosis. "I see Derek and his new wife go places and do things with the kids," Becky commented. "When their new baby comes, I think he's going to be a good dad. Why wasn't he like that for the girls and me?" If Becky and her mother felt like outsiders observing the seemingly happy second marriages of their ex-husbands, their own lives were remarkably full. The doorbell at Becky's house rang often. Tania and Renee, daughters of the single mother across the street, often visited and stayed for meals, while the answering machine accumulated messages from friends at the plant.

For Becky, the time her ex-husband now spent caring for their daughters was a symbol of his larger obligation to them and to her. Derek, on the other hand, claimed that since he took the children while Becky worked the day shift (a shift during which the girls were awake, and so had to be actively watched) as well as every other weekend, he was fulfilling his half-time obligations to them and should not have to pay child support. Becky countered (reasonably enough, it seemed to me, though since Derek declined to be interviewed, I never heard his side of the story) that childcare for one week out of four was not half-time, and half-time childcare did not, in any case, exempt him from paying half the child support. Since he was unemployed at that moment and his second wife was expecting a baby, the issue may have been more symbolic than real. Quite real, though, was the overtime Becky was working to pay $573 a month toward the mortgage on the house she and Derek had bought together, so the girls would have a nice backyard with room for a slide and a swing. Now Derek was telling her that the girls didn't need a yard.

To Derek, time spent with his daughters was evidence of his devotion to them and of his status as a caring father (which only improved his standing in the eyes of his second wife). For her part, Becky felt that Derek's time with his daughters was good for them but—with child support money lacking—also a "weapon against her." His time was to her only a small token of what she was owed for eleven years of tending a home and six years as the primary parent feeding and clothing their children. It meant Derek was cheating on her yet again. But as he had more time than money at the moment, her arguing got her nowhere.

Like Derek, Becky wanted to be recognized for spending time with their daughters. In this sense the lure of home was stronger for her than the lure of work. But her world at home was filled with tremendous tension and half-expressed regret for a life that was no longer—perhaps never had been—hers. So Becky dreaded her phone calls to Derek, the quarrels over child support, and the strong attachment she still, despite her best intentions, felt to him. As we were walking along one day, Esther, Becky's stormy, bright, willful older daughter, finding her shoes too tightly knotted, sat down to retie them and suddenly burst into tears. "I can't tie them!" she moaned. Becky listened warmly, patiently, but was not overly solicitous. Half an hour later, back at home, Esther plopped into her mother's lap in despair, complaining that Tania, her friend from next door, had taken her kit of glitter, stars, sequins, and glue. Becky believed Esther tended to get upset after she heard her parents quarrel on the phone about child support. Her younger daughter, Tiffany, seemed reserved, orderly, resilient. "Tiffany is Daddy's girl," Becky observed. "Esther is nobody's girl, because she reminds Derek of me."

The tensions at work, by comparison, only enhanced Becky Winters's sense of self. Life at Amerco, in her descriptions, sounded almost like an extension of the high school prom, the local bar, the neighborhood—a world where she felt attractive and liked. At the factory, she began telling me, she had more men friends than women:

> When I first walked into the factory, the only other young woman on my assembly line hated me because she thought I was taking male attention away from her. The men called me "honey," "babe," "beautiful." The guys talk with you in double meanings. There's a computer in the factory where you bid on different jobs, and I was on the computer and a very nice-looking guy came along and said, "What are you going to do?" I told him, "I'd like to try something different." He looked at me real hard and said, "Yes, I'd like to try something *different*, too." I turned scarlet.

Becky knew she was gossiped about by certain older women who kept an eagle eye on the flirtations at the plant. While she ostensibly disapproved of them talking about her, she also seemed just a little pleased. In a context where occupational mobility was unlikely, perhaps sexual desirability, quite apart from marriage, became the focus of ambition in its own right. If Becky half-avoided the women who complained about her sexual "oversuccess," she nevertheless had good women friends at the plant. Five of them, she told me, were just then planning a weekend trip to another state to catch a country-western jamboree. Another friend from work had children exactly the ages of Esther and Tiffany, and her husband fixed Becky's car when it broke down.[8]

Gossip passed through the plant as if through a village community, and much of it was about matters at home. When Becky's sister-in-law, who worked in the same plant, left her husband to have an affair with a coworker, the jilted husband wrote an article in the local paper about women who selfishly abandon their families for "greener pastures." He then xeroxed the article and taped it up all over the plant for everyone to read. Becky typed a reply and someone pinned *that* up on lockers and bulletin boards. Becky's sister-in-law soon replied to both of them. Names were never mentioned, but everyone knew who was meant. To some extent, work was where people learned about and judged what went on outside of work.

For Becky and her friends, work was a more predictable, safer, more emotionally supportive and relaxing place to be than home. This was not so much because cultural engineering had enhanced the pleasures of working at the plant. Assembly line work was still assembly line work.

Life at work was more pleasant or, at least, less painfully disappointing in large part because life at home, at the moment, was a torment. It wasn't that Becky regretted her split-up with Derek. If anything, she took a certain satisfaction in living out her mother's unfulfilled wish—to get out of an unhappy marriage with enough time left to live a full life. Nevertheless, from childhood on, she had pinned great hopes on marriage, and her divorce made her wonder whether those hopes had ever been realistic. Even now, two years after their split-up, she still kept the brightly painted "Winters Family" sign that Derek had carved hanging on the front porch. Still displayed along her dining room walls, too, were a series of plates, each portraying a scene from *Gone With the Wind*. While eating lunch there one day, I looked from plate to plate: on one, Clark Gable as Rhett Butler is embracing Vivian Leigh as Scarlett O'Hara; on the next, Rhett carries Scarlett up the grand staircase of Tara; on a third, Rhett and Scarlett are happily married with two children; on a fourth, Rhett poses proudly beside his growing daughters; on the final plate, Scarlett stands windblown and alone outside her homestead. Perhaps Becky saw her own life in this stormy love story with its unhappy ending. Yet the plates put an odd twist on the movie, showing Rhett as a stable, happy father.

The wedding album that was kept on the coffee table, the painted plates, the "Winters Family" sign, all were votes for a stubborn dream of blissful marriage in a land where divorce was common. All were reminders of how eager Becky had once been to marry, of how powerful that dream had been, of how incidental Derek may even have been to its fulfillment. They reflected a familial version of the rags-to-riches myth, which persists despite declining emotional wages and episodic familial layoffs. All her "wedding" furniture, after all, had been purchased before Becky's engagement to Derek. It had been she who had saved money to make a down payment on their freshly painted house on a tree-lined street in town. In their wedding album, which she laid across our two laps, were numerous photos of a luminous Becky and a slightly sullen Derek. Both bride and groom were twenty. In one photo, Derek stood in a lineup of six brothers, his cheeks rosy, his eyes bleary—she now saw—with drink. Indeed, Derek, while married, had regularly shared late evening drinking bouts with his brothers, who teased him for being "whupped" at home and egged him on to defy Becky's increasingly exasperated requests that he come back for dinner at "six—okay, seven. All right, no later than eight."

His drinking worsened until he lost his job; then to save his pride he lied about being fired. When Becky learned of this, she became enraged, and that was when Derek first hit her. Furious, and eager to break her sense of dependency on Derek, she had an affair with an attractive man she met at work who was looking for solace on his way down the management ladder. Becky also encouraged her sister-in-law Dana to end her faltering marriage with a workplace affair as well. So the two women "did their divorce together," for which Derek's family bitterly blamed her.

For Becky and Derek, as for at least half of all couples nationwide, marriage was not a safe haven. Of the smiling young relatives and friends in Becky's album, half—exactly the national average—had since divorced. Derek's younger brother Sam, twelve years old in the album, had already married and divorced, and then called the Social Security Administration asking them to order his wife to stop using her married name. Jay, then seventeen, had married, divorced, and remarried his ex-wife Barb, who also appeared in the album. Each divorce had had its own ripple effect on the extended families involved. For Becky's and Derek's families, as for so many others in their social class in a region hit hard by waves of unemployment, it seemed a daunting task to make a marriage last as long as the idea of it did.

Instead, Becky and her friends talked about "good" divorces, "all-right" divorces, and "bad" divorces. Dana's husband had taken her to court, claimed she was an unfit mother, sued for custody, and married a woman who aggravated the conflict. So Dana had a bad divorce. Because Derek's new wife wasn't mean, Becky thought that she had an all-right divorce. Becky had no plans to remarry. As she explained,

> I don't want the "Where-have-you-been?" and "Where-is-the-laundry?" and "What's-for-dinner?" routine. Once you get involved with another person, you're the mother whether you choose it for yourself or not. I don't want to take care of somebody else. Because, underneath, they'll get to know everything about you, and if they leave, they'll take all that with them.

In Becky's life, marriage had ceased to function as a basis for financial and emotional security. For what tenuous security she could now muster she looked to her mother, her children, and her job.

But in her world, jobs, like marriages, were nothing to rely on either. Becky reflected,

> I don't know if we'll get family-friendly policies here in the plant. You always get the sense that you can be replaced. The company doesn't say that to us. They don't have to. We hear a lot of rumors that Amerco may take the operation out of the country and pay fifty cents an hour to Mexican workers to do our jobs. That means that high-seniority people will bump people like us out of the plant.

The job could "divorce" you, too. But if Becky had given up on marriage, she hadn't yet given up on work.

A Gypsy Life

Driving along a ribbon of freeway that led away from Amerco head-quarters over miles of rolling hills, it was easy to miss the small sign announcing Treemont Village. A turnoff led up a narrow, winding paved road to a trailer court at the top of a hill. The village superintendent was chatting amiably with a resident. When I told him I was looking for Sue Carpenter, he said laconically, "She's here, *he's* gone. I don't know what the trouble is."

Sue was late for our interview. As I perched on a step leading up to her front door, I saw elderly people and children coming and going from tidy trailers, a dozen on either side of a paved roadway. Under an awning, an overweight woman sat in a folding chair, legs crossed, holding a child by the hand. Somewhere a baby cried and a woman called out. An old, low-slung Ford pulled in slowly, mindful of toddlers and tricycle riders. Soon after, a truck marked "Frank's Hauling" brought in a new blue-and-white mobile home, a "wide-load" sign dangling from its rear bumper. A dozen or so overweight middle-aged onlookers, in shorts and sunglasses, cigarettes dangling from their mouths, appeared to welcome the diversion.

Between small, well-tended plots of grass, each family trailer made a unique statement. From one hung two baskets of pink and blue plastic flowers. Another had a large pot of red geraniums over the trailer hitch. Yet another was brightly decorated with bursts of blue lupine and yellow pansies and had a small greenhouse attached to the side. On one of the mini-lawns that fronted each trailer sat a row of plastic ducks. Another had a model windmill and a large American flag. Indeed, half a dozen tin American flags formed a doll-sized parade along a row of metal mailboxes in front of the homes. If the monotonous work at the factory offered little range for free expression, the grounds of this trailer court seemed to offer a great deal.

Sue Carpenter's yard was less cheerfully done up. Two plastic bikes leaned against the railing of her porch; next to a broken chair, a couch covered in plastic exuded stuffing. Sue herself arrived in a large, tan Chevrolet, her children in the back. Like Becky, she wore her long blond hair in a high-standing flip. She was short, lithe, pretty, and slightly withdrawn. A single mother of two daughters, five and two, she worked with Becky on the rotating shift. Inside, the house was decorated in pink and blue. We sat down to talk in the living room. Lillian, Sue's curious two-year-old daughter, padded back and forth between Sue's lap, the bedroom, and a hole in the front screen door that led out to the babysitter's trailer across the road. Five-year-old Michelle appeared at one point with the mail and proudly read a form letter aloud: "SUE CAR-PENTER, Congratulations! You have just won a grand prize. . . ."

Sue's tall, muscular nineteen-year-old stepbrother, Brian, was splayed on the couch, an injured knee elevated. He was watching wrestling on television. Laid off three months before, he'd been staying with Sue ever since. He babysat when Sue left for her 3 P.M. shift. By Brian's head was a Barney doll, the same purple dinosaur that democratically populated the homes of children at every rung of the Amerco occupational ladder. At the gap in the screen door, a small child appeared asking, "Can Michelle come out to play?" After responding to the visitor, Sue turned to me saying, "She visits all the time."

The living room couch faced a large television console. Beside it sat an equally large framed photo of Sue in a flaming red, ruffled blouse in front of a vase of roses, giving the viewer a sultry glance over a bare shoulder. "A photo shop at the mall had a 'gypsy' offer," she explained. "They do your hair, makeup, and dress, and then take the picture." In the presence of this image of herself as a gypsy, solo in an exotic world of adventure, Sue leaned back on the living room sofa and began to tell me a sad, complicated story of unraveling family ties.

Unlike most of the managers and professionals I spoke with, Sue Carpenter felt herself surrounded by a sprawling, disjointed network of relatives. Her mother had eight children from her first marriage; her father, two from his. Sue was one of four more children her parents had together. Contrary to a common stereotype of working-class life, however, Sue's expanded, extended family did not provide much social or emotional support. In fact, she received most support from an older woman, a nonrelative she'd met at work.

When I asked Sue to tell me something about herself, she was not inclined to talk about her present-day life or her work at Amerco. Instead she turned immediately to relatives she didn't see, rarely called, and, by and large, didn't trust, as if she were still largely caught in the disappointing world of her childhood:

> My mother was the one who held everything together. But she passed away when I was nineteen. She and I never got close until probably a year before she died. There were so many of us, we didn't have that closeness you should have with your kids.

> My mom used to work the 5 P.M. to 1:30 A.M. shift as a waitress. My dad was in contracting. He's a loner. Work wasn't that plentiful, and independent contractors can't compete with the big guys. So my dad worked long hours and my older sister babysat me. My parents both liked to drink on weekends, and with that came arguments. My father has a very short fuse and he'd get violent when he drank. Outside of that, he was an excellent person. He wasn't afraid to tell us he loved us, unlike most men.

Over the course of her twenty-seven years, Sue's large family had slowly shattered and scattered. She inventoried them:

> Two of my half-brothers and one of my real brothers live right here in town, but I'm not close to them. My oldest brother, my real brother, is unemployed, I think. My younger brother is a carpenter in Florida the last I heard. He's a wanderer. He and his wife split up and he came back and stayed with me for four months, but I couldn't let it go on because he never baby-sat. I felt like he was taking advantage of me. He's a taker, not a giver. And my sister and I aren't

very close like sisters should be. She tried to take my mom's place when Mom died but she was too bossy. As for my dad, I don't go and ask him for advice. I'm much closer to Brian, the one that's living with me now for a while.

Sue described her family largely in terms of how close they weren't, how often they didn't get together, the siblings' birthdays she didn't remember, what meaning their relationships should have had but didn't. "We don't get together for Christmas. We don't get together for Thanksgiving or birthdays," she said. "It's just me and my kids."

As Sue Carpenter said this, Brian looked up from the TV and remarked with a twinkle. "So I guess we come from a dysfunctional family, right?" They smiled at each other affectionately and laughed. "No family values," he added. In fact, both seemed ready to compare their family to a quasi-medical notion of "functional" families cycled through television's daytime talk shows that bring family sociology to trailer courts and working-class suburbs across the land.

In her third year in high school, Sue worked as a part-time shampoo girl at a hairdresser's. That year she met a shy boy named Michael Carpenter, himself a refugee from the chaos of family life. Sue and Michael began to date and, soon after, to live together. Neither of them believed in marriage, but at Michael's stepmother's insistence, they married anyway in a little church on a rainy November day. They had two children and stayed together for seven years before getting a divorce, an act that Michael and Sue (somewhat more hesitantly) regretted. They still spoke of each other as "best friends."

On the patio outside Michael's apartment several miles from Treemont Village five or six dolls lay scattered about, part of a colorful mosaic of toys strewn across a dozen apartment patios in the development where he lived. Toddlers trundled out into the hot morning from doors left ajar. Michael's apartment was spare and neat, the living room dominated by the stuffed head of an eight-point buck that gazed abstractedly over the goings-on. "Even the venison I sent Sue two-thirds of," he said proudly. Tacked up on a bulletin board between the buck and a mounted twenty-inch northern pike (a fly stuck in its open mouth) was a collection of recent snapshots of his daughters.

Michael Carpenter, twenty-six, an athletic, tanned blond man, moved to fetch coffee with muscular grace. The owner with his half-brother of a racing stock car, he landscaped and repaired lawns and yards for Amerco. He began his story this way:

> I was raised on a farm. By the time I was eighteen, I felt ready to retire. That was how hard we worked. Sometimes my dad was nice, but three-quarters of the time he was mean. He hauled cattle for a living and drank brandy and beer all day from bottles under the front seat of his truck. He swore at us. "Dumb little bastards, you don't know shit!" That's what we heard the whole time we were growing up. His dad treated him mean, but that's no excuse to treat us that way. I don't treat *my* kids mean. I turned that around.
>
> My real mom and dad split when I was three, and my real mom moved with me to Florida. My dad came down, kidnapped me, and hid me at my aunt's. When my mom came up to get me, my dad threatened to kill her. So she gave up. I didn't see her again until I drove down to Florida when I was seventeen. She didn't call. She didn't write. She didn't bother. Once when I was five, she came to visit me and didn't recognize me. That hurt.

Michael's dad then married Elizabeth, a woman who adopted and raised him as if he were her own son. Elizabeth drove a bus, cleaned houses, and became "a super mom, *my* mom." As time went on, though, Michael's father began to accuse his wife of taking money from him. He would shout at her and pull her hair. Finally, when Michael was thirteen, they too divorced. Michael soon was diagnosed with an ulcer, and because of vivid, recurring memories of their frightening fights slept poorly even now. In the divorce settlement, Elizabeth took Michael's two younger brothers but,

Michael said, "She didn't dare take me—she'd heard what my dad did the first time. After that, I just said I don't care if anything else bad happens." His father married for a third time to a woman who, together with her daughters, "more or less ran me right out of the house." Now a grown man and a father himself, Michael said, "I haven't seen my father in five years."[9]

Refugees from postmodern family life, Sue and Michael seemed, in their divorce, to be following uncomplainingly in their parents' footsteps. But unlike their parents, they remained good friends. "I won't ever be able to love anyone as I loved her and love her now," Michael told me. "I don't know if I know what love is. But it's real strong. I can't even picture meeting another girl and feeling the same way."

Both dated other people, but these relationships had not yet interfered with their powerful "friendship." Michael recently broke up with a girl who wanted to "get between me and Sue." Though more interested than Michael in having a serious lover, Sue didn't want her daughters to become attached to her current boyfriend "in case he dumps me and that upsets my kids." (She described her current lover as someone who "calls me when there's nothing else to do.")

Marriage seemed to Michael like a hollow public ritual, but then so did divorce.

> If I go down to Sue's to get the kids, she may have fixed us something to eat. I can sit down on the couch and we don't have to say anything to each other for half an hour. We're just relaxing.

They reminded each other of upcoming events, took turns with the kids so the other could take a vacation, and spent a certain amount of scarce leisure time together.

"Who do you think has a good marriage?" I asked Michael.
He paused a long while and then said,

> A lot of my coworkers come to work just to get away from home. I think that's because husbands and wives don't allow

each other enough time away from each other to go to the mall, or whatever. They have to be together all the time. Also, when the sex part of marriage slows down, a lot of guys thrive on seeing other women at work, because they lack excitement and sex life at home. None of the men I know cheat on their wives, but I'm not saying they wouldn't. The way they flirt I think they would if they could get away with it, not that they wouldn't regret it.

"So, looking around, who has a marriage that seems to work pretty well?" I asked again. Michael smiled and replied, "Me." Michael, who had lost two mothers and divorced his wife, nonetheless had an animating vision of a small haven of kin ties, a good divorce in a heartless world.

All I ever wanted was a family and kids. I love my kids. They are my life. I spend all the time I can with them. My youngest one sticks to me like glue. They are my first priority in life.

In contrast, he didn't care much about work.

To me, a job is just a job. If I lose it tomorrow, I lose it. If I have enough money to pay the bills, it doesn't matter what my job is. But if I still have my family at home, that feels best.

Sue didn't feel quite the same way. When I asked her what she wanted for her daughters, she said, "I want the girls to be independent, to go to college, to be able to support themselves. I want them to be good, strong, single mothers."

Becky Winters's mother had experienced a bad divorce. Becky had gone through a "better" divorce. Her children might look forward to the best divorce yet. Though she continued to feel there was "good" in marriage, she was passing on to her girls as their cultural capital the idea that a girl should expect to divorce. Given a divorce rate that starts high and rises as social class goes down, this legacy makes a certain sad sense.

Whether the girls of the next generation marry, as Becky Winters wants hers to do, or become strong single mothers, as Sue Carpenter wants hers to do, they face a new emotional economy at home. For caring now seems to move around like financial capital to new investment opportunities wherever they appear. This liquidity makes life frightening for those divested from, even as it creates new possibilities elsewhere. Some men like Becky's father and her husband invest love and care in their children, then move their investment to a new family enterprise where conditions seem better. Even Sue Carpenter, whose ex-husband had diverted none of his emotional capital from their family, felt the precariousness of her home life. For now, at home, there is an atmosphere of emotional "deregulation," which is creating a basic crisis of security. People wonder: Where do we feel the safest? Even among those with lousy jobs, the answer is sometimes "at work."

CHAPTER 12

The Overextended Family

If work was sometimes a refuge from troubled family lives, it was also a place where conflicts originating in the home were discussed, debated, and subjected to sympathetic scrutiny and where possible solutions were devised and tested. A case in point was Vivian Goodman, a slow-speaking, dignified woman of forty-two whom I interviewed in the breakroom one night. She lowered herself into a chair opposite me, as if before a judge, and immediately began to describe why she was struggling to free herself of the 11 P.M. to 7 A.M. shift and get on the 7 A.M. to 3 P.M. shift. At stake was a rekindled love affair with another Amerco worker, Emmanuel, who was holding down a 5:30 A.M. to 1:30 P.M. shift. Both worked ten to fifteen hours a week of overtime.

To begin with, everything she said was about time:

It's not easy. Emmanuel comes home at two-thirty in the afternoon, and I'm already gone to work. If I work overtime, that means I work until 10 A.M. and come home when he's gone.

Having divorced her husband ten years earlier, Vivian had been building a new life with the recently divorced Emmanuel for ten months. "He is my life," she said simply. "He's very kind. We seldom quarrel." But only weeks before, her plans had taken a disastrous turn. Emmanuel moved out because, as she explained it, "my children made it hard for him to be there. I live with my two children from my previous marriage. They should be on their own, but they aren't."

Though Vivian separated from her first husband when her son Tim, now nineteen, was small, Tim continued to cling to memories of his father and of moments of family vacation fun long forgotten by Vivian. She had reconciled with her husband several times, each time raising her son's hopes. "Of course, Tim doesn't know about the affairs his father had with other women, the terrible fights we had. I can't convince Tim that we will never be that family again." Tim had rejected a series of his mother's boyfriends, and most recently, Emmanuel. When Emmanuel was around, Tim became moody and pugnacious. Emmanuel was understanding, but the boy's persistent rudeness finally wore him down.

Vivian's daughter, Tracy, twenty-one, had gradually come to accept Emmanuel. They had even planted a vegetable garden together behind Vivian's trailer; and for her birthday, Emmanuel had given her a blue jacket he knew she coveted. Tracy liked the idea of Emmanuel's moving in, until she learned Emmanuel wanted to incorporate Emerald, his own daughter from a previous marriage, into their family. As Vivian described the situation,

> Having missed her real dad, she wanted Emmanuel to be her new dad, a dad for herself. She was jealous. She thought Emmanuel treated Emerald like a queen. We were building two new rooms onto the trailer, and Tracy says to me, "You're just building the extra rooms so you can bring *Emerald* in."

Vivian had been protective of Emmanuel's relationship with his daughter and had tried desperately to include her in a blended family. "Emmanuel only got to see Emerald every other weekend, so I didn't want to make plans that interfered with that," she explained. Once when she, Emmanuel, and Emerald went to a restaurant, Emmanuel sat on the same side of the table as Vivian. Noting that Emerald felt pushed away, Vivian prompted Emmanuel, "Go sit next to Emerald."

In the same gentle spirit, Vivian tried to blend into her contentious fold tattered pieces of her own extended "family." She took in Tracy's jobless boyfriend, who according to the hard-working Emmanuel, lolled about the house "doing nothing." She also took in her ex-husband's adopted sister, who had been sexually abused by her ex-husband's father. For six months, she housed two nephews who were avoiding their drunken father. Soon after, she also took under her wing Tracy's closest friend, a young woman who had been abused by her mother's boyfriend. In effect, Vivian was running a refuge to protect the young against the old, children against parents or parent surrogates. She carried a heavy caseload of broken hearts, opening her home to those who needed a safe place, a bed, a meal, or a sympathetic ear. So she worked one shift plus overtime at the plant, a second as a housewife-mother at home, plus overtime as Mother Teresa for a troubled circle of family and friends.

Emmanuel loved Vivian for her big heart and claimed to share her vision of home as a shelter for loved ones in need. But he had little patience for the long waits for the bathroom on rushed mornings, the beer missing from the refrigerator when he was about to watch a game on TV, the tools mislaid from his own workbench when he had a few rare hours for the projects he loved, and, most of all, the lack of time with Vivian.

He simply didn't feel up to sharing Vivian's caseload. He admired her for it but increasingly wanted to assert his own needs, to come first—or at least second—in her community of needy relations. Amid the mad traffic of refugees at home, and with Vivian spending even more hours at Amerco, Emmanuel felt there was little left for him.

So he began to stop off a bit longer at the neighborhood bar after work—and that turned out to be only the beginning. "I thought he was with his brothers and sisters," Vivian told me, "and they were there some of the time, but so was a certain other somebody."

> Eventually, he had an affair with her. One time the mistress called me and tried to justify what she'd done by saying, "*You're* never home." It was true. I *was* never home. I took all the overtime I could get. I wasn't home because I didn't want to be home. The problem was that I was trying to take care of us all and I couldn't.

From childhood on, Emmanuel had had a lot of relatives around the house; he was used to that. What was hard, he claimed, was seeing the "lost lambs" Vivian brought in take advantage of her in her own house while he felt powerless to intervene. "Emmanuel says the kids mistreat me. Well," said Vivian, "they do have their whiny little tantrums, but I've learned to live with them." When Emmanuel finally moved out, his last words to her were "I can't stand to see you wash Tracy's boyfriend's dirty socks."

The problem seemed to be threefold. First, many people, including Emmanuel, came to Vivian in need of help. Second, Vivian herself didn't really have anyone at home to turn to when life became too much for her. Third, Emmanuel's own long hours took him out of the show at home, though no one defined this as a problem. Without Emmanuel to rely on, Vivian turned to friends at work instead. And Emmanuel eventually retreated into an affair. Vivian was devastated. As she recounted,

> I haven't talked to Emmanuel about his affair and I don't think I will. If it happens again, it happens again. It's over and Emmanuel told me that it would never happen again. Well, my ex told me that, too. But this time, it was more than I could bear. I lost thirty-six pounds. The doctor gave me nerve pills. I took them, went into the bathroom at work, and zonked out for two hours at a stretch. I missed my overtime. My coworkers knew Emmanuel was seeing someone.

They see. They know. I had girls come back and tell me, "The whole department is worried about you."

My kids realized how much his leaving hurt me. I felt like I had no control. The kids were making decisions. Emmanuel was making decisions. Amerco was making decisions for all of us. I felt I was being buried. In the middle of all this, I had to come to work. I had to function. But you know, coming to work helped.

Work was the one place where Vivian could feel supported in her misery. She was surrounded by an audience of coworkers who offered sympathy, warnings, tales of their own—who gave rather than took. Coworkers told her to eat more, to change her medication, to tell Emmanuel off, to have (or not have) a fling herself. At lunch, on breaks, or over beers after work, coworkers talked among themselves about whether a carousing louse like Emmanuel deserved a kind-hearted woman like Vivian, or whether Vivian had pushed Emmanuel out by paying too much attention to too many other people. It was so unfair that men did so much damage, some said, and then when a few good women like Vivian tried to repair it, they got left for their trouble. Whatever the point of view, these were the conversations—which once might have taken place in a neighbor's kitchen or over the backyard fence—that helped Vivian weather her crisis at home.

Feminine Community and Company Policy

Many of the men I interviewed took pride in helping others, but no one told a story remotely similar to Vivian's. At work and at home, most Amerco men saw themselves primarily as wage earners, and their care of others was likely to seem "extra." In general, offering and receiving personal help in and outside of the office, reaffirming bonds of friendship, or building community were more common activities for women than for men. As Amerco hired more women, it adapted to, and built upon, the female culture women brought to work. Just as Vivian Goodman took in needy people at home, so too did Vicky King feel it natural to take them in at work. Vicky's informal caseload was made up of management trainees, secretaries in her office, and other workers in trouble. Even as home was being "masculinized," managed as an efficient "workplace" where personal needs were to be displaced, repressed, or deferred, the workplace was being "feminized" through a management philosophy that stressed trust, team building, and courtesy to the internal customer.

There was a key difference, however, in the extent of workplace "feminization" between top-tier salaried workers and factory wage laborers. Asked about their family lives, top executives, male and female, scarcely mentioned grandparents, aunts, uncles, or cousins. "Family" to them meant the *nuclear* family—mother, father, and children. In interviews with factory workers, male and female, a vast array of relative's names—extending far beyond the nuclear family—popped up all the time. Partly, this was because Amerco factory workers generally came from the Spotted Deer area while most Amerco managers had moved to Spotted Deer from somewhere else. Partly, working-class family ties simply seemed to connect a wider circle of kin.[1]

If one could speak of family and friends as an informal domestic "welfare system," there were more welfare workers among factory personnel than among managers. At the top, "family needs" were likely to be taken care of by paid services—babysitters, summer camps, retirement communities—or by housewives. At the factory level, family needs were likely to be met by family members, and usually by working women like Vivian. So the temporal "cutbacks" at home caused by ever longer workdays at Amerco caused more obvious suffering for those at the bottom than at the top.

The changes at Amerco in recent years only exacerbated this situation. Total Quality, which emphasized cooperation and mutual aid within the workplace, was extended to the factory floor; family-friendly policies that emphasized these same goals at home were not. These corporate decisions, when added to increasing amounts of required (and often desired) overtime, created the framework within which Vivian's terrible dilemma was being played out.

Improving work-family balance was not an issue easily raised on the factory floor. After all, for a lone individual to contest the terms of the "normal" workday, given the company's power, was unlikely, and few were doing it. Even the harshest policies went unchallenged. According to the rules on absenteeism in Amerco plants, if a worker was late for any reason, familial or otherwise, a note went into her file. If she was late again, she would be punished with unpaid days off. It may seem paradoxical that Amerco punished workers who needed time by giving them more time, but punitive suspension was only the first of three steps that led inexorably toward dismissal. Three such suspensions in one year and a worker was fired.

Many mothers of young children came up against these absentee rules when medical emergencies arose. As one described it,

> The kids have been sick all winter. Todd has the chicken pox now. Two weeks ago, Teddy got pneumonia and they put him in the hospital. We called up my supervisor and asked for some time off so I could stay with Teddy. But he said no. I took three sick days and then some vacation days, and they put a note in my file. But I can't take my kids to my mom or my mother-in-law every time they get sick. They both work, too. And besides, when Teddy is sick, he wants me, not anyone else.

In another case, the son of a single mother needed surgery, but because she had already used up her sick days and her vacation days, she chose to wait six months to schedule the surgery so she could arrange a day off. In response to this delay, her son's doctor threatened to press charges of child abuse. In another instance, the coworkers of a single father at Amerco covered for him each night during fifteen-minute extensions of his thirty-minute break so that he could drive to his house and put his ten-year-old daughter, home alone, to bed. On discovering this arrangement, his supervisor stopped the practice. The supervisor in a third case threatened to fire a mother who left work to care for a daughter with a dangerously high fever.

One factory-employed mother was written up for absenteeism for quite a different reason:

> I had to take a day off to go to family court to help my husband get custody of his two daughters [by a previous marriage]. Between us, we have five. Family court is like a green-stamp store, you wait all day. It was two-thirty before we got out. All the days I came into work late because of court, my boss wrote me up. I lost three days of pay. I went through the chain of command in the plant and out of the plant to an executive in Industrial Relations at headquarters. They all told me, "We're sorry, but you took the time off."

Nine out of ten examples of work-family balance crises that came up in my interviews with hourly working parents concerned sick children. But while medical emergencies were fairly clear-cut, the difficult issue of what might be called semichronic problems—children who were depressed, failing in their studies, isolated, or hanging around with the wrong kids—which cried out for more time and parental attention, were rarely raised at all.

Outside emergencies, however, most working parents were not complaining much about the encroachments of work time. For one thing, parents needed the money. But for Becky Winters, work was also a way of avoiding quarrels.[2] For Vivian, it was a way of distancing herself from her demanding "caseload" at home. And for one of their coworkers, Dolores Jay, work was an escape route from family violence. One day she pointed to the wood-trimmed wall of the small office in the plant where I was conducting interviews and said,

See the boards along the wall here? My husband would check if there was dust on them and beat me if he found any. He'd measure the space between the coffee table and the wall, and if it wasn't exactly twenty-one inches on each side, he'd get violent. One time he came home on leave from the navy. He hadn't seen me or our year-old baby. I was taking a shower and my husband came into the bathroom, pushed back the shower curtain, and handed me the baby. He'd beaten him. I laid the baby on the bed. He didn't cry for hours. My husband wouldn't let me out of the house. He sat on the front porch, so I couldn't get help. I just sat there over the baby because I didn't have a phone, didn't have anyone I could call. I couldn't go anywhere! After a few hours, my son started moving. I think he thought I did it. I've had problems with my son ever since.

Help for Dolores came through her husband's workplace. A coworker of his called the navy chaplain, who in turn called Dolores's father. He then sent Dolores a one-way ticket back home.

As it was for Dolores Jay, work can become a place to hide and recover from traumatic experiences, and home the place where the trauma takes place. Another woman who worked in the plant discovered that her husband was having an affair long known to her best friends. "That's what I do all day at work," she said. "Toss it back and forth in my mind. How could he? And why didn't they tell me?" In such cases, work became a "recovery room" in which to heal from or at least contemplate with some degree of calm the bruises of life suffered outside. In other cases, work can be a means of trying to avoid the trauma in the first place. For example, the wife of one man was taken to the hospital, half-dead from hemorrhaging with a stillborn child. The distraught husband called his wife's friend from the hospital to tell her the news and then drove back to work. His wife's friend marched up to his workstation, clapped him firmly on the shoulder, and said, "She *needs* you. Go!" Embarrassed at himself, the husband later humbly thanked his wife's friend for helping him do the right thing at such an important moment.

The structure of work time with its rotating shifts and its overtime exacerbated the very problems people thought they were fleeing home to escape. With Amerco's help tens of thousands of individual "time scarcity" cycles were being set in motion. The more overtime Vivian Goodman took, for example, the more demands her children made and the more Emmanuel withdrew. The more they demanded and he withdrew, the harder it became for Vivian to be home, and the more overtime she worked. Only when Emmanuel moved out, precipitating a crisis, did Vivian even begin to imagine that there was a cycle to be broken and to explore ways out.

Joann Redman, another of Vivian's coworkers, experienced an extreme version of this cycle. The mother of a four-year-old, she worked nine-hour days, six days a week, to pay for seventy-seven acres of land, a camper truck, and a $40,000 boat the family had been out on once all summer. As Joann explained,

> My father sometimes worked twenty hours at the plant and would be back four hours later. My mother worked a lot of doubles, too. So I had to cook and take care of my brother, which I hated. Now, I guess I'm doing the same. This past year, I worked twelve hours a day for eight months, rotating shift.

Her husband Paul often found these hours hard to handle. Since they had so little time together, she didn't want to waste it cooking at home.

> We take the kids to Burger King, McDonald's, Friendly's. We went out last night because my sisters were in town. We had some drinks and dinner. That was the first time we'd been out with no kids in over a year. Paul really loosened up. He was surprised. He said, "I . . . am . . . having . . . a . . . good . . . time!"

Most of all, her long hours were hard on her four-year-old son, Lewis. Given her schedule, Joann saw Lewis only one day a week for any length of time, and that changed how she treated him.

> I'm not going to spend that day being the bad guy. So I let Lewis get away with a lot. I'm paying for it now, because he's become a rude brat. Not to Paul, just to me.

Joann had herself been alternately neglected and indulged by workaholic parents. Just as she'd been given toys and ice cream instead of parental time, so she gave gifts to Lewis to substitute for missing time. Complicating matters further was the fact that Paul's two children, aged eleven and nine, lived with the Redmans every other weekend.

> There are days I resent paying for Paul's two kids. I resent being the "dad" who works long hours. I felt guilty that I went back to work when Lewis was six weeks old, back to twelve-hour days, six-day weeks. I'm like my dad who missed a big part of my growing up. But maybe it's worth it. I want to give this seventy-seven acres to Lewis and my stepchildren.

What worried Joann about her overwork, about being "the dad," was that she didn't quite know why she was doing it. None of her explanations satisfied her. "The money's nice; but it's not worth it when you live at work," she concluded. But at the same time, she wasn't changing her hours. For a while, as she brooded about this, she fell into a private after-work ritual:

> When I work the 3 P.M. to 11 P.M. shift, Paul and Lewis are asleep by the time I'm home. I went through a period when I'd stop at the store to buy a six-pack of beer, put it in the car, and drive around for an hour on old country roads, pull up a half-mile from the house, sit and drink maybe two beers. I'd ask myself, "Is this really what I want? Do I want to

uproot Lewis and be a single mother? Do I want to be free?"
Paul didn't know I did this, and I got scared on those country
roads by myself. I'd forget about it until the next time, and
then I'd do it again. For a long time, I thought I was losing
my mind.

At work, Becky Winters found some solace from the pain of her
traumatic divorce. Vivian Goodman found relief from her rescue
missions at home. But Joann Redman, who worked an even longer
day, couldn't figure out why she was working so hard. It made me
wonder how many other people were driving around their own
"country roads" at midnight, asking themselves why their lives are
the way they are, never quite grasping the link between their desire
for escape and a company's desire for profit.

CHAPTER 13

Overtime Hounds

I love this job because I get to work Christmas.

Factory worker

As I listened to the lunchtime banter of the women and men who work the Demco assembly line, two themes—long hours and the equality of the sexes—kept coming up. Deb Escalla, mother of three and quality control worker on Line 5, believed in the equality of the sexes. In a good-natured way, her husband, Mario, did not. He was an overtime hound who liked to have fun, something a man's entitled to.

On a languid weekday morning, I drove through a neighborhood of modest homes surrounded by small, scorched lawns to reach the Escallas' two-story wooden house. I saw two boys peering under the hood of a large, rusty pick-up truck, and an elderly man out on a walk, but otherwise, few people were around. I rang the Escallas' doorbell and was greeted instantly by three frolicking children—Gina, a five-year-old, in charge; Gordon, a one-and-a-half-year-old who circled around us as if tying us up with invisible string; and Hunter, a winsome three-year-old, who wanted to know if I'd come to play with her.

Deb Escalla, twenty-seven, led me to a well-worn couch in their downstairs den from which all our eyes were drawn to the flickering images on a huge TV screen. Gina was playing a Nintendo game on it while baby Gordon stared at the gaudy illustrations in a Nintendo instructional pamphlet. Hunter, up on her tiptoes, was reaching to insert a cherished *Pinocchio* tape into the VCR, but a *Dumbo* tape, already there, frustrated her. There were no books in the room.

The children darted here and there like a school of fish. They didn't exactly share toys, but often the same toy excited all of them at once, so it fell to Deb to repeatedly adjudicate their struggles for the toy of the moment. They all wanted to play fry-an-egg, or they all wanted to sing the Barney song into my tape recorder. They all wanted Hunter's bottle. Gordon lurched from the divan to the plastic play-kitchen sink to the VCR control box and back again. Their dog, Cakes, jumped into my lap, rolled on his back and looked up with devoted eyes.

Becky Winters and Sue Carpenter were disappointed with their families, each in her own way. The Escallas weren't disappointed, they were overwhelmed, and both turned to work to escape the exhaustion of a hectically happy life at home. In a low monotone, Deb, a brown-eyed, dark-haired beauty, began by describing members of her family by their hours of work:

> I work a rotating seven. Mario works 9 A.M. to 5 P.M. steady. My father works a steady 2 P.M. to 10 P.M. My mother's on the 8 A.M. to 5 P.M.

She recounted how her parents, too, raised three children while working two factory jobs and then described in loving detail her own rotating seven-day shift—similar to Becky Winters's. On top of this, she averaged five hours of overtime a week. Mario, who worked a regular day shift, took all the overtime he could get, some months averaging up to twenty hours a week.

The house was divided into a place for sleep and a place for wakefulness. Although Deb ultimately got less leisure than Mario, the diurnal rhythms of the Escalla home seemed to revolve more around Mario, since he worked longer hours. "Sometimes Daddy is up. Sometimes Daddy is asleep. Other times Daddy is up but tired," the five-year-old explained.

Only Deb understood the byzantine weekly schedules of the

whole family. Like a railroad switchman, she described how each child's time was sorted out, given the work schedules of the seven adults who regularly alternated caring for the children, and the several others who occasionally did:

> When I work the 7 A.M. to 3 P.M. shift we start the day about quarter to five. I can't bring the children to the sitter until 6:30 A.M., but I have to punch in at the plant by 6:45, so I race. On weekdays, I have two sitters because Melody, our main babysitter, can't take all three kids. On the weekends, I take them to my mom, to Mario's cousin, or to my mother-in-law. Usually, I bring one child to each house, because when Gina and Hunter are together, they're monsters. When Mario and I both work the same hours, the kids get to spend the night at their grandparents' for the whole week.

On the days when Deb worked the night shift, the children's schedules depended on Mario's overtime. If Mario was working a double shift (the equivalent of two eight-hour days) that carried through the night, the children went to Mario's mother's to sleep over, and then to the sitter's early the next morning. After five nights of the 11 P.M. to 7 A.M. shift, Deb got five days off. On those days, she would take care of the children. If Deb was really desperate for help with a sick child, she would call her mother, a secretary at Amerco, who used accumulated paid sick days to help out. Three of her five days off, Deb was adjusting her sense of time to that of the rest of the world. For two days, she felt adjusted. Then the cycle began again.

Half of hourly men and women at Amerco regularly work weekends. Sixty-five percent of the women and 73 percent of the men regularly work overtime. Recently, for the first time, an hourly worker—a woman who cleaned the cafeteria and needed to take care of an ailing parent—was allowed to work part time. But neither Deb nor Mario were interested in shorter hours.

Instead of describing an intricately calibrated system of work and

childcare, Mario Escalla began his interview by telling me his philosophy of life and only then turned to his schedule. He was a
friendly thirty-two-year-old Italian American who, the first time we
met, was dressed in a Pittsburgh Pirates baseball uniform, his baseball
cap on backward. He was seated at the dining room table eating
breakfast, which he offered to share. As soon as our interview
ended, he bounded out the door, bat and glove in hand, headed for
practice. He plays first base on a team sponsored by the Blue Dot, a
bar in town. A fifty- to sixty-hour-a-week worker on a steady day
shift, he said,

> I look at it this way. If I'm working and then I'm babysitting
> and not doing anything else, I'm miserable. I hate it. So I
> have to do other stuff. I cheat myself out of sleep to do the
> other stuff. Sometimes I come home from a double shift,
> drink a pot of coffee, and go out to play baseball.

For Mario Escalla, being home was work too. He looked for his fun
elsewhere. To get that fun, he stole time from himself. Five hours
for his body, three for himself: that was the deal.

Mario took fierce pride in being a "sixty-hour man" like his dad
and talked of the custom of working long hours as if it were a patri-
mony, passed from generation to generation:

> I take all the overtime I can get and all the doubles I can
> stand. I'm an overtime hound. There's a rule against work-
> ing more than fifteen consecutive hours, but once in a
> while I'll pop a twenty-hour or a twenty-five-hour at a go.
> I've driven off the road going home after doing overtime.
> Once I walked right into a locker at work. I worked seven
> doubles in a row one time. I like to get a hundred hours
> a week between Deb and me. I've woken up before and not
> even known what day it was. Other times, I've sprung
> out of bed and said, "Wait a minute, it's night." Maybe
> I'm a workaholic, but not as much as a lot of people
> around here.

With a sigh, Deb said of her husband,

> Mario loves overtime. He wants at least sixty hours a week. He calls himself a machine. Sometimes I think he likes it, and other times I think he does it because he thinks he has to. He says he feels guilty if he turns overtime down.

Actually, Mario was a warm, vital man, anything but a machine. His job was to stack and load boxes, tasks that called for little skill and that he happily admitted bored him. Hours were his source of pride.

> Most of my buddies will settle for forty hours and say, "See you later." But they're buddies without kids. If I had no kids, I'd work forty hours, too.

> People look at the hours I work and say, "What, are you crazy?" I earned $40,000 last year, and Deb normally earns $23,000. An older woman in my department is taking all the overtime she can get to retire and go on a trip. I kid her, "That's *my* overtime. You're taking food out of my kids' mouths." I don't just work for the money, though. We could live on one salary. In fact, I've asked Deb to quit. I work 50 percent for need, 25 percent for greed. A lot of it is greed. And 25 percent is getting away from the house.

Mario liked the idea of having extra money so as not to be caught short. "If I had no kids and two forty-hour checks, I would have a gold mine. But that's not how it is. So I want to be prepared if my van or water heater breaks down. I want to be able to go to Pittsburgh to see the Pirates and not use up family money."[1]

"How much money would you need to live the life you want to live?" I asked. As if he'd thought about this question before, Mario quickly replied: "One million wouldn't be enough. If I just had one

million I'd still work. I just wouldn't do overtime. To quit completely, I'd need two plus." But when I asked how he might use
such money, his answers were hardly grandiose. "I'd own two
vehicles, a boat. I'd remodel," was all he could think to say.

Mario's desire for unlimited money seemed to be fueled less by
consumer lust than by fear of losing his job. In 1982, he had experienced a traumatic eight-month layoff from Amerco. "I washed
dishes for a fiver, I cut lawns, I helped my cousin remodel his bedroom." But if some of Mario's eagerness for overtime work came
from an all too realistic assessment of an uncertain future, that wasn't
all of it. He also wanted, he sheepishly confessed, to escape the
house:

> Many times I've said that if I knew it was going to be like
> this, I never would have had kids. None! I still would have
> married Deb. But three kids? Maybe one. We had to have
> that boy, though. That's how we got three. We planned on
> two, but I was very depressed when I found out our second,
> Hunter, was a girl. But now we're happy with the three
> of them.

Mario's long-hours machismo meant that whatever time he did
spend with the children came on top of a very long workday.

> When I come home, the kids want to see me. They missed
> me. So even though I'm exhausted, I'll go downstairs and lie
> on the floor. They enjoy getting on top of me and pounding
> me. They make me give them rides like an elephant. So I
> play the game for half an hour before I go to bed.

> My dad never went to school events, and I'm not interested
> in making it a habit either. But I can see myself doing a
> double in the future, and then going to watch one of my kids
> play a ball game. I would cheat myself out of sleep to see
> their games.

Even when Mario wasn't in a state of exhaustion as he played with his children, he found being with them hard work. Certain times were worse than others. He explained,

It's not the mess, it's the screaming. I have sensitive ears, especially when I haven't slept much, and Gordon can go "WAAAAAAAHHHHH!!!" And do you know about zwieback toast? . . .

He rose from the dining room table, marched into the kitchen, opened a cupboard, and indignantly held up a box of zwieback.

This is supposed to be good for kids who are teething. Right? Well, Hunter crammed zwieback down her throat and thought it was funny. Then it clogged her throat. She was going, "ACCCHH, ACCCHHH, ACCCHHH." I panicked. I slapped her in the middle of the back and pulled up on her stomach. It came out. Then I sat down and smoked twelve cigarettes.

Mario thought of himself as "baby-sitting" the kids for Deb, but when he described them it was from the perspective of a highly involved parent. Unlike Amerco's male managers, he did not discuss his children's possible future career tracks or assess how they "were doing" in school; he talked about the everyday process of raising them. "As for discipline," he explained, "I scream. I don't hit, except on the back end." He laid out for me in graphic detail what he liked and didn't like about raising children:

I didn't do diapers to begin with, but I have no choice now, and I don't like it. Hunter is the nastiest doer I've ever seen. She has it up her back. Unbelievable. Gina wasn't so bad, because me and Deb did it back and forth, back and forth. Then, we only had one kid, and it was easy. But Gordon kicks his legs and gets it all over you.

Raising the children surely bound Deb and Mario closer together, but it also worsened incipient tensions between them.

> Sometimes kids make you argue and scream. They are probably 80 percent of our arguments. I fell with Gordon under the hose sprinkler outside, and he landed on his face and screamed, and she says, "Oh, good one!" We're both sarcastic toward each other. It comes from watching *Married . . . with Children*, *The Honeymooners*, and *Archie Bunker*.

But for all that, Mario and Deb seemed to have settled into a happily adversarial marriage.

> When I first married Deb, she was very shy. After two years, she'd figured out that I wanted to go have fun, that I was just going to be miserable working a double and coming home to housework. So I'd go to the bar and hang out. Our third year of marriage, I was a real drinker, even at work. It was all new to me, the two kids cramped into a little apartment. After work, I just didn't want to go back home, so I'd go party, and I got involved with the wrong guys. I'd go to strip joints like Belini's or the Bulldog Grill. I'd come home and she'd been with the kids all day with no break. I really was to blame. But somehow, she stuck through all that. I said to myself, this has to be the right woman to put up with this. She never once threatened me, though she did pack my bags once.

> Then she started giving it back to me. Going to work helped her do that. I realized I have a tough little Italian here. Now I go to a bar where sports are on TV. I don't go to pick-up bars anymore. She knows where to find me. In fact, if she gets tired of hearing me scream she says, "Go to the Blue Dot. Play ball."

Like legions of men before him, Mario was playing hooky from home in company with other men doing the same thing. But this leisure was not given to him by Deb; it was leisure Mario *took.* He was stealing time from her just as he stole time from his own sleep. So Deb put Mario on notice. After taking time off for the birth of their third child, Deb went back to work in a new way—piling on the overtime herself. She thus found a way of stealing time back from Mario and forcing him back into the home.

If Mario had his way, he and Deb would be like his parents, a long-hours man and a housewife. But if Deb had her way, she and Mario would each work regular hours *and* care for their children. Unable to earn a higher hourly wage than his wife—as his father or grandfather had—Mario worked more *hours* than Deb and in that way outearned her. The earnings gap he created (which was really an hours gap) gave Mario an economic rationale for asking Deb to cut back at work and attend to domestic life. It was this rationale that Deb rejected.

Mario's explanation for why he worked twenty hours of overtime a week—"50 percent for need, 25 percent for greed, and 25 percent is getting away from the house"—did not touch on their struggle over Deb's work. But through his sixty-hour week, Mario seemed to be saying to Deb, "I can earn enough so that you can stay home the way my mother did, and we can be a real family." By insisting on her own overtime, Deb seemed to be replying, "When we first married you were out with the boys drinking and who knows what else on your time off. The only way I'm going to get equal respect and equal time in this day and age is to do paid work, and lots of it."

This "conversation" was very much in both their minds during my stay in Spotted Deer. Once, I had arranged to be with Deb as she got the children up, took them to the sitter, and drove to her job at the plant. Instead, she called me at eleven o'clock the night before to say that the opportunity had arisen to do "a double" and she was already at work. So, I met her at 1 A.M. at the plant, and Mario, who was also on break, joined us. Deb would not get off

work until 3 P.M. that afternoon. She seemed subdued—or was it
just tired? The three of us and a friend of Deb's assembled around
four Cokes in the plant breakroom, and even before I could ask a
question, a conversation between Deb and Mario sparked to life.

"Why did you take the double?" Mario asked Deb goadingly.
"You don't *need* to take it." Deb's response, though unemphatic,
almost overlapped his question: "Well, you don't need to take overtime either, do you?"

Then Deb turned to me to explain, "Whichever one takes overtime, the other one complains. Neither of us wants the other to
work a double." Then Deb laughed a light laugh and elaborated:

> Mario wants me to quit. I said there's no way I'm going to
> quit. He wants me to stay home like his mom did. Some-
> times I really think he likes to work overtime so I'll do
> everything at home, and he can come and go as free as he
> pleases. But my dad always helped out around the house, and
> I'd rather be working.

To Deb it was clear enough. Mario was balking at doing his part
of the second shift. Sociologist Harriet Presser has found that when
wives go to work outside the home, a third of husbands do more
housework and childcare to compensate; a third don't change; and
a third actually do less.[2] Mario, as it happened, was one of those
men who did more at home and was around more when Deb
worked, and that was a big reason why she worked the hours
she did.

But Deb normally put the matter to Mario as an issue not of
time but of money, as a pragmatic matter of self-sufficiency in case
someday it turned out she couldn't depend on him.

> If we split up, or if something happens to him, where are we
> going to get the money if I don't have a job? He tells me,
> "You'd get the money from Amerco." You know, his insur-
> ance, if he died on the job. But I want a regular income.

When I asked Deb as we drove home together the next afternoon if she really thought they might split up, she replied matter-of-factly, "No, it's just something I bring up as one of my reasons to keep my job."

Like most of the other hourly mothers I talked to, Deb had no intention of cutting back at work. She knew that while she was away doing her extra time, Mario would be home cooking Beef-a-roni, Spaghetti-o's, or tuna noodle casseroles for the kids. If she cut back, he'd be gone more. Though it wasn't something she'd say directly to him, she believed her work kept him home.

Mario Escalla was following in his father's footsteps. But Deb wasn't following in her mother's or her mother-in-law's. Deb's mother went to work only after her last child was in first grade, and even then reluctantly. Mario's mother had stayed home to care for six children, and only got a job after they were grown. Deb had taken three months, four months, and then six months off with each successive birth. But none of these breaks left her with a taste for life as a housewife. "I thought about staying home with the kids," Deb explained, "but they drove me nuts."

> Maybe it's just my kids, but they are a wild bunch. Gina whines an awful lot. Hunter is a very stubborn girl. I think I'd rather be working. When I took a few months off, I just felt like I had to get away. If work's what you have to do to get away, so be it. Plus, I'm getting paid for it.

Mario understood how she felt.

> Deb doesn't want to be considered a baby-sitter for the rest of her life. She saw what her mom and my mom went through as housewives. She doesn't want that. That's why she won't quit. This job of raising three children is three times harder than a job at the factory. I know that. That's why I understand why she doesn't want to quit. I don't blame her. I couldn't stand being in this house with three kids continuously. It's

very stressful mentally, and I get sick of hearing myself scream. I hate it. "Stay *away* from the glass cabinet! Stay *away* from the stove!" The kids are like water. They find the first opening and out they go.

I asked Deb whether she or Mario would like to work shorter hours. "No," she answered, "because I like the money. It's good money." This reason was real enough. Deb, even more than Mario, marked time in debt payments: "We have fifteen years to go on the house; two years on the van . . ."

But when I asked her my usual question, "What if you had all the money you needed?" she persisted, "I'd probably still work just for the extra money." But what if she already had the extra money?

I would probably work part time. I don't like being trapped in the house. Neither does my husband. For a while, I worked the steady 4 P.M. to midnight shift. My mother-in-law helped Mario get the kids ready for bed. It was great: I didn't have to put the kids to bed, I didn't have to feed them dinner. I know that sounds terrible.

Another time when Deb and I were in the breakroom with several of her friends, she said,

I always tell people here that I come to work to relax. I know to some people this sounds mean, but to me it's eight hours of relaxation. I can go to work and the kids aren't right in front of me to worry about. Mario, too, will tell you it's relaxing to work. At work, I can do more of what I want. At home, I have to do what the kids want.

Her friends nodded knowingly.

If home felt to Deb and Mario like work, could a factory job by any stretch of imagination seem like home? I could understand how Bill Denton, behind his oak desk in a carpeted office, with family photos on the wall, might say that his workplace was pleasant, even homey. But what of a job on an assembly line, where work can be dirty, ill lit, and unsafe and where noise and the fast pace of the line make it hard to talk?

To be sure, terrible workplace conditions still exist in the United States. But at Fortune 500 companies like Amerco, one is more likely to find a plant like Deb's: well lit, fairly quiet, relatively pleasant. At Deb's plant, workers wore safety glasses and had fifteen-minute breaks every three hours. They earned eleven or twelve dollars an hour for unskilled or semiskilled work. They enjoyed health benefits and access to a wide range of mental health services, including psychological and alcohol abuse counseling. In addition, Amerco had introduced both monetary and nonmonetary incentives to encourage workers to participate in cross-training programs meant to expand their skills and give them an overview of the whole production process. The workforce of eight hundred at Deb and Mario's plant had also been reorganized into self-managed production teams of twenty-seven people each, responsible for deciding among themselves how to do their tasks.

It was perhaps this sense of "ownership" that accounted for Mario's ambassadorial pride as he greeted me with a lively wave at the entrance to the plant one midnight. He had gotten ahead folding his boxes, which left him some spare time, he told me, to show me around the plant. He took me through the many steps in the production process. Along the way, he introduced me to his buddies at various workstations around the plant and set up a series of interviews for me in the breakroom. Once I was known as Mario and Deb's friend, workers spelled each other to allow time for interviews.

As Mario walked me around, he offered a running commentary. Pointing to a lean man in his fifties, he said, "Chuck works 119 pay-hours a week, $60,000 a year, but he lost his family a decade ago. He *lives* here." Motioning toward a man in his twenties driving a forklift truck, Mario said, "That's Joey. Watch out for him. He drinks two six-packs of Oly [Olympia beer] a night, but so slowly it doesn't show. On the break, he goes across the street to the bar and gets tanked up." Indeed, at the Dance N' Shout, where each worker sat on his favorite bar stool, as if at the dinner table at home, the bartender knew all their regular drinks: a double whiskey for Hank, a Dos Equis for Rick, a Bud for Mike.

Continuing his commentary, Mario pointed to a young woman working a lathe:

> She's a marriage buster. That's what we call them, "marriage busters." They make a sport out of getting men to fall for them and leave their families. Watch out for them!

(He said this emphatically, even though the men in the breakroom regularly took bets, Mario had also told me, on how long it would take one of them to get a "marriage buster" into bed.)

> A lot of single girls will come on to you. They don't care if you're married or not. Probably a good five of the girls here are into that. They're evil. I flirt too, but I try to stay away from them, which isn't that hard, since I know Deb is coming in the next shift. I do my share of flirting, and they flirt back, but it means nothing. Once I got hammered at a Christmas party, and a female coworker had to drive me home. Deb tosses that at me even still.

Among hourly workers at the company, a quarter of the women and 18 percent of the men were divorced or unmarried. Often, older women would come to work early to gossip about the cut of a young woman's jersey or her new hair coloring—or like the men, they would consider the latest bulletins from the "marriage busting" front.

For Mario, Deb, and their coworkers, strong social bonds developed "on the line." There were friends to joke with and confide in. Coworkers would often shop and drink together or go fishing and hunting. Then there were the blood ties—spouses, fathers, mothers, brothers, sisters-in-law, ex-brothers-in-law, the siblings or parents of an ex-sister-in-law working somewhere in the plant.[3]

Both the stability of the workforce (64 percent of the men and 59 percent of the women had been at the plant for twenty years or more) and the unusual hours of shift labor undoubtedly intensified these bonds. The odd-hours employees kept the plant open twenty-four hours a day, which meant that they shared a sense of night and day, week and month with their fellow workers that they did not share with neighbors, kin, friends outside the plant, or even sometimes spouses. While other people came home from school, ate dinner, and watched TV, the 3 P.M. to 11 P.M. shift was hard at work. While others slept, the 11 P.M. to 7 A.M. shift was wide awake. While others went home on Friday at 5 P.M., many in the plant had just reached the middle of their workweek. Meanwhile, such shift work put tremendous stress on friendships outside the factory. This was especially true for married women at the plant. Mario still had his baseball buddies, but Deb was too busy with her second shift of housework and childcare to go out for chicken wings at the Neon Chicken with the neighborhood "girls" the way she once had.

Often, it seemed equally hard for Deb and Mario to get a night out together. There was simply too little overlapping time at home. They sometimes talked to each other about the ways in which time at work affected their marriage, but they seldom asked each other how this time scarcity was affecting their children. When asked, Mario and Deb both responded that the children were doing as well as they had themselves done as children. Nevertheless, Mario thought the children needed Deb at home. Deb reflected,

He thinks the kids need me all the time. I think they get enough of everyone. They get their aunts, their grandparents. It's good for them to do without me sometimes.

The Escalla children were lively and appealing. They were skilled at entertaining themselves and seemed to expect kindly attention from adults. Hunter had a speech impediment, the result of an infected eardrum not diagnosed early enough, which left her slightly deaf and sometimes made her cranky. Both parents seemed harder on her than on either of her siblings. ("Oh, Hunter's such a cry-baby.") But Deb and Mario's treatment of Hunter perhaps derived less from their shift work and long hours than from the fact that Mario had wanted a boy so badly the second time around. Such misplaced parental blame is hardly unusual. The more difficult question was whether (and, if so, in what ways) Deb's and Mario's long work schedules affected their children over and above all that. Mario, inadvertently perhaps, offered some clues:

> The kids have no idea where they're going next. They love it at Grandma's. They're fine about going to Melody's. They're not shy. They enjoy themselves. But when they are seven or eight, they're going to realize, "I don't want to go from Grandma's to Melody's."

Deb and Mario were loving parents, and the extended family Deb had constructed to care for their children was for the most part loving, too. But, in truth, the children were on an elaborate Rube Goldberg assembly line of childcare, continually sent from one "workstation" to the next. Their lives were full of comings and goings: "It's time to go. Get your coat on," and "Here we are. Take your coat off." To each of these locales the children's stash of cherished toys and blankets traveled as well. But the children were quick to learn that pleasing their series of childcare workers meant being good sports about having one or more of their vitally important objects—Gordon's blanky or Gina's paper dolls—left behind, or about being interrupted in the middle of games or television shows they did not want to leave, or about waiting—often a long time— before getting to be with whomever they most wanted to be with. It was Hunter, more than the compliant Gina, who was getting difficult about these transitions as she began to grasp the idea that this time was—or should be—hers. She was learning how to protest against the childcare conveyor belt, and the fact that for every hour of overtime her parents took at work, she was having to log an extra hour of overtime at a makeshift version of home.

Deb and Mario's situation was hardly unique. Everywhere in Amerco's factories parents were working long hours while their children put in long hours at daycare. Everywhere parents were having the same problems meshing schedules and creating their own versions of the Escallas' childcare conveyor belt. Everywhere there were children who in their own way were living on corporate time, though for them there would be no Total Quality systems of care, no recognition ceremonies, and no empowerment.

For workers like Deb and Mario, no one was promising a future of family-friendly planning. For their children there was no company support for a round-the-clock childcare center. No one was handing them cheery brochures about flextime. The only part time or flextime they were ever likely to get would have to come—as it did already—from their private schedules, and would be taken at the expense of home and children.

In the absence of company help, over three-quarters of hourly parents who answered a 1990 Amerco survey and used some childcare agreed with the statement "It is hard for me to manage my work and family/personal responsibilities." Women felt the strain more than the men probably because, like Deb, they were the guardians of family time—and any stoppages on the childcare conveyor belt fell to them to repair. Half of hourly women and a third of hourly men said they had a "great deal of difficulty" monitoring the activities of children home alone. Seventy-one percent of these women and 59 percent of the men said they had a great deal of difficulty finding childcare that conformed to their work hours.

But the fact remained that even if on-site childcare, flexible schedules, and shorter-hour jobs were available, and even if money was no issue, the Escallas were not interested in shorter hours: Deb said she "sort of likes" the rotating seven-day shift; Mario was a self-confessed "overtime hound"—and between them, a gender war for time was underway in which the real losers were their children.

Implicit in this war was the devaluation of the work of raising children. Deb and Mario Escalla surely wouldn't have struggled so to escape their children were the work of raising them more valued. Hunter's crisis with the zwieback, Gordon's messy diaper, and the children's loud screams were, in themselves, no more reason to avoid parenting than a difficult equation was a reason to avoid a career in mathematics. "Women's work" has always been devalued, however, and under the pressure of the new time-math of corporate America its value is sinking lower still. It is this devaluation that was at the root of the Escallas' flight-à-deux.

The politics of time has been almost totally personalized in recent decades. A giant public issue appears to us as millions of individual problems, each to be solved privately at home.[4] Companies have far more power over families than families have over companies. So time demands at work come to seem implacable while those at home feel malleable. Workers focus on that aspect of the whole scene that they feel they can control—constantly organizing and reorganizing odd fragments of increasingly fractured domestic time, while long hours in the plant and the organization of shift work go unchallenged. Mario wasn't asking for time from Amerco; he was demanding it from Deb. Parents didn't challenge the company; they stole time from their children.

When I asked Mario and Deb what the company could do to improve their family life, Mario couldn't think of anything. Deb wanted to see steady day shifts for working mothers, or a system whereby one could bargain with coworkers to trade shifts as family needs came up. Other factory workers I asked wanted on-site childcare, and some spoke vaguely of "slowing down" or living "like in the country."

If workers downplayed the effects of their marathon shifts on their children, they ignored entirely the effects on themselves. A sixty-year-old ex–overtime hound, a man who had worked a "rotating seven" and all the overtime he could get for fifteen years and who had "almost lost my family" on account of it told me with great feeling, "You don't know it at the time, but rotating shift work ages you. When I was doing it, I didn't think it was bad. *Now* I know it's bad."

In the meantime, Mario had found a classic way to escape the endless conflicts over time, at least in his fantasies. He lost himself in dreams of a better age to come. "I can't wait until I turn forty-five," he exclaimed one day. "My kids will be grown and my house will be paid off." When he thought about the thirteen years between now and then, however, all he could imagine was more of the same—more screaming kids, more overtime, more time stolen from Deb and from his own sleep to do the things he liked to do.

For now, though, he was going to have to wait, because Hunter had just knocked something over in the kitchen, and Deb was nowhere to be found. She was doing another double at the plant.

PART III

*Implications
and Alternatives*

CHAPTER 14

The Third Shift

Amerco, a highly profitable, innovative company, had the budget and the will to experiment with new ways to organize its employees' lives. Its Work-Life Balance program could have become a model, demonstrating to other corporations that workforce talents can be used effectively without wearing down workers and their families. But that did not happen. The question I have asked is: Why not? The answer, as we have seen, is complex. Some working parents, especially on the factory floor, were disinclined to work shorter hours because they needed the money or feared losing their jobs. Though not yet an issue at Amerco, in some companies workers may also fear that "good" shorter-hour jobs could at any moment be converted into "bad" ones, stripped of benefits or job security. Even when such worries were absent, pressure from peers or supervisors to be a "serious player" could cancel out any desire to cut back on work hours. The small number of employees who resolved to actually reduce their hours risked coming up against a company Balashev. But all these sources of inhibition did not fully account for the lack of resistance Amerco's working parents showed to the encroachments of work time on family life.

Much of the solution to the puzzle of work-family balance appeared to be present at Amerco—the pieces were there, but they remained unassembled. Many of those pieces lay in the hands of the powerful men at the top of the company hierarchy, who had the authority and skill to engineer a new family-friendly work culture but lacked any deep interest in doing so. Other pieces were held by the advocates of family-friendly policies lower down the corporate ladder, who had a strong interest in such changes but little authority to implement them. And the departmental supervisors and managers, whose assent was crucial to solving the puzzle, were sometimes overtly hostile to anything that smacked of work-family balance. So even if the workers who could have benefited from such programs had demanded them, resistance from above would still have stymied their efforts.

But why *weren't* Amerco working parents putting up a bigger fight for family time, given the fact that most said they needed more? Many of them may have been responding to a powerful process that is devaluing what was once the essence of family life. The more women and men do what they do in exchange for money and the more their work in the public realm is valued or honored, the more, almost by definition, private life is devalued and its boundaries shrink. For women as well as men, work in the marketplace is less often a simple economic fact than a complex cultural value. If in the early part of the century it was considered unfortunate that a woman had to work, it is now thought surprising when she doesn't.

People generally have the urge to spend more time on what they value most and on what they are most valued for. This tendency may help explain the historic decline in time devoted to private social relations,[1] a decline that has taken on a distinctive cultural form at Amerco. The valued realm of work is registering its gains in part by incorporating the best aspects of home. The devalued realm, the home, is meanwhile taking on what were once considered the most alienating attributes of work. However one explains the failure of Amerco to create a good program of work-family balance, though, the fact is that in a cultural contest between work and home, working parents are voting with their feet, and the workplace is winning.

In this respect, we may ask, are working parents at Amerco an anomaly or are they typical of working parents nationwide? In search of an answer, I contacted a company called Bright Horizons, which runs 125 company-based childcare centers associated with corporations, hospitals, real estate developers, and federal agencies in nineteen states.[2] Bright Horizons allowed me to add a series of new questions to a questionnaire the company was sending out to seven thousand parents whose children were attending Bright Horizons Children's Centers. A third of the parents who received questionnaires filled them out. The resulting 1,446 responses came from mainly middle- or upper-middle-class parents in their early thirties.[3] Since many of them worked for Fortune 500 companies—including IBM, American Express, Sears, Roebuck, Eastman Kodak, Xerox, Bausch and Lomb, and Dunkin' Donuts—this study offers us a highly suggestive picture of what is happening among managers and professional working parents at Amerco's counterparts nationwide.

These parents reported time pressures similar to those Amerco parents complained about. As at Amerco, the longest hours at work were logged by the most highly educated professionals and managers, among whom six out of ten regularly averaged over forty hours a week. A third of the parents in this sample had their children in childcare forty hours a week or more.[4] As at Amerco, the higher the income of their parents, the longer the children's shifts in childcare.

When asked, "Do you ever consider yourself a workaholic?" a third of fathers and a fifth of mothers answered yes. One out of three said their *partner* was workaholic. In response to the question "Do you experience a problem of 'time famine'?" 89 percent responded yes. Half reported that they typically brought work home from the office.[5] Of those who complained of a time famine, half agreed with the statement "I feel guilty that I don't spend enough time with my child." Forty-three percent agreed that they "very often" felt "too much of the time I'm tired when I'm with my child." When asked, "Overall, how well do you feel you can balance the demands of your work and family?" only 9 percent said "very well."

If many of these Bright Horizons working parents were experiencing a time bind of the sort I heard about from Amerco employees, were they living with it because they felt work was more rewarding than family life? To find out, I asked, "Does it sometimes feel to you like home is a 'workplace'?" Eighty-five percent said yes (57 percent "very often"; 28 percent "fairly often"). Women were far more likely to agree than men. I asked this question the other way around as well: "Is it sometimes true that work feels like home should feel?" Twenty-five percent answered "very often" or "quite often," and 33 percent answered "occasionally." Only 37 percent answered "very rarely."

One reason some workers may feel more "at home" at work is that they feel more appreciated and more competent there. Certainly, this was true for many Amerco workers I interviewed, and little wonder, for Amerco put great effort into making its workers feel appreciated. In a large-scale nationwide study, sociologists Diane Burden and Bradley Googins found that 59 percent of employees rated their family performances "good or unusually good," while 86 percent gave that rating to their performances on the job—that is, workers appreciated *themselves* more at work than at home.[6] In the Bright Horizons national survey, only 29 percent felt appreciated "mainly at home," and 52 percent "equally" at home and work. Surprisingly, women were not more likely than men to say they felt more appreciated at home.

Often, working parents feel more at home at work because they come to expect that emotional support will be more readily available there. As at Amerco, work can be where their closest friends are, a pattern the Bright Horizons survey reflected. When asked, "Where do you have the most friends?" 47 percent answered "at work"; 16 percent, "in the neighborhood"; and 6 percent, "at my church or temple." Women were far more likely than men to have the most friends at work.[7]

Some workers at Amerco felt more at home at work because work was where they felt most relaxed. To the question "Where do you feel the most relaxed?" only a slight majority in the Bright Horizons survey, 51 percent, said "home." To the question "Do you feel as if your life circumstances or relationships are more secure at work or at home?" a similarly slim majority answered "home." I also asked, "How many times have you changed jobs since you started working?" The average was between one and two times. Though I didn't ask how many times a person had changed primary loved ones, the national picture suggests that by the early thirties, one or two such changes is not unusual. Work may not "always be there" for the employee, but then home may not either.

I should have asked what arena of life—work or family—was most engrossing. Amerco parents loved their children but nonetheless often found life at work more interesting than life at home. The workplace, after all, offered a natural theater in which one could follow the progress of jealousies, sexual attractions, simmering angers. Home, on the other hand, offered fewer actors on an increasingly cramped stage. Sometimes, the main, stress-free, "exciting" events at home came during the time Americans spend watching television. (According to one study, Americans spend about 30 percent of their free time in front of the television.)[8]

For this sample, then, we find some evidence that a cultural reversal of workplace and home is present at least as a theme. Unsurprisingly, more people in the survey agreed that home felt like work than that work felt like home. Still, only to half of them was home a main source of relaxation or security. For many, work seemed to function as a backup system to a destabilizing family. For women, in particular, to take a job is often today to take out an emotional insurance policy on the uncertainties of home life.

The Bright Horizons parents—middle- and upper-middle-class employees of large corporations who had children in childcare—are a good match for many Amerco parents, and the results of the survey confirm that much of what we have seen in Spotted Deer is in fact happening across the nation. Obviously, however, many working parents do not resemble those in the Bright Horizons group. What kinds of families might be omitted from this sample, and what are *their* experiences of work and home and the relation between the two? As a start, we need to recognize at least four other models of family and work life, each based on the relative emotional magnetism of home and work. Most real families, of course, blend aspects of more than one of them.

There would be a "haven model," for instance, in which work *is* a heartless world and family still a haven. Amerco workers who fit this traditional "haven model" to any extent tended to be factory hands, who did jobs that were relatively unpleasant and lacked on-the-job community. For many blue-collar men and even more women, home is still often—though as Deb and Mario Escalla's story indicates not always—far more of a haven than work. When I asked women whether they would continue to work if they did not need the money, the proportion who answered "no" rose as occupational level fell. This, in part, may reflect the fact that, over the last decade as the rich have become richer and the poor poorer, those with "desirable" jobs have generally found their jobs to be ever more inviting (with more carefully engineered workplace cultures and more impressive corporate perks). Those with "undesirable" jobs, on the other hand, have generally found them ever less welcoming (with little cultural engineering, growing vulnerability to technological displacement, greater insecurity, and declining pay). Many of these "have-nots" may still look to home as a haven, no matter what the realities of their actual home lives.

Bill and Emily Denton fit another "traditional" model, in which home and work each exhibit gender-specific pulls. Bill, and men like him at the top of the corporate ladder, flee neither a dismal workplace nor a stressful home. They make pleasurable "homes" for themselves at an office to which they devote most of their waking hours, while their real homes become like summer cottage retreats. Wives like Emily are then left to manage home and children. For them, home is not a refuge from the workday world, but a potentially fulfilling world in its own right. This old-style model of work-family balance in which each sphere of life is given to one gender is on the decline even among top executives at corporations like Amerco. The magnetic pull of work is drawing some executive wives out of the house; while for those who remain the appeal of housewifely and motherly duties and pleasures has probably diminished.

There is also a "no-job, weak-family" model, in which neither work nor home has any strong attraction for the individual. Poor people who can't find work and to whom a job may be the economic and emotional prerequisite for a reasonable family life would fit this model. In his book *When Work Disappears*, focusing on the plight of African Americans, the sociologist William Julius Wilson has argued that without a New Deal–style national public works program many blacks will find themselves living in a spreading economic desert.[9] Inner city street corner and gang life, buoyed by an underground economy, loom ever larger as substitute sources of appreciation, relaxation, and security, while drugs help provide the temporary illusion that these ideals are really within one's grasp.

Finally, there is the "work-family balance" model in which parents take advantage of family-friendly options at work and do not crave time on the job so much that they are tempted to steal it from time allotted to their children. Such parents might begin to break the time-deficit cycle and so escape the need for a third shift at home. This model was a reality for a small minority at Amerco, and probably a larger minority nationwide.

If families matching the "haven" and "traditional" models are on the decline, and families matching the "no-job, weak-family" model fluctuate with the economic times, families that fall into the reversal model in which home is work and work is home have been on the increase over the last thirty years. But what social conditions have been fostering this change? The takeover of the home by the workplace is certainly an unacknowledged but fundamental part of our changing cultural landscape.

Behind Reversing Worlds

Although work can complement—and, indeed, improve—family life, in recent decades it has largely competed with the family, and won. While the mass media so often point to global competition as the major business story of the age, it is easy to miss the fact that corporate America's fiercest struggle has been with its local rival— the family. Amerco company officials worry about their battles for market share with companies in Asia and Europe. But they take for granted their company's expanding share of domestic time. For where the workplace invests in its employees, as at Amerco, it often wins the emotional allegiance of its workers—and so ever more of its workers' time.

The ascendancy of the corporation in its battle with the family has been aided in recent years by the rise of company cultural engineering and, in particular, the shift from Frederick Taylor's principles of scientific management to the Total Quality principles originally set out by Charles Deming.[10] Under the influence of a Taylorist worldview, the manager's job was to coerce the worker's mind and body, not to appeal to his heart. The Taylorized worker was deskilled, replaceable, cheap, and as a consequence felt bored, demeaned, and unappreciated.

Using more modern participative management techniques, companies now invest in training workers to "make decisions" and then set before their newly "empowered" workers moral as well as financial incentives. Under Taylor's system, managers assumed that workers lacked the basic impulse to do a good job. Under Total Quality, managers assume workers possess such an impulse. Under Taylorism, the worker was given no autonomy. Under Total Quality, the worker has a certain amount of autonomy and is drawn further into the world of work by the promise of more.

As the Amerco work environment illustrates, the Total Quality worker is invited to feel recognized for job accomplishments. The company publishes a quarterly magazine, *Amerco World*, that features photos of smiling workers credited with solving problems, anticipating bottlenecks, inventing new products, reducing errors, and otherwise "delighting the customer." In describing its application of the Total Quality system before the House Subcommittee on Science, Research, and Technology, an Amerco vice president noted that the company preferred to reward quality work with personal recognition rather than money. Personal recognition, he pointed out, has proved an extremely effective motivational tool, one far less likely to create the jealousies that often result from giving financial rewards to some workers and not others. Company surveys confirm this.

At Amerco, employees are invited to feel relaxed while on the job. Frequent recognition events reward work but also provide the context for a kind of play. Amerco's management has, in fact, put thought and effort into blurring the distinction between work and play (just as that distinction is so often blurred at home). Fridays during the summer, for instance, are "dress down" days on which employees are urged to dress "as though" they are at home; and the regular rounds of company picnics, holiday parties, and ceremonies are clearly meant to invest work with celebratory good feeling. For white-collar workers at Amerco headquarters, there are even free Cokes, just as at home, stashed in refrigerators placed near coffee machines on every floor.

Amerco has also made a calculated attempt to take on the role of helpful relative in relation to employee problems at work and at home. The Education and Training Division offers employees free courses (on company time) in "Dealing with Anger," "How to Give and Accept Criticism," "How to Cope with Difficult People," "Stress Management," "Taking Control of Your Work Day," and "Using the Myers-Briggs Personality Test to Improve Team Effectiveness." There are workshops in "Work-Life Balance for Two-Career Couples" and "Work-Life Balance for Single Adults." At home, people seldom receive anything like this much help on issues so basic to family life. At home, there were no courses on "Coping with Your Child's Anger over the Time Famine" or "Dealing with Your Child's Disappointment in You or Yours in Him."

As a result, many Amerco managers and professionals earnestly confessed to me that the company had helped them grow as human beings in ways that improved their ability to cope with problems at home. Even in the plants, training in team building sometimes instills similar feelings in the workers. One Amerco handout for its managers lists a series of "qualities for excellence at work" that would be useful at home—an employee would be judged on whether he or she "seeks feedback on personal behaviors," "senses changes in attention level and mood," or "adapts personality to the situation and the people involved." Amerco is also one of about a hundred companies that enrolls its top executives in classes at the Corporate Learning Institute. There, managers learn how to motivate and influence others and manage conflict. The Institute offers an open-ended "personal focus program designed for people from all walks of life who have a genuine desire to explore and expand their unique possibilities." One can, at company expense, attend a course on "Self-Awareness and Being: The Importance of Self in the Influence Process."[11]

The Total Quality worker is invited to feel committed to his company. When, in *Modern Times*, a speedup finally drives the Taylorized Charlie Chaplin crazy, he climbs into a giant complex of cogs and belts and is wound around a huge wheel. He has become part of the machine itself. How could he feel committed to a company that had turned him into a machine part?

Under Total Quality at Amerco, the worker is not a machine; he's a believer. This became clear to me when I witnessed a "Large Group Change Event," held in a high school cafeteria one summer morning in 1992. The event, Amerco's response to losing customers to a growing competitor, was staged somewhat like a revival meeting. Its purpose was to convince each worker to renew his commitment not to his spouse or church but to his workplace. It was one of a series of such events held at underproducing plants in the valley. Two banners hanging at the entrance said, "Show Our Commitment." Four hundred workers, most of them white men between the ages of twenty and forty, were assembled eight to a table. They tended to sport tee-shirts, blue jeans, and baseball caps worn back to front. One young man in sunglasses casually lifted his leg over the back of his chair as if mounting a horse and sat down to join his group. "What's frustrating about your job?" the group leader asked.

"A few supervisors don't have anything to do but watch for you to make a mistake," one man responded. "Why don't they just get to work themselves?"

Talk soon turned to the effect the morning's proceedings might have on life at home. George, twenty-two, his hair in a Mohawk, volunteered, "Me and my wife just got back together. We were going down to New Orleans for a trip; but now this event comes along."

"If we keep this plant open," another worker replied wryly, "that will help keep your family together more than going on some trip."

The organizer of the event then introduced three people, a plant manager, an investor, and a union representative, each emphasizing the need to improve production in the next six months. As a revivalist minister might plumb the depths of sin, the plant manager described how "low down" plant production had sunk, how many fewer defects per million parts Amerco's competitors had, and how many more employee-initiated ideas (or, as they were calling them, Corrective Action Requests) their plants were generating each year. He went on to bemoan Amerco's declining share of the market.

The union representative, who had been a mold maker at another company for twenty-six years, told how his plant had merged with another, then closed. "We lost over 400 jobs in a town of 2,000," he said. "This is what American industry and labor face today." To think up good ideas, to concentrate harder, to be more careful, to cooperate with the coworkers on your team—these were, he suggested, patriotic as well as pro-labor acts.

Workers were then handed pads of Post-its and asked to write down good ideas, which would be stuck on a large wall in the cafeteria under the heading, "Action Ideas." Typical Post-its read: "Don't throw safety goggles away." "Recycle the water." "Don't need to wax the floor three times a day—save money." Each eight-person group was then given twenty-one adhesive gold stars and asked to vote for the best suggestions by sticking stars on the wall next to the action ideas of which they most approved. Back at their tables, workers discussed the stars their groups, now renamed "Worker-Manager Improvement Teams," had given out.

Each team was then asked to consider the question "What am I willing to commit to?" Men at one table talked about quitting their horseplay, their back talk, their slowdowns. They vowed to "cast out the devil" of taking petty revenge on the company for the tediousness of their jobs.

The event organizer then asked all the workers to take a Meyers-Briggs Personality Test using pamphlets and pencils set out on the tables.[12] This test focuses on one's capacity for teamwork, one's tendency to lead or follow, to stand up or hide, to work fast or slow. "Who here is an introvert? Who is an extrovert?" People volunteered and were then asked, "Is your personality getting in the way of committing yourself to improvement?" As was the intent of the whole meeting, the test tacitly invited these blue-collar workers to take on a managerial viewpoint in which people skills matter more than brawn, in which you and the company both should care about what type of personality you have and how it best suits the workplace. They were invited to leave their individual fates behind and try, like any executive, to envision, care about, and plan for the fate of the company.[13]

At the end of the event, to signify their new "commitment," workers inscribed their names on one of the immense red banners that hung at the cafeteria entrance. They signed with fancy long *g*'s and tall *t*'s, with lines under their names, and curlicued *s*'s. Under some names they bracketed nicknames, others as in a high school yearbook were cleverly written inside one of the banner's larger letters that corresponded to the beginning letter of a name.

The event had climaxed with a promise of redemption. Workers had offered themselves up, name by name, to be "saved" from unemployment, and to save the company from falling profits. Amerco, too, wanted these workers to be saved, not laid off. It had already spent four million dollars to get the "mission" of Total Quality out to the plants—and now it was spending even more to save plants and jobs. That said something in itself, the workers felt: Amerco cared.

This sense of being cared for encouraged workers to adopt a more personal orientation toward work time. If, in *Modern Times*, Chaplin, like millions of real factory workers of his era, found himself the victim of a company-initiated speedup, Amerco's professionals, managers, and even factory workers were being asked to envision themselves as their own time strategists, their own efficiency experts. They were to improve their own production, to manage their own intensified work pace at their own plants, even in their own lives. Under the moral mantle of Total Quality, however, workers weren't being asked to consider the speed of their work— not directly anyway—only its "quality." Meanwhile at home, the same workers were finding that quality was exactly what they had to let go of in order to do a certain quantity of chores in the few hours left to them.

The Taylorized Family

If Total Quality called for "reskilling" the worker in an "enriched" job environment, capitalism and technological developments have long been gradually deskilling parents at home. Over time, store-bought goods have replaced homespun cloth, homemade soap and candles, home-cured meats and home-baked foods. Instant mixes, frozen dinners, and take-out meals have replaced Mother's recipes. Daycare for children, retirement homes for the elderly, wilderness camps for delinquent children, even psychotherapy are, in a way, commercial substitutes for jobs a mother once did at home. If, under Total Quality, "enriched" jobs call for more skill at work, household chores have over the years become fewer and easier to do.

Even family-generated entertainment has its own mechanical replacement—primarily the television, but also the video game, VCR, computer, and CD player. In the Amerco families I observed, TV cartoons often went on early in the morning as a way to ease children into dressing and eating breakfast. For some families in the evening, CNN or network news lent an aura of seriousness to the mundane task of preparing dinner. After dinner, some families would sit together, mute but cozy, watching sitcoms in which *television* mothers, fathers, and children talked energetically to one another. TV characters did the joking and bantering for them while the family itself engaged in "relational loafing." What the family used to produce—entertainment—it now consumes. Ironically, this entertainment may even show viewers a "family life" that, as in the sitcoms *Murphy Brown* and *Ink*, has moved to work.[14]

The main "skill" still required of family members is the hardest one of all—the ability to forge, deepen, and repair family relationships. Under normal circumstances the work of tending to relationships calls for noticing, acknowledging, and empathizing with the feelings of family members, patching up quarrels, and soothing hurt feelings.

In the wake of the "divorce revolution," this sort of emotional work, always delicate, has become even more complicated and difficult. Two-thirds of the marriages that end in divorce involve children. In *Second Chances*, Judith Wallerstein and Sandra Blakeslee report on a fifteen-year study of sixty middle-class parents and children. Within ten years, half of the children whose parents had divorced had gone through a parent's second divorce; typically, one parent happily remarried and the other did not. Only one child in eight saw both parents remarry happily. Half the women and a third of the men were still intensely angry at their ex-spouses a decade later.

The study provided other insights as well. For one thing, parents and children often saw divorce differently. Two-thirds of the women and half of the men claimed they felt more content with the quality of their lives after divorce, but only one in ten children felt the same way. Three out of four children felt rejected by their fathers. Yet Wallerstein and Blakeslee found, poignantly enough, that these "rejecting" fathers often maintained phantom relations with the children they didn't see or support, keeping their photographs near at hand. One national study found that half of children aged eleven to sixteen living with a divorced mother had not seen their fathers during the entire previous year.[15]

Family life can be baffling under the best of circumstances. But in a society based on the nuclear family, divorce creates extra strains. Blending and reblending people into remarriage "chains" can be much harder than the word "blend" implies. Stepsiblings in such families are rarely as close as biological siblings—and that's only one of many problems such new families face. One divorced Amerco employee complained that his stepchildren refused to obey him and instead confronted him with the challenge "You're not my *real* Dad!" On the other hand, many divorced mothers also deeply resented the ways their remarried ex-husbands favored their new families. One divorced wife, for instance, observed bitterly that her ex-husband had managed to buy a new car and boat while remaining in arrears on his child support payments. Faced with such issues and in need of emotional "reskilling" few parents at home have the faintest idea where to look for "retraining."

At Amerco, successful completion of on-the-job training is rewarded with a recognition ceremony, a Total Quality pin, and possibly even a mention in the company magazine. At Amerco, large sums of money are spent to stage "commitment ceremonies" between the company and its workers whenever a "divorce" seems to threaten. But who rewards a difficult new kind of emotional work or watches for declining profit margins at home?[16] Who calls for renewed vows of commitment there?

The Hydro-Compressed Sterilized Mouth Wiper

Working parents often face difficult problems at home without much outside support or help in resolving them. In itself time is, of course, no cure-all. But having time together is an important precondition for building family relations. What, then, is happening to family time?

Working parents exhibit an understandable desire to build sanctuaries of family time, free from pressure, in which they can devote themselves to only one activity or one relationship. So, for instance, the time between 8 and 8:45 P.M. may be cordoned off as "quality time" for parents and child, and that between 9:15 and 10 P.M. as quality time for a couple (once the children are in bed). Such time boundaries must then be guarded against other time demands—calls from the office, from a neighbor to arrange tomorrow's car pool, from a child's friend about homework. Yet these brief respites of "relaxed time" themselves come to look more and more like little segments of job time, with parents punching in and out as if on a time clock. When Denise Hampton read *The Narnia Chronicles* to her two sons at night, for instance, she made a special effort not to think about the e-mail piling up for her in cyberspace and the memos she might soon have to compose and e-mail back. Thus, for her, "relaxed" quality time actually took special discipline, focus, and energy, just like work. Even when Denise was at home, even when her mind was on domestic matters, she often found herself approaching time in a quasi-industrial way.

Paradoxically, what may seem to harried working parents like a solution to their time bind—efficiency and time segmentation—can later feel like a problem in itself. To be efficient with whatever time they do have at home, many working parents try to go faster if for no other reason than to clear off some space in which to go slowly. They do two or three things at once. They plan ahead. They delegate. They separate home events into categories and try to outsource some of them. In their efficiency, they may inadvertently trample on the emotion-laden symbols associated with particular times of day or particular days of the week. They pack one activity closer to the next and disregard the "framing" around each of them, those moments of looking forward to or looking back on an experience, which heighten its emotional impact. They ignore the contribution that a leisurely pace can make to fulfillment, so that a rapid dinner, followed by a speedy bath and bedtime story for a child—if part of "quality time"—is counted as "worth the same" as a slower version of the same events. As time becomes something to "save" at home as much as or even more than at work, domestic life becomes quite literally a second shift; a cult of efficiency, once centered in the workplace, is allowed to set up shop and make itself comfortable at home. Efficiency has become both a means to an end—more home time—and a way of life, an end in itself.

A surprising amount of family life has become a matter of efficiently assembling people into prefabricated activity slots. Perhaps the best way to see this is to return to a classic scene in the film *Modern Times*. A team of salesmen is trying to persuade the president of Electro Steel, where Charlie Chaplin works on an assembly line, to install a J. Willicomb Billows Feeding Machine, which, as the mad inventor explains, "automatically feeds your men at work." The sales pitch, an automated recording, continues: "Don't stop for lunch. Be ahead of your competition. The Billows Feeding Machine will eliminate the lunch hour, increase your production, and decrease your overhead." In scientific-looking white lab coats, two sales demonstrators—with the muted smiles and slightly raised eyebrows of French waiters—point to the "automatic soup plate with the compressed air blower" ("no energy is required to cool the soup"); to the "revolving plate with automatic food pusher"; to the "double knee-action corn feeder with its syncro-mesh transition, which enables you to shift from high to low gear by the mere tip of the tongue"; and finally to the "hydro-compressed sterilized mouth wiper," which offers "control against spots on the shirt front."

The hapless Chaplin is chosen to test the machine, and a salesman straps him into it, his arms immobilized. The machine begins to pour soup into his mouth and, of course, finally down his shirt. Chaplin keeps a doubtful eye on the automatic mouth wiper, which periodically spins in to roll over his lips and, if he doesn't stretch up, his nose. Buttered corn on the cob appears, moving automatically back and forth across his mouth. As a deskilled eater, his only job is to bite and chew. However, the corn, like the factory's conveyor belt, soon begins to speed up, moving back and forth so fast that he has no time to chew. The machine breaks. Impassive white-coated salesmen try to fix it, but it only malfunctions again, feeding Chaplin bolts with morsels of sandwich and splashing a cream pie in his face. The mouth wiper leaps out wildly to make a small, clean stripe across his smeared face, and Chaplin drops away from the machine in a faint.

The CEO of Amerco didn't have to introduce a Billows Automatic Feeding Machine. Many of his employees quite voluntarily ate lunch quickly at their desks to save time. This pattern is by no means unique to Amerco. A recent report commissioned by the

National Restaurant Association found that these days business lunches are faster and fewer in number. Only 38 percent of adults polled in 1993 said they ate lunch out at least once a week, compared with 60 percent in the mid-1980s. According to Wendy Tanaka, an observer of San Francisco's business district, people take less and less time out for lunch, and many restaurants are being turned into take-out businesses to make ends meet. Customers who do sit down to lunch are more likely to bring work with them. As Tanaka observes, it is no longer unusual for someone to walk in with a laptop computer and have lunch opposite a project not a partner.[17]

Perhaps more significant, though, a feeding-machine atmosphere has entered the home. *Working Mother* magazine, for example, carries ads that invite the working mother to cook "two-minute rice," a "five-minute chicken casserole," a "seven-minute Chinese feast." One ad features a portable phone to show that the working mother can make business calls while baking cookies with her daughter.

Another typical ad promotes cinnamon oatmeal cereal for breakfast by showing a smiling mother ready for the office in her square-shouldered suit, hugging her happy son. A caption reads, "In the morning, we are in such a rush, and my son eats so slowly. But with cinnamon oatmeal cereal, I don't even have to coax him to hurry up!" Here, the modern mother seems to have absorbed the lessons of Frederick Taylor as she presses for efficiency at home because she is in a hurry to get to work. In a sense, though, Taylor's role has been turned over to her son who, eager for his delicious meal, speeds *himself* up. What induces the son to do this is the sugar in the cereal. For this child, the rewards of efficiency have jumped inside the cereal box and become a lump of sugar.

A Third Shift: Time Work

As the first shift (at the workplace) takes more time, the second shift (at home) becomes more hurried and rationalized. The longer the workday at the office or plant, the more we feel pressed at home to hurry, to delegate, to delay, to forgo, to segment, to hyperorganize the precious remains of family time. Both their time deficit and what seem like solutions to it (hurrying, segmenting, and organizing) force parents, as shown in earlier chapters, to engage in a third shift—noticing, understanding, and coping with the emotional consequences of the compressed second shift.

Children respond to the domestic work-bred cult of efficiency in their own ways. Many, as they get older, learn to protest it. Parents at Amerco and elsewhere then have to deal with their children, as they act out their feelings about the sheer scarcity of family time. For example, Dennis Long, an engineer at Amerco, told me about what happened with his son from a previous marriage when he faced a project deadline at work. Whenever Dennis got home later than usual, four-year-old Joshua greeted him with a tantrum. As Dennis ruefully explained,

> Josh gets really upset when I'm not home. He's got it in his head that the first and third weeks of every month, he's with me, not with his mom. He hasn't seen me for a while, and I'm supposed to be there. When a project deadline like this one comes up and I come home late, he gets to the end of his rope. He gives me hell. I understand it. He's frustrated. He doesn't know what he can rely on.

This father did his "third shift" by patiently sitting down on the floor to "receive" Josh's tantrum, hearing him out, soothing him, and giving him some time. For a period of six months, Joshua became upset at almost any unexpected delay or rapid shift in the pace at which events were, as he saw it, supposed to happen. Figuring out what such delays or shifts in pace meant to Joshua became another part of Dennis Long's third shift.

Such episodes raise various questions: If Josh's dad keeps putting off their dates to play together, does it mean he doesn't care about Josh? Does Josh translate the language of time the same way his father does? What if time symbolizes quite different things to the two of them? Whose understanding counts the most? Sorting out such emotional tangles is also part of the third shift.

Ironically, many Amerco parents were challenged to do third-shift work by their children's reactions to "quality time." As one mother explained,

> Quality time is seven-thirty to eight-thirty at night, and then it's time for bed. I'm ready at seven-thirty, but Melinda has other ideas. As soon as quality time comes she wants to have her bath or watch TV; *no way* is she going to play with Mommy. Later, when I'm ready to drop, *then* she's ready for quality time.

A busy doctor married to an Amerco executive offered a similar description of the disruption of her well-laid plan to have "special time" with her children:

> Normally, we pay our neighbor to drop Sam and Grace off at childcare at eight in the morning. Wednesday mornings I give the kids a supposed special treat. I drive them myself and stay and watch them for half an hour. I think of it as a great treat, but usually it's a disaster. Normally, they're pretty happy to be dropped off. But when I do it, they cry. They cling. They get hysterical. And here I am, thinking, "Isn't this great? 'Quality time.' "

In such situations, pressed parents often don't have time to sort through their children's responses. They have no space to wonder what their gift of time means. Or whether a parent's visit to daycare might seem to a child like a painfully prolonged departure. Is a gift of time what a parent wants to give, or what a child wants to receive? Such questions are often left unresolved.

Time-deficit "paybacks" lead to another kind of difficult emotional work. For example, like many salespeople at Amerco, Phyllis Ramey spent about a fifth of her work time traveling. She always kept in touch by phone with her husband and their two children—Ben, three, and Pete, five—and at each sales stop, she bought the boys gifts. Ben enjoyed them but thought little about them; Pete, on the other hand, fixated anxiously on "what mommy's bringing me"—a Tonka truck, a Batman cape, a bubble-making set. As Phyllis put it,

> When I call home and Pete gets on the phone, that's the first thing he'll ask me, "What are you bringing me?" Then he'll tell me what he wants, and he gets disappointed or mad if I don't bring just the right toy. I don't like Pete to care that much about toys. I don't like him to *demand* toys.

Phyllis believed that Pete "really needed more time" with her, and she sensed that she was buying him things out of guilt. Indeed, she talked and joked about guilt-shopping with coworkers. But in Pete's presence she had a hard time separating his anxiety about gifts from his relationship with her.

Amerco parents like Phyllis are not alone, of course. Spending on toys has soared from $6.7 billion in 1980 to $17.5 billion in 1995. According to psychologist Marilyn Bradford, preschoolers looking forward to Christmas ask for an average of 3.4 toys but receive on average 11.6.[18] As employers buy growing amounts of time from employees, parents half-consciously "buy" this time from their children. But children rarely enter into these "trades" voluntarily, and parents are tempted to avoid the "time work" it takes to cope with their children's frustration.

Part of modern parenthood now includes coping with children's resistance to the tight-fitting temporal uniforms required when home becomes work and work becomes home. Like Janey King, some children don't finish their dances, and like Vicky King, some parents try desperately to avoid appeasing their children with special gifts or smooth-talking them with promises about the future.

But even the best of parents in such situations find themselves passing a systemwide speedup along to the most vulnerable workers on the line. It is children like Josh and Pete who signal most clearly the strains in the Taylorized home. Just as a company that is good to its workers need not worry about strikes, so a family without speedups could be less concerned about time-tantrums and might find little need for third-shift work. Of course, some children adapt quietly to the reversal of home and work, as do adults. But many children want more time with their parents than they get, and they protest the pace, the deadlines, the irrationality of "efficient" family life. Parents are then obliged to hear their children's protests, to experience their resentment, resistance, passive acquiescence, to try to assuage their frustrations, to respond to their stubborn demands or whining requests, and in general to control the damage done by a reversal of worlds. This unacknowledged third shift only adds to the feeling that life at home is hard work. Parents are becoming supervisors with stopwatches, monitoring meals and bedtimes and putting real effort into eliminating "wasted" time. If Charlie Chaplin's mechanized dance evoked a speedup in the Taylorized workplace, it is Janey King's interrupted dance that reveals the strains of the Taylorized home.

Children dawdle. Children refuse to leave places when it's time to go, or they insist on leaving places when it's still time to stay. Surely, this is part of the stop and go of childhood itself, but is it also a plea for more control over family time?

CHAPTER 15

Evading the Time Bind

Most Amerco working parents held on to some fantasy of a more leisurely and gratifying family life. Their wishes seemed so modest— to have time to throw a ball with their children, or to read to them, or simply to witness the small dramas of their development, not to speak of having a little fun and romance themselves. Yet often even those modest wishes seemed strangely out of reach. So many of these parents had come to live in a small town and work for a family-friendly company precisely because they thought it would be a good place to raise children. They had wanted some kind of balance. As Amy Truett commented with a chuckle, "No one ever said on his death bed, 'I wish I'd worked harder at the office.'"

Still, family-friendly Amerco put steady pressure on its employees to lead a more work-centered life, and while some working parents resisted, most did not. As a result, they were giving their children, their marriages, their communities, and themselves far less time than they imagined giving. They were, in a sense, leading one life and imagining another.

As Jimmy Wayland, the middle manager who was raising a small son, expressed it, "I'm not putting my time where my values are."

His idea of time outside of work lived on—but only in his head. Like other Amerco employees, he was in a time bind, and he felt bad about it—worse in fact than a number of his colleagues who had simply ceased to value personal time. Indeed, Jimmy was laboring under a strange burden of time-debt. In the public marketplace, he had, like many of his peers, developed a "credit card mentality" and borrowed money to buy now. He bought a car in the present, drove it in the present, but paid for it later. Similarly, in his personal life, he borrowed time from his family in order to work longer hours at Amerco and, like other working parents, built up time-debts at home. Always swearing to pay time back to his son or to his partner or even to redeposit it in his own account in the future, he lived with a self "on loan."

As one Amerco mother of a nine-year-old girl described her own time bind,

> I used to be an activist, leading the recycling movement in Spokane, Washington. I helped get out the vote for local environmental candidates. And I always thought when I had children, I'd work on a community garden with them planting, working in nature, and I'd throw out our TV. I wouldn't want them to be exposed to all that junk, ads, and violence.
>
> But now that I'm working these hours, Diane watches TV after school, plays with her Barbies—I hate those dolls—and we're not doing a thing about recycling or gardening. It takes *time* just to protect my kid from what all the advertisements throw at her. It takes more time to do anything else. I don't *see* that time. Maybe when Diane's older . . .

Instead of trying to arrange more flexible or shorter work schedules, Amerco parents applied themselves to evading the time bind, and so avoided facing it. Three strategies were common. Some developed ideas that minimized how much care a child, a partner, or they themselves "really needed." In essence, they denied the needs of family members, as they themselves became emotional ascetics. They made do with less time, less attention, less fun, less relaxation, less understanding, and less support at home than they once imagined possible.[1] They emotionally downsized life.

Some time-poor Amerco parents readjusted their ideas about how to meet the family needs they did acknowledge.[2] Instead of trying to meet these needs themselves, they paid others to do it for them and detached their own identities from acts they might previously have defined as part of being "a good parent" or "a good spouse." As with many efficient business operations, they outsourced ever larger parts of the family production process.

Finally, many parents divided themselves into a real and a potential self, into the person each of them was and the person each of them would be "if only I had time." Often the real self had little time for care at home while the potential one was boundlessly available.

Emotional Asceticism

Responding to overwhelming demands on their time, some Amerco parents decided that everything seemed fine at home, that families simply did not need as much time or attention as had once been imagined. Take, for example, the issue of children who stayed home alone. According to a 1990 Amerco survey, 27 percent of its employees with children aged six to thirteen (and no spouse at home) described their primary type of childcare as "stays alone."

On this question men and women tended to answer the survey differently. Among top managers, 61 percent of fathers—but not one mother—responded that their children thirteen and under routinely stayed alone. Furthermore, 18 percent of fathers in top management—but again no mothers—reported routinely leaving their six- to nine-year-old children home alone. Among middle-manager parents of children under thirteen, 34 percent of fathers and 22 percent of mothers marked the "stays alone" box; among administrative workers, 40 percent of fathers and 23 percent of mothers; and among hourly workers, 18 percent of fathers and 18 percent of mothers.[3]

What is to be made of this gender gap in reporting on children home alone, and why is it so pronounced among top managers while it barely exists among hourly workers? Is it that working mothers at the top actually leave children home alone less than working fathers at that level, or is it that they underreport it? And if they underreport it, why do they do so?

Based on my research at Amerco I suspect that women who left their children home alone were less likely than men to check off the "stays alone" box because they felt more guilty about it. They probably believed that the response to that question said more about a "good mother" than it did about a "good father." And perhaps top women managers were especially protective of their identities as mothers because their private lives were more closely scrutinized at work by their male colleagues, and of all the women, they were the ones who worked the longest hours. More perplexing was the apparent candor the men showed. Though top male managers with full-time working wives were few in number, perhaps those men adopted a macho attitude about leaving children home by themselves—"My child can tough it out alone"—that prevented them from feeling guilty. Such well-paid men could, after all, have afforded to hire an after-school sitter. In contrast, blue-collar men for whom the hiring of a sitter would be more of a sacrifice seemed less "macho" on the subject.

DeeDee Jones, a middle manager and forty-year-old mother of four, had reluctantly checked "stays alone" on the survey, and I wanted to understand in greater detail why she'd hesitated to do so. DeeDee began our interview by recounting a series of stories about fighting for her right to be an involved mother in the world of business. She recalled ignoring skeptical looks when, as a graduate student, she arrived in classes at the Wharton School of the University of Pennsylvania with a baby in tow. At Amerco, she had taken a year off after each child's birth, so that on paper her career looked "checkered." She had objected to evening sales meetings because they cut into family time, and she unashamedly considered herself "family oriented." (Although she did admit to me once, "When the kids are driving me nuts, I come into the office. In all honesty, I just come in to drink coffee. Work can be a real escape.")

She described the afternoon schedules of her four children in detail. The fourteen-year-old played basketball after school. The six- and two-year-olds were at a babysitter's house. But between 3 P.M., when her ten-year-old daughter Janet got out of school, and 5:30 P.M., when DeeDee made it through the front door, Janet stayed home alone. The Joneses didn't live in a dangerous neighborhood but on a pleasant tree-lined street in Spotted Deer, and DeeDee's workplace was a mere five-minute walk away. Still, DeeDee had confused feelings about Janet's afternoons alone, which she described to me:

> I tell Janet that she can't have her friends over. If she wants to play, she is to go to somebody's house where there is adult supervision, because I just worry about her. Often she will come down here [to DeeDee's office] and watch television in the lounge downstairs. She gets lonely. I suppose I could let her have her friends over to play, but I worry about fires. It's a big house. She could be switching things off and on. I just don't want her to get hurt. I certainly don't want another child in there to get hurt. So I tell her she can play outdoors with a friend in our yard, but not indoors. I worry about liability too. I discourage mothers from letting their kids come over. Janet can go out and ride bikes with somebody, but ordinarily I tell her to go home and get her homework done.
>
> Janet says she's bored. She doesn't say so, but I'm sure she's lonely too. I guess what I try to do is force my kids to be independent. I think it's good for Janet to be on her own. It's not the best setup. But I would rather she be on her own than have someone come over and watch her. I would rather

224 THE TIME BIND

she just do her homework, which she has plenty of, or read a book. But Janet tends to turn on the television, which I don't think is great for her.

DeeDee claimed she wanted Janet to become "independent" but felt ambivalent about how she was to do so. For her part, Janet was not happy with her situation but didn't openly protest it. Perhaps she reasoned that if she could manage her loneliness, she could win her mother's approval. Besides, she got to watch whatever television shows she wanted.

When she sat at home, Janet was not the only child home alone. Nationwide, estimates range from 1.6 million latchkey children in 1976 to 12 million in 1994.[4] Some researchers point to the cheery news that children like Janet often do become more self-sufficient than those not left home alone. But most researchers agree that what was once melodramatically called "the plight of latchkey kids" is now, in fact, a major problem. A study of nearly five thousand eighth-graders and their parents found that children who were home alone for eleven or more hours a week were three times more likely than other children to abuse alcohol, tobacco, or marijuana. This was as true for upper-class as for working-class children.[5] Research on adults who had been left home alone as children suggests that they run a far higher risk of "developing substantial fear responses—recurring nightmares, fear of noises, fear of the dark, fear for personal safety."[6]

Many parents in minimum wage jobs cannot afford to hire sitters or enroll their children in after-school programs. But at Amerco it was largely not the minimum wage parents who left their children home alone; they generally called on relatives or neighbors for help. It was professional and managerial parents who did so and who explained their decision by talking about a child's need to be self-sufficient.

Were such parents simply affirming a value deeply embedded in the Protestant ethic and the American way of life? Certainly DeeDee Jones believed that self-sufficiency was an important char-

IMAGES OF THE TIME BIND

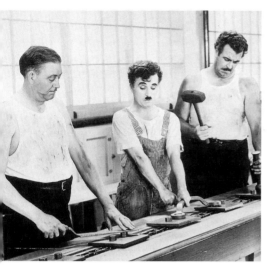

In his 1936 classic *Modern Times*, Charlie Chaplin depicts a speedup on the factory floor. The hapless Charlie fastens bolts onto machine parts at a faster and faster rate. In an era when few women worked outside the home, the speedup was confined to the workplace. Now that the majority of women and mothers are employed, the speedup extends to the home.

Ever want to be in more than one place at once?

Then you'd have enough time for everything. It's a thought, but just a thought. That's why Whirlpool® makes refrigerators with EZ-VUE™ Design. The see-through bins and up-front lighting make every-thing easy to find. And unique lateral adjustable shelving means you can even custom-create storage. At Whirlpool, we know you've got a lot to do. That's why we make refrigerators for the one of you.

Whirlpool
Home & Appliances

How To Make A Home Run.™

Learn more about how you and Whirlpool can make your home run.
Call 1-800-253-1301. Any day. Anytime.
©1994 Whirlpool Corporation ®Registered trademark/TM Trademark of Whirlpool Corporation

In *Modern Times* Charlie is strapped to the Billows Automatic Feeding Device, a machine introduced to save work time by feeding workers more "efficiently." Here, an automatic fork rapidly feeds the startled Charlie steel bolts for lunch. The feeding device applies to the act of eating the principle of efficiency introduced to the factory floor by the time and motion expert Frederick Taylor. Today, workers efficiently eat lunch at their desks or at fast-food delis. They even begin the day at home in the spirit of the Billows machine. In a recent advertisement for Quaker Oatmeal, a working mother feeds her child "in just under 90 seconds."

If the Billows Device hurried the factory worker, it is the mother who hurries her child, and indeed it is the child who hurries himself. The virtue of "hurry" becomes internalized.

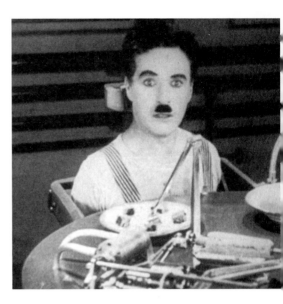

In the film, the speedup drove poor Charlie crazy. He began dancing around, chasing a secretary, and tightening imaginary bolts on her dress. He is at last carted off in disgrace to the insane asylum. But no one today is hauling the speeding worker off to a mental hospital. Indeed, in modern life, speed and efficiency are not associated with insanity and disgrace, but with sanity, pride, and heroism. When a boss reminds workers to quit at five, they think *he's* gone mad.

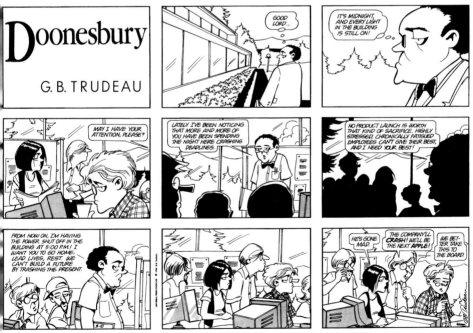

Take a lunch break with Lunch Express®

Enjoy eleven mouth-watering dishes, like our tangy Oriental-style Rice and Chicken Stir-Fry, our delicious Broccoli and Cheese Baked Potato, and our flavorful Cheese Lasagna Casserole, mixed with tender vegetables. The same satisfying portions as our Lean Cuisine entrees, they're all ready in about 5 minutes and designed to eat right from the box. Even better, they cost under $2.00. With choices like these, you'll never look at lunch the same way again.

Time To Treat Yourself Right.

From 0 to fajitas in 8 minutes flat.

Now you can make great tasting fajitas at home in just minutes. That's because we've done all the work. Tyson's Fajita Kits have everything you'll need. Fully cooked strips of tender white meat chicken, crisp garden vegetables and Mexican Original® soft flour tortillas. Whip up a fiesta tonight. It takes only minutes, with Tyson's Chicken or Beef Fajita Kits.

FAJITA KITS FROM Tyson

Feeding you like family.

A cult of efficiency moves from the workplace to home. Foods are advertised according to how little time they take to cook—a five-minute lunch or an eight-minute fajita feast. Another ad features a computer service that allows a customer to order groceries by e-mail. An iron called Handy Xpress is touted as going so fast it gets a speeding ticket. The allure of speed enters the culture. Doing something "fast" becomes a virtue in itself.

"I'm going out to log some face time with the dog."

Today, it's not simply the premium on efficiency and speed that has been transferred to the home; corporate ways of thinking about time have become part of home life, too. Even in leisure, time is divided into carefully measured segments, a domestic version of "office hours" allocated to each member of the family. If the man in the first cartoon logs "face time" with his dog, the man in the second Taylorizes his sex-life, allotting a little "Kama Sutra time" to his wife before the opera. Meanwhile, in recent workaholism humor, men don't simply transfer a

"I can't play squash tonight, Ed. I promised Linda I'd put in a little Kama Sutra time with her before the opera."

"You know Daddy has a very important job and he has to be very careful. Now sit down and put on your I.D. card."

work orientation to the home, they forget they have a home. In one cartoon, a hard-working man, wearing his ID card at the dinner table, forgets the names of his children; in another, a man forgets he *has* children. In yet another, a workaholic man, briefcase in hand, walks past his wife into his office-home. What we don't see in these cartoons is the source of work's attraction—though its effects are clear. In *Modern Times* the speedup drove Charlie Chaplin crazy—but not *that* crazy.

Doonesbury

BY GARRY TRUDEAU

"*Hello, dear. I had a very hard day at the office, and grabbed a bite on the way home. I've brought home some work, which I'll be doing in my study. See you in the morning. Good night.*"

acter trait to develop, but the spirit in which she imposed it on her daughter was more doubting than zealous. Was her affirmation of self-sufficiency, then, just a cover-up for her feelings of negligence? Actually, it would be hard to claim that DeeDee was either forgetting or ignoring Janet. She thought a great deal about her daughter's situation, even brooded about it. It seems more likely that DeeDee was half-consciously falling back on a strategy of needs reduction to resolve a larger conflict between the structure of work and the demands of home—then using the value of self-sufficiency to stress the positive side of her "emotional downsizing." It was the way she explained to herself why she was denying her daughter's need for companionship and closeness.

Much in modern American culture supports this inclination to minimize, if not deny, a child's need for security. Self-help books, for example, provide a fascinating window onto such trends in emotional asceticism. In the preface to *Teaching Your Child to Be Home Alone*, Earl Grollman and Gerry Sweder, two psychotherapists, explain that they wrote their book to "allay parents' sense of guilt and uncertainty," and to help "youngsters gain fresh insights and appreciation of how hard their parents are trying to balance work and family life." In a part of the book that parents are evidently meant to share with their children, they advise,

> The end of the workday can be a difficult time for adults. It is natural for them to sometimes be tired and irritable. . . . Before your parents arrive at the Center, begin to get ready, and be prepared to say good-bye to your friends so that pick-up time is easier for everybody.[7]

The authors focus on the case of ten-year-old Ben, who must be home alone from 7:30 A.M. until school opens an hour later. Ben's parents worry that he will become engrossed in TV, forget to take his lunch, or not leave on time. To address these concerns, the two specialists suggest that Ben reassure his parents by not arguing with them in the morning because it "will upset your mom or dad for a

good portion of the day." The authors further caution the child
reader,

> Don't go to school early just because you don't like staying
> home alone. Teachers are busy preparing for the day, and
> they are not expected to care for youngsters until school offi-
> cially begins.[8]

Principals interviewed by the authors reported that at least a
quarter of their students were already at school when they arrived
for work. Reviewing the situation for the child home alone,
Grollman and Sweder calmly present a variety of possible situations—unexpected noises, a stranger at the door, a stranger on the
phone, disturbing phone calls, misplaced keys. They then discuss
"emergencies"—a stomachache, a cut, a burn. Finally, they proceed
to "alarming situations"—a fire, a burglary, being pursued by a
stranger. Toward the end of the book, the authors note that acci-
dents, not childhood diseases, are the leading cause of death among
children in the United States. More than half of the children they
interviewed, thirteen or younger, they report, did not know how to
act appropriately in times of crisis. *Teaching Your Child to Be Home
Alone* bravely ends with a "readiness" test a parent can administer to
a child. The reader is asked to focus on the readiness of the child,
not on the world for which that child is being readied.[9]

In a similar vein, *I Can Take Care of Myself*, a booklet by Work-
Family Directions, a Boston company that conducts applied research
for corporations, is designed for working parents who leave their
children in what is now euphemistically called "self-care." Its title
appeals to a child's natural desire to grow up, and it begins in a comforting, authoritative tone: "While there is no magical age which is
the right age to leave children alone, most experts agree strongly
that children under the age of nine years are not ready to be left
alone on a regular basis."[10] It advises parents to write down the TV
programs they would like their children to watch when home
alone, and to check electrical cords and inform children that they
shouldn't use the telephone while in the bath or shower. It further

suggests that parents install safety locks on handguns, remove bolts from rifles, lock all guns in a safety box, store bullets in a separate location, label poisons, make sure smoke detectors work, and store sharp knives and power tools properly. It warns children that they should always accept deliveries without unlocking the door, slipping any paper needing a signature back and forth under the door. It warns parents that certain family pets, such as cocker spaniels and male rottweilers, have a tendency to be aggressive. It urges families to make out a list of "family self-care rules" and suggests that parent and child sign a written "self-care agreement." The booklet explains:

> Some parents like the idea of a written arrangement between parents and children concerning self-care.

The agreement has a curiously formal look to it, borrowing from legal documents its air of authority. At the same time, it is bordered by a quaint, old-fashioned lace design as if to soften the legal aspects of the deal with a hint of the personal, the feminine. In this denuded system of "care," real people—neighbors, relatives, friends, baby-sitters, teachers in after-school programs, and parents with flexible work schedules—have disappeared, while MTV, the "new neighbor" for the latchkey child, remains only the press of a button away.

Home Alone, a blockbuster film of 1992 in which a child left by himself emerges as a heroic everyboy, masks the anxiety that infuses the subject of children home alone with upbeat denial. In the movie, a bright, confident boy of about eight (played by Macaulay Culkin) is accidentally left behind by parents off on a vacation in France. At home alone, the boy triumphs over adversity. He breaks open his brother's piggy bank, buys himself frozen pizzas, and frightens off burglars who hear the menacing soundtrack of a gangster movie he plays on his VCR. His abandonment is, of course, reassuringly temporary and aberrant; his parents are away on a short vacation, not working at long-term jobs; and once they discover their mistake, they rush home. The film also places the boy in a

large house implying safety and support, and the robbers menace
him in comically improbable ways. Most important, the boy is the
embodiment of the confident, innovative, independent-minded
superkid DeeDee Jones might in her fantasies have wanted her
daughter to become. He is the emotional ascetic's dream child. He
doesn't really *need* care.

In the grip of a time bind, working parents redefine as nonessen-
tial more than a child's need for security and companionship. Pressed
for time, many two-job couples I've studied questioned a variety of
other kinds of familial needs. One husband told me, "We don't
really need a hot meal at night because we eat well at lunch." A
mother wondered why she should bother to cook greens when her
son didn't like them. Yet another challenged the need for her children's daily baths or clean clothes: "He loves his brown pants. Why
shouldn't he just wear them for a week?" Even though each of these
might seem an understandable revision of old-fashioned ideas about
"proper care," such lines of questioning can lead to the minimizing
of emotional needs as well. Of a three-month-old child in nine-hour
daycare, a father assured me, "I want him to be independent."

Humor sometimes moves in where sociologists fear to tread.
The new parent-free child is portrayed in Barbara and Jim Dale's
Working Woman Book. "Don't be alarmed if your children don't recognize you or refer to you as 'that lady,' " they warn parents. A *New
Yorker* cartoon shows a child in bed watching a TV video of his
father whose recorded voice is saying, "Now Daddy is going to read
you your favorite bedtime story." Somewhere between unintended
humor and the new familial reality is the line of Hallmark cards for
parents who are too busy to see their children. One reads, "Sorry I
can't be there to tuck you in." Another says, "Sorry I can't say good
morning to you."[11]

If, in the earlier part of the century, many middle-class children
suffered from overattentive mothers, from being "mother's only
accomplishment," many of today's children may suffer from a
parental desire for reassurance that they are free of needs.
Throughout the second half of the nineteenth century, as women
were excluded from the workplace and the woman's role at home

expanded, the cultural notion of what a child needed at home expanded as well. As Barbara Ehrenreich and Deirdre English point out in *For Her Own Good*, doctors and ministers once argued strongly that a woman's place was at home because her children needed her there.[12] As economic winds have shifted, so has the idea of a woman's proper place—and of a child's real needs. Nowadays, a child is imagined to need time away from Mother with other children or to need "independence training" (just as the elderly are often seen as "content on their own"). Like their hurried parents, Taylorized children are being asked, in essence, to "save time" by growing up fast.

Parents minimize not only the needs of their children but their own needs as well. In *The Culture of Narcissism*, Christopher Lasch remarked critically on the growth of a "narcissistic" personality, a label that later came to be associated with the supposedly self-centered 1980s.[13] For many working parents in the 1990s, however, "narcissism" has taken an odd turn. Adapting to the rigors of time-bound lives, they steel themselves against both the need to care for others and the need to be cared for. Emotional asceticism, then, is one defense against having to acknowledge the human costs of lost time at home. If we can't see a need as a need, how can we imagine we need time to meet it? As the Amerco survey on leaving children home alone suggests, more men than women probably favor this attempt to escape the time bind. They adapt to being time-poor, and their adaptation helps to crank the great wheel of Taylorism one more turn.

Women's Uneasy Love Affair with Capitalism

A second way of trying to evade the time bind is to buy oneself out of it, an approach that puts women, in particular, at the heart of a contradiction. Like men, women absorb the work-family speedup far more than they resist it; but unlike men, women are the ones who shoulder most of the workload at home. Naturally, then, they are more starved for time than men. It is women who feel more acutely the need to save time and women who are more tempted by the goods and services of the growing "time industry." They are the ones who shop for time. What the speedup takes away, the new time industry sells back in time-saving goods and services, many of which are geared to appeal to eager working women, especially of the urban middle and upper classes. But at what point does this infatuation with consumerism become a problem?

There are many substitutes for family services—summer camp for children or retirement homes for the elderly, to mention two—that have already become acceptable features of modern life. Increasingly, though, new products and concepts are being developed to extract smaller and smaller bits of time and effort from family life and return them to the family—for a price—as ready-made goods and services.

Some of these replace the practical activities of a 1950s housewife. In some parts of the country, a family can now phone in a dinner order to a child's daycare center in the morning and pick up both the child and the meal (in an ovenproof container) in the evening. Bright Horizons offers a dry-cleaning service based on the same principle. According to one news report, some daycare centers will schedule your child's extra time, arranging for and making sure that children get to swimming or gymnastics classes, for example. As the president of Bright Horizons notes, "At Christmas we even have vendors come in and set up displays so parents can buy gifts."

A mail-order company called Extended Family Food From Hane allows people to order a week's worth of dinners, $64.95 plus shipping. Meals are cooked, flash-frozen, and delivered two days later in an insulated box. A week's worth of prepared breakfasts can be shipped out in brown paper bags. Merry Maids, an Omaha-based company with six hundred franchise offices nationwide, will regularly clean the house, or for a special price do the annual spring cleaning.

A Centreville, Maryland, service called Kids in Motion gets children from school to after-school activities. Beck and Call, an errand-running service based in Warren, New Jersey, does "just about any errand you can think of" for $25 an hour. As the owner explained, "I've watered plants, brought a kid's forgotten homework to school, even picked up a cat at the airport."[14] There are now businesses that, for families with little time to make repairs, can schedule the services of a "handyman," who will fix a broken toilet or a leaky roof, and can also arrange your dental appointments. Fel Pro, an automotive parts company in Chicago, offers its employees income tax preparation and in-home tutoring of children.

Other companies edge a bit further into conventional parenthood by offering even more personal services. Playground Connections, a Washington, D.C., area business started by a former executive recruiter, matches playmates to one another. It is "like a dating service for children," the owner explained. One mother hired the service to find her child a French-speaking playmate. Another wanted a play group made up exclusively of twins or triplets.[15] In several cities children home alone can call a 1-900 number for "Grandma Please!" and reach an adult who has time to talk with them, sing to them, or help them with their homework.

An ad for KinderCare Learning Centers, a for-profit childcare chain, pitches its appeal this way: "You want your child to be active, tolerant, smart, loved, emotionally stable, self-aware, artistic, and get a two-hour nap. Anything else?" It goes on to note that KinderCare accepts children six weeks to twelve years old and provides a number to call for the KinderCare nearest you. Kindercare also stays open one Friday night a month until 9:30 P.M. for an extra $5 per youngster. "Pizza and a movie keep the kids content," the brochure promises. Kinderberry Hill Center in Minneapolis invites in local barbers and hairdressers. "Parents are encouraged to leave instructions like 'cut bangs to the eyebrow.'" Another typical service organizes children's birthday parties, making out invitations ("Sure Hope You Can Come . . ."), as well as providing party favors, entertainment, a decorated cake, and balloons.[16] The San Francisco Yellow Pages, for instance, carries such entries as "Already Taken Care Of: Party Planning and Event Consultant" and "A Whim Agency—A Complete Party Planning Resource, Children's Parties a Specialty, Same Day Service."[17]

The list goes on. Virginia-based Precious Places helps parents decorate their children's rooms. Creative Memories puts family photos in albums. As Jacqueline Salmon, a reporter who wrote a story on such services in the *Washington Post*, described it,

> Brent Lloyd . . . is glad he turned over a hundred years worth of family photos stuffed in shoe boxes and crumbling scrap-books to Marilyn Anderson, the owner of Creative Memories in Fairfax Station. Six weeks later, for about $600, Lloyd got back three photo albums with descriptive captions and decorative touches, one for his elderly mother and two to share with his wife and three children.

Yet another service offers help to quarreling spouses. As Salmon explained,

> When those less tender family moments arise, you can call Helga Abramson at Alexandria Mediation. After a dozen years of mediating business conflicts, Abramson now wades into family fights for $120 an hour. Most of the time she's immersed in divorce battles, Abramson said, but her three-year-old company also has settled disputes between a demanding parent and a disobedient child.[18]

The time-starved mother is being forced more and more to choose between being a parent and buying a commodified version of parenthood from someone else. By relying on an expanding menu of goods and services, she increasingly becomes a manager of parenthood, supervising and coordinating the outsourced pieces of familial life.

This trend toward the commodification of home life appears to be reinforcing itself. The fastest-growing sector of the American economy is the self-employed, a majority of whom are now women. Many of their small businesses have been set up to take various tasks out of the hands of busy working mothers. So some of the women consuming items produced by the time-industry do so in order to go to work selling more of the same to other women in similar situations.

The Amerco women I interviewed, in a small town in a rural area, were hardly pioneers on the commodification frontier. For the most part, they consumed little from the time industry. Many of them still cooked a Thanksgiving turkey, prepared their children's Halloween costumes, and organized birthday parties themselves. Even in Spotted Deer, though, this was beginning to change, and Amerco mothers found themselves confused when trying to sort out how much of that change was a blessing and how much a curse. Despite their uncertainty, it seemed to fall to women more than men to set limits on commercial "violations" of domestic life. If a woman like DeeDee Jones left her ten-year-old alone hour after hour with only a TV set for company, she risked compromising her identity as a good mother. For to most Americans the mother still represents the heart and soul, the warmth and human kindness of family life, a brake on the forces of capitalism, and a protector of the family haven in what is still generally imagined as a heartless world. It is a woman's symbolic role to preserve time for personal bonds, not to spend money substituting for them.

As one task after another is surrendered to the realm of time-saving goods and services, questions arise about the moral meanings people attach to doing such tasks. Is it being "a good mother" to bake a child's birthday cake (alone or together with one's partner)? Or can we gratefully save time by ordering it, and be a good mother by planning the party? Or can we save more time by hiring a planning service, and be a good mother by watching one's child have a good time at the party? "Wouldn't that be nice!" one Amerco mother exclaimed, responding to this scenario with a laugh. As the idea of the "good mother" retreats before the time pressures of work and the expansion of "motherly" services, actual mothers must continually reinvent themselves.

An overwhelming majority of the working mothers I spoke with recoiled from the idea of buying themselves out of parental duties. A bought birthday party was "too impersonal"; a ninety-second breakfast, "too fast." Yet a surprising amount of lunchtime conversation between women friends at Amerco was devoted to expressing complex, conflicted feelings about the lure of trading time for one service or another. The temptation to order flash-frozen dinners or to call a 1-900 number for a homework helper did not come up because such services had not yet made their way to Spotted Deer. But many women dwelled on the question of how to decide where a mother's job began and ended, especially with regard to baby-sitters and television. For example, one working mother told another in the breakroom of the Demco Plant,

> Damon doesn't settle down until ten at night, so he hates me to wake him up in the morning and I hate to do it. He's cranky. He pulls the covers up. I put on cartoons. That way, I can dress him and he doesn't object. I don't like to use TV that way. It's like a drug. But I do it.

The other mother countered,

> Well, Todd is up before we are, so that's not a problem. It's after dinner when *I* feel like watching a little television that I feel guilty, because he gets too much TV at the sitter's.

Another pair of parents discussed how much babysitter "coverage" they felt was *too* much. One declared forcefully,

> Nicky is in daycare from eight to five, and by five he's ready to come home. Now, I would like to work out at the gym twice a week, so I get my husband or sister to pick him up on those days. Letting him stay till six is *too* much. I don't see why some parents *have* kids if they don't want to take care of them.

I often heard this scolding refrain about "neglectful" parents— "Why do they even *have* kids?"—from Amerco mothers. I heard it used to defend or attack even the smallest differences in boundaries between work and family life, personal and paid-for services. One parent said, "My neighbor went back to work full time when her baby was six weeks old. Why do parents have children if they don't want to take care of them?" The speaker herself had taken three months off after her child's birth and then returned to a nine-hour-a-day job, leaving her child in the hands of a sitter. And her neighbor privately made the same remark about her.

Men, as well as women, acknowledged the attraction of the time industry, but in general they were slightly less tempted to suggest buying services, since it was less often they who were responsible for doing the housework and babysitting or for symbolizing the "hearth."

The Potential Self

A third way of trying to evade full recognition of the time bind is to imagine that we could and would meet the needs of our loved ones if only we had the time. In doing so, we neither wish away those needs, nor buy goods and services to meet them. Instead, we do something directly about those needs ourselves—in theory. We split our identities into actual selves and potential ones.

As we become aware of the fact that we have more things to do than time to do them, our potential selves fill the vacuum. A potential self is a set, not of imagined present alternatives—activities one "might have done" or ways "one might have been"—but of imagined future possibilities. Often, we visualize what we might do in the future in order to prepare ourselves for that future. But the potential selves that I discovered in my Amerco interviewees were substitutes—not preparation—for action. They were fantasy creations of time-poor parents who dreamed of being time-millionaires.

Phillip Domincini, a gifted fifty-five-year-old engineer in Re-search and Development at Amerco, had done well by most measures of success; but, as his wife told me, he still felt a certain disappointment that he had not accomplished more professionally. And although he took great pleasure in his daughters, eight and ten, their demands on his energies exhausted him, and he was disturbed by his inability to balance those demands with his desire for more work time. In addition, his forty-two-year-old wife, a high school mathematics teacher, had recently decided to take an evening course in psychology as part of a plan to return to graduate school. Though Phillip gave the plan his blessing, he secretly felt it strained the family's—and his—temporal pocketbook.

He was already convinced that he gave his children far less time than he should, yet he resented a change that might force him to devote more time to them. When he spoke of his life with his daughters, however, he hit a more hopeful note. "I've had this idea," he told me one day, "that I'll take Bonnie and Cheryl camping in the Poconos."

> I bought all the gear three years ago when they were five and seven, the tent, the sleeping bags, the air mattresses, the backpacks, the ponchos. I got a map of the area. I even got the freeze-dried food. Since then the kids and I have talked about it a lot, and gone over what we're going to do. They've been on me to do it for a long time. I feel bad about it. I keep putting it off, but we'll do it, I just don't know when.

Phillip's potential self was the architect of numerous everyday adventures, always ready to forge exciting plans for himself and his girls. The camping trip was only one of many projects taking shape in his imagination. The problem was that his actual self had no time to carry out any of them. His were not the escapist fantasies of a Walter Mitty, James Thurber's fictional character who imagines himself in impossibly glorious roles—a brilliant surgeon, a great warrior, a romantic lover. But no matter how "practical" his projects were, Phillip found himself planning and delaying, planning and delaying. He had become an armchair father. This was not a simple matter of procrastination. Even as his actual self moved his plans to ever more distant points in time, his potential self gained powerful emotional satisfaction from having made them.

The potential self fills an empty space where in years past was a wealth of ritual and convention. A hundred and fifty years ago, as families moved from farm to factory, social occasions—such as holiday celebrations and family meals—came to take the place of working together planting the corn, harvesting the wheat, shearing the sheep. As the historian John Gillis notes,

> One could say that the family was put into cultural production, representing itself to itself in a series of daily, weekly, and annual performances that substituted for the working relationships that had previously constituted the everyday experience of family life.[19]

Now a second substitution is in progress. The very rituals that once replaced working together are themselves being replaced by the *promise* of rituals that only the potential family will ever carry out. The family gathering is slowly losing its actuality and becoming like a phantom limb, there only in memory or fantasy. Sometimes, potential gatherings are simply postponed, as when a busy parent of three overscheduled teenagers told me, "We'll all eat a relaxed meal together when we finally get our schedules coordinated." Sometimes, such plans are removed to a more distant future. Many Amerco parents, for instance, spoke of going places and doing things "when the children are older."

Joined to these imagined future events were imagined potential selves. "I'll be more relaxed after this project is done," one Amerco engineer remarked. "I look forward to getting back my sense of humor—I'm so wound up, it's gone now. I'll get back into doing duets with my daughter and feeling free like I felt in college."

Many of the Amerco workers I interviewed were openly struggling with the time bind in which they found themselves. But most were evading conflict by scaling back on what they thought family members really needed, by buying time-saving goods and services, by developing potential selves, or by some combination of the three. While Total Quality management at Amerco was extolling the virtues of "just-in-time" production, in which needs were satisfied almost before they were felt, at home family members began to deal with time pressures by recasting their understanding of what being a householder, a parent, a husband, a wife really meant. Once parents understood the problem as one of efficiency and began "retooling" the home accordingly, their everyday solutions to the scarcity of time in their Taylorized homes opened the way for yet a little more Taylorization.

Chapter 16

Making Time

One morning in January 1995, Dorothy Myers was summoned to the office of the head of the Human Resources Division, who told her that she was being "internally de-hired" because the Work-Life Balance program in which she was employed as a psychologist was being "downsized." She could remain at Amerco, he said, if within a year another division "re-hired" her. But Dorothy was not rehired, so nine months later she took down the colorful photos of her daughter that had caught my eye when I first visited Amerco, and left the company, stunned and humiliated.

Dorothy's departure was one of many that followed the implementation of a "reengineering process" called Amerco Competes. All employees were sent to workshops to learn about the fierce global competition for market share that Amerco was facing—an implicit justification for the decision to downsize. Amerco also set up a two-month-long Stress Reduction Workshop for salaried employees to attend weekly. Its offerings included yoga, tai chi, and half-hour massages, all available on company time.

Some workers were "internally re-hired." Others were invited to accept generous retirement packages. Employees politely refrained from calling the layoffs "layoffs"; but when the smoke had cleared, one out of every ten employees had been laid off, and the other nine had seen colleagues, sometimes close friends, disappear from their work lives. Meanwhile, Amerco's profits continued to rise; its current CEO, appointed two years earlier, was earning a salary, including bonus and stock options, that came to over $1.5 million—more than a third of the annual cost of the company's Work-Life Balance program.

In fact, that program was virtually dismantled. What remained of it was folded into the Benefits Department under the supervision of a man known to be indifferent to the idea of alternative schedules. Many employees came to fear Amerco Competes and to resent the loss of the Work-Life Balance program, but as quietly as they had watched the program come, they watched it go. There was nothing that resembled a protest in response.

Yet a momentous event had occurred. Amerco had only a few years earlier boosted its productivity in part by dangling a carrot; now it was wielding a stick. To be sure it was using that stick in a kinder way than many other companies might have. Employees were, after all, being given a year to search for another job at Amerco or being helped on their way elsewhere by solicitous workers in the Outplacement Office. Still, layoffs were layoffs.

Such layoffs were deeply unsettling in two ways. They threatened people's sense of economic security, and they also called into question the wisdom of making work a haven. Amerco Competes was reengineering a workplace that, for many, had come to feel like home; so even employees who had kept their jobs were often disconcerted by the changes.

In the wake of Amerco Competes, Bill Denton's responsibilities expanded to absorb the job of one of his superiors, who took early retirement. His hours increased only a bit, but his work pace underwent a radical speedup, and his job came to include the distinctly unfamilial task of earmarking who else among the two hundred employees under him would have to go.

Vicky King was offered a big promotion, a change that thrilled her, accelerated her work pace, and led her to ask her secretary to answer the phone in a "less laid back" way. "Vicky wants my voice to reflect the new persona she's having to project," her secretary explained. At home, the pressure increased, and Vicky was beginning to worry not about Janey, who was doing well in school, but about Janie's previously outgoing "good" brother Kevin Jr., who had become more reserved both at school and at home. At work, Vicky, who had fought bravely year after year for workplace flexibility of all sorts, began to speak less of a family-friendly workplace and more about "keeping the stockholders happy." But many close friends who had fought by her side for a family-friendly Amerco were now gone. She did not say so directly, but it was clear that something deep inside hurt at this turn of events.

Denise Hampton, the mother who, unable to relax from her work pace, had sped through the Narnia books with her children, was relieved to discover that she had been spared but devastated to learn that the mentor she so admired, her "company mother," was forced to leave. Denise's husband, Daniel, was transferred to another, less pleasant job, but his hours did not increase, and the children were beginning to read on their own.

Sam Hyatt, the first man to ask for paternity leave, was transferred to a plant in another state where he became so absorbed in his new work project that he threw himself into the long-hours life he had once so ardently declared he would resist.

Amy Truett (who'd headed up the Work-Life Balance Program) had been diagnosed with cancer, and for several years worked part time. One day, I was told, she collapsed at the office and was taken to the hospital, where her husband, son, friends, kin, and minister kept a vigil. But it was a coworker and friend, Jane Cadberry, who held her hand as she died.

Connie Parker, who'd sparred with Arney Stolz for the right to work part time, was fired and now works for a temporary agency for much less money. She has more time off but not necessarily when she needs it. Now, if her son requires a new round of asthma shots, the odds are that she would not be able to take him.

Eileen Watson, the engineer who struggled to arrange a part-time schedule, finally succeeded in getting it. She works 80-percent time now, though with overtime it's more like 90. She takes most Fridays off and volunteers in the computer lab of her son's preschool. But Amerco colleagues treat her as an anomaly ("Are you still working?" they keep asking.) Using flextime, her husband Jim starts work at 6 A.M. and picks up the children around 4:00.

Mario Escalla, the overtime hound who stole sleep from himself, doesn't do that so much now. He's loading material onto kiln cars at the plant, but recently passed a test for math and dexterity that enables him to bid for a job in another plant where pay is lower but work more secure. Mario coaches baseball more than he plays it now, and Deb works steady days.

Becky Winters, the single mother who left the wedding photos out for her daughters to see, has remarried. When I called, she was separated from her new husband though about to reconcile. "It's been rough." she confided. "My husband says I'm doing to him what my second husband did to me, escaping. And maybe there's something to that," she mused. "We're in therapy to work it out." Her ex-husband found a thirteen-dollar-an-hour job as a welder, working permanent days at another company. When Becky sued for child support, he countersued Becky for joint custody of the two girls. "His lawyer argued I was an unfit mother because I work a rotating shift and the girls stay with their grandma when I work nights. He argued the girls would be better off with his new wife." Now the children have one week with my ex-husband and his new wife, and one week with me."

Meanwhile Frederick Taylor is making a reappearance at the plant. "They've taken the stools away so we have to stand at the conveyer belt," Becky explained, "and now the ware moves twice as fast." They've cut back our morning and afternoon breaks from thirty to fifteen minutes, and they're using fewer people. Now the talk is that we're competing with our own nonunion plants that pay eight dollars an hour in right-to-work states in the South. If those plants are more efficient than ours, they get the work.

For many workers earning less in new jobs, shorter hours were out of the question. Even for those who kept their jobs and pay levels, family time often fell toward the bottom of their list of priorities With jobs in peril and fewer employees around to do the work that remained, ever longer hours were a given, and family time was, more than ever, something one could wish for now but, at best, plan for later.

Even as they experienced the bad news of a rising "industrial divorce rate" firsthand, most Amerco working parents remained blind to the enormous constraints they lived under. Like most Americans they tended to believe that because they enjoyed so many constitutionally protected rights—to a free press, to freedom of travel, to life, liberty, and the pursuit of happiness—that they were, in fact, free themselves. They thought they were free, but they didn't *feel* free; in reality, many of them were living, as Michael Ventura has noted, in "temporal prisons."[1]

For the inhabitants of Spotted Deer, at least, there seemed to be no way out—no time off for good behavior, no parole, and no possibility of a jailbreak. There were also no special groups outside of work with whom to develop a new vision of how work life and home life could be balanced. Many of Spotted Deer's community groups and voluntary organizations were, if anything, also showing signs of a time scarcity—with no idea of what to do about it. Libraries, childcare centers, schools, houses of worship, and after-school programs were relying on dwindling bands of "old regulars" to help with outings, new projects, and fund raising.

Community organizations in Spotted Deer were hardly atypical in this regard. According to Harvard political scientist Robert Putnam, the proportion of Americans reporting that they had attended a public meeting on town or school affairs in the previous year fell from 22 percent in 1973 to 13 percent in 1993.[2] A declining percentage of eligible Americans vote. Union membership has fallen from 32 percent of all workers in 1953 to 16 percent in 1992. Membership in Parent–Teacher Associations, the League of Women Voters, the Red Cross, the Boy Scouts, the Lions Club, the Elks, the Jaycees, the Masons, and most other major civic organizations has also fallen.

Should we conclude, then, that the time bind is leading us toward not only the parent-free home, but also the participant-free civic society and the citizen-free democracy? If the question were put to them in this way, most Amerco parents—still dreaming of potential communities inhabited by potential selves—might reluctantly agree and shake their heads in disapproval.

But how are working parents at Amerco—or any of us—to face the time bind? And once we face it, what are we to do about it—not just in our imaginations but in real life? One course of action is to deal with the time bind as a purely personal problem, and to develop personal strategies for coping with it in one's own life. At Amerco the most common response by far was to try to limit the pull of home by needs reduction, outsourcing, and dreams of a potential time-rich self, but these strategies merely avoided, and even exacerbated, the time bind.

There are also strategies to limit the pull of work. One could, in the language of author Amy Saltzman, "backtrack" at work (demote oneself), or "plateau" (stay in place intentionally by turning down promotions), or transfer from a high-pressure to a low-pressure field.[3] Or one could start a new business, though that usually introduces powerful new time pressures of its own. (All such strategies assume, of course, some level of bargaining power at work or the financial ability to look elsewhere and so are available mainly to middle-class professionals, not to most service, clerical, or factory personnel.)

Another option might be to "migrate" away from companies like Amerco—and so from the time bind itself—by joining a tiny if growing movement toward "voluntary simplicity." In their best-selling advice book *Your Money or Your Life*, Joe Dominguez and Vicki Robin outline a program to end the "addiction" to long hours and high spending. "The movement is about dumping what doesn't make you happy," the authors say, "in order to have some time for what does."[4] Simple-living study circles have sprung up, especially in the Northwest.

More unusual still is a small "back to the land" movement. Scott Savage, a thirty-five-year-old Quaker librarian, the cofounder and director of the Center for Plain Living in Chesterhill, Ohio, advocates a life as bare of modern technology as that of the Amish. The

Center's bimonthly magazine suggests beginning by throwing out the television and the computer. While each may be an interesting option, voluntary simplicity or a move back to the land is unlikely to attract large numbers of Americans, or if it does, may rapidly be transformed into a consumer category as the *New York Times* suggests:

> By the end of the decade, 15 percent of America's 77 million baby-boomers will be part of a "simplicity" market for things like low-priced, durable gardening and home products that are short on slickness and status. They will be joined . . . by youngsters now in their early teens. They are going to buy into the idea that we are over-consuming. . . . This is the first group that's been indoctrinated green.[5]

A more daunting yet ultimately more promising approach to unknotting the time bind requires collective—rather than individual—action: workers must directly challenge the organization, and the organizers, of the American workplace. For this to occur, Amerco employees and their counterparts across the country would have to become new kinds of political activists who would—to borrow a slogan from the environmental movement—"think globally and act locally." Together, they might create a time movement. For the truth of the matter is that many working parents lack time because the workplace has a prior claim on it. It solves very little to either adapt to that claim or retreat from the workplace. The moment has come to address that claim, to adjust the old workplace to the new workforce. As history has shown us, the only effective way to bring about such basic change is through collective action.

Movements to limit work time are not new. From 1825 on, groups of people have banded together to demand first a ten-hour and later an eight-hour day. In 1886, according to the historian Paul Avrich, "the Furniture Workers Union rigged up a wagon, drawn by six white horses" called the "Eight Hour Car." A bell mounted on the cart pealed forth, eight rings at a time, while a sign on the back bore the words "IT WILL STOP OVER-PRODUCTION.

IT WILL TAKE AWAY THE TRAMPS, IT WILL GIVE THE
IDLE BROTHERS WORK." The first national law establishing a
ten-hour workday for federal workers was signed by President
Martin Van Buren in 1840. The eight-hour day for federal workers
was signed into law by Ulysses S. Grant in 1868. Ten-hour days
continued to be a commonplace for nonfederal workers for many
more decades, however. Only in 1935 did Franklin D. Roosevelt
sign a bill making the eight-hour day the national standard.[6]

The struggle for the eight-hour day was spearheaded mainly by
unionized male workers. A new time movement would have to be
made up of a wider range of stakeholders and the organizations that
represent them. Male and female workers, labor unions, child advocates, feminists, as well as work–family balance advocates and even
the leaders of some progressive companies would act as the van-
guard. Supporters of the eight-hour day strove to expand the leisure
time of workers but said little about families per se. Perhaps this was
because most unionized workers at that time were men and therefore not responsible for the direct care of children. But now that
most mothers are on the job, work time is inextricably linked to
family life. A new time movement must differ from its predecessors
by focusing far more on the nature of this linkage. On the other
hand, corporations that do provide family-friendly programs tend to
associate these programs only with middle-class women, leaving out
middle-class men as well as the working class and poor of both gen-
ders. Clearly, although women would be a significant constituency
of a time movement, men have just as much to gain. Male workers,
who often average longer hours than women and whose presence is
often sorely missed at home, need a time movement at least as much
as women do.

But we know from previous research that many men have found
a haven at work. This isn't news. The news of this book is that
growing numbers of working women are leery of spending more
time at home, as well. They feel torn, guilty, and stressed out by
their long hours at work; but they are ambivalent about cutting back
on those hours.

Women fear losing their places at work, and having such a place has become a source of security, pride, and a powerful sense of being valued. As the Bright Horizons survey indicates, women are just as likely as men to feel appreciated at the workplace, as likely as men to feel underappreciated at home, and even more likely than men to have friends at work. Cutting back on work hours, to such women, means loosening ties to a world that, tension-filled as it is, offers insurance against even greater tension and uncertainty at home. For a substantial number of time-bound working parents, the stripped-down home and the community-denuded neighborhood are simply losing out to the pull of the workplace.

Many women are thus joining men in a flight from the "inner city" of home to the "suburbs" of the workplace. In doing so, they have absorbed the views of an older, male-oriented work world about what a real career and real commitment mean to a far greater extent than men have been willing to share "women's" responsibilities at home. One reason women have changed more than men is that the "male" world of work seems more honorable and valuable than the "female" world of home and children. Deb Escalla, who worked the rotating shift at the factory, didn't want to stay home and be "just a housewife" like Mario's mother; while, by contrast, Mario still wanted to be an overtime hound like his father.

Women now compose nearly half the American labor force. The vast majority of them need and want to be there. There is definitely no going back. The difficulty is not that women have entered the workplace but that they have done so "on male terms." It would be fine for women to adopt the male model of work, to enjoy privileges formerly reserved for men, if this model were one of balance. But it is not.

All of this is unsettling news, in part, because Cassie, Timmy, Jonathan, Jarod, Tylor, and all the other children of working parents are being left to deal with the time bind—and all of its attendant consequences—more or less on their own. It is unsettling because while children remain precious to their parents, the "market value" of the world in which they are growing up has drastically declined.

One need not compare their childhoods to a perfect childhood in a mythical past to conclude that our society needs to face up to an important problem.

A time movement would have to face certain fundamental issues. As a start, since the corporation absorbs increasing amounts of family time, it is *there* that the organization of time most needs to change. Furthermore, research on Amerco and other large companies indicates that it is hardly prudent to rely on company executives as our architects of time. Whatever their stated goals, whatever they believe they are doing, they are likely to exacerbate, not relieve, the time bind of their workers. Therefore, a time movement would need to find its center *outside* the corporation, however important it may also be to cooperate with advocates of family-friendly policies inside the company.

But a movement to reform work time should not limit itself to encouraging companies to offer policies allowing shorter or more flexible hours. As this book has shown, such policies may serve as little more than fig leaves concealing long-hour work cultures. A time movement would also need to challenge the premises of that work culture. It would ask, Are workers judged mainly on the excellence of their performance, or mainly on the amount of time they are present in the workplace? Is there a "culture of trust" that allows workers to pinch-hit for one another as needs arise?[7] Is there job security? The answers to these questions are crucial, for there can be little appeal to shorter hours when employees fear that the long hours they now work may disappear entirely.

To start with, a time movement should press to restructure corporate incentives. For example, the Commerce Department could be pressured to broaden the criteria for receipt of its coveted Malcolm Baldrige Award (annually given to companies for outstanding performance in meeting the standards of Total Quality) to include the successful implementation of family-friendly programs as measured by the number of employees who actually use them. Indeed, Total Quality systems are so effective in part because they focus on the ultimate *result* of work. Instead of asking, How many man-hours did we put into this project? the question under Total Quality becomes: Is the customer pleased? It would not seem so odd, then, to urge companies to measure success in work–family balance by outcomes at home. How many working parents at a given company report they have time for their families? How many go to PTA meetings? How many volunteer in the schools? These could be signs of a company's success in establishing work–family balance.[8]

A time movement cannot stop at the company level, however. In the long run, no work–family balance will ever fully take hold if the social conditions that might make it possible—men who are willing to share parenting and housework, communities, that value work in the home as highly as work on the job, and policymakers and elected officials who are prepared to demand family-friendly reforms—remain out of reach. And it is by helping foster these broader conditions that a social movement could have its greatest effect.

Any push for more flexible work time must confront a complex reality: many working families are both prisoners and architects of the time bind in which they find themselves. A time movement would have to explore the question of why working parents have yet to protest collectively the cramped quarters of the temporal "housing" in which they live. It would have to force a public reckoning about the private ways out of the time bind—emotional asceticism, the love affair with capitalism, the repeatedly postponed plans of the potential self—that only seem to worsen the situation.

Then, too, a time movement must not shy away from opening a national dialogue on the most difficult and frightening aspect of our time bind: the need for "emotional investment" in family life in an era of familial divestiture and deregulation. How much time and energy ought we to devote to the home? How much time and energy do we dare subtract from work? Current arguments about what should and should not count as "a family" do little to help the families that already exist. What is needed instead is a public debate about how we can properly value relationships with loved ones and ties to communities that defy commodification.

Finally, a time movement would compel us to face the issue of gender. In the early stages of the women's movement many feminists, myself included, pushed for a restructuring of work life to allow for shorter-hour, flexible jobs and a restructuring of home life so that men would get in on the action. But over the years, this part of the women's movement seems to have surrendered the initiative to feminists more concerned with helping women break through the corporate glass ceiling into long-hour careers. A time movement would have to bring us all back to the question of how women can become men's equals in a more child-oriented and civic-minded society.

Such a movement would need to tackle a number of other tough questions as well. How many hours a day, a week, a year should people work? How can we press for better work environments without inadvertently making them havens from life at home? How can both partners in a relationship achieve a stable and compatible understanding of work–family balance? In an era of growing income inequality, how can more time be made available to the working poor as well as to the better off?

Opponents of a time movement will undoubtedly criticize it from many points of view. To anticipate some of their objections we need only look back at debates over the once revolutionary transition to the eight-hour day. In May 1886, for instance, one opponent of the eight-hour day argued in the pages of the *New York Tribune* that while eleven or twelve hours of daily work

> were beyond the capacity of man for the most efficient labor, . . . [n]o such claim is made or can with reason be made regarding a further reduction. Honest and faithful labor ten hours is not in fact beyond the capacity of the human frame for the most efficient work in most employments.[9]

Similarly, opponents today will certainly argue that the eight-hour day (even with overtime) is a perfectly reasonable use of human energy. They may also object that, under pressure from a time movement, American productivity and competitiveness will both suffer declines. The same argument was raised in that *Tribune* article over a hundred years ago:

> [With the eight-hour day] there would be fewer things pro-
> vided by labor and therefore fewer things to divide as the
> rewards of labor. . . . So there would be fewer houses built
> and fewer chairs and tables and fewer carpets and fewer
> tools. . . . It comes to this, then, that in order to work fewer
> hours we must all be content with one fifth less results of
> labor, less food, clothing, tools, traveling, cigars or beer.[10]

Some critics focused on the quality of labor, arguing that limiting work hours would open up new jobs to "idlers" who would
prove inferior workers. Even some labor activists insisted that good,
reformist intentions would lead only to disaster for the very workers
whom the eight-hour day was meant to benefit, by making the
United States a magnet for cheaper immigrant labor. There was
concern as well that employers would pass on the costs of offering
ten hours' pay for eight hours' work by raising the prices of goods,
or that freed-up workers would prove incapable of doing anything
useful with their extra time. The eight-hour day, wrote one wag,
was only "a charitable scheme for the benefit of saloon keepers."[11]

Of course, that time movement finally won, and none of those
fears were realized. But, as Juliet Schor has argued in *The Overworked
American*, in recent decades the victories of that bygone era have
been rolled back—and this has happened just as the weakened
family structure is least able to absorb new time pressures from the
world of work. Critics of a latter-day time movement are likely to
sound many of the same alarms as did their nineteenth–century
counterparts: shorter, more flexible hours, more part-time work,
and more elastic schedules will mean lower production, higher
prices, work by less able workers, loss of markets for American corporations, misuse of free time by workers, and so on. Whatever
critics may say, however, many of the basic reforms a time movement would support have already been tried with success. Norway,
Sweden, and Germany, for example, have all developed inventive

alternative architectures of time. Each has maintained a thriving economy for decades, even though many sectors rely on a thirty-five-hour workweek. Swedish and German workers average six weeks of paid vacation a year; Dutch workers five weeks. (Americans, by contrast, average only two and a half weeks.) "Global competition" hasn't prevented the German government from requiring employers to offer a three-and-a-half-month paid leave for new mothers and an eighteen-month job-protected leave for all parents of newborn children. Since this can obviously be hard on smaller companies, the government reimburses those with fewer than twenty employees for 80 percent of this cost. Employed parents are also entitled to five paid days a year to care for sick children.[12]

In Sweden, a global competitor long held up as a model of work–family balance, parents are allowed ten days of leave in a child's first sixty days—and half of Swedish fathers take it. In addition, Sweden offers temporary paternal leave for the care of sick children, at 80 percent pay for the first fourteen days, and 90 percent thereafter. (Travelers in Sweden quickly sense that they are in a child-friendly environment. Even trains have children's play areas with little slides, crawl spaces, and tables.) Swedish family policy specifies that children have the right to be looked after properly while their parents work. The Swedish government subsidizes childcare, maintaining high standards for secure and stimulating environments at childcare centers nationwide.

In the 1990s, Sweden has become a model in a more unexpected way as well. Pressured by more conservative members of the European Union, Sweden has taken tentative steps to cut back on family benefits for working parents. In response, grassroots protest groups have sprung up across the country. The Children's Lobby, established in 1991, is fighting cuts in children's benefits as is the Support Stockings, a group formed by women from all of the main political parties. Members of Support Stockings have even threatened to create a separate party if politicians don't work harder in support of family-friendly issues. In opinion polls, a third of Swedish women indicated that they might vote for such a party.[13]

Three American Experiments
in Time

Time activists need not go abroad for ideas about how to proceed, however. We could start by looking at modest, practical time innovations being carried out in various corners of the American corporate world. To begin with, there's "work sharing," an idea that began as a way to equalize the pain of layoffs. According to an AFL-CIO study, if American business simply reduced overtime to 1982 levels, three million new jobs could be created. One executive, Doug Strain, the vice chairman of ESI, a computer company in Portland, Oregon, saw the link between reduced hours for some and more jobs for others. At a 1990 focus group for CEOs and managers, he volunteered the following story:

> When demand for a product is down, normally a company fires some people and makes the rest work twice as hard. So we put it to a vote of everyone in the plant. We asked them what they wanted to do: layoffs for some workers or thirty-two-hour workweeks for everyone. They thought about it and decided they'd rather hold the team together. So we went to a thirty-two-hour-a-week schedule for everyone during a down time. We took everybody's hours and salary down—executives, too. But Strain discovered two surprises.

> First, productivity did not decline, I swear to God we get as much out of them at thirty-two hours as we did at forty. So it's not a bad business decision. But second, when economic conditions improved, we offered them one hundred percent time again. No one wanted to go back!

Those who worked four eight-hour days became the heart of his organization. He noted,

Never in our wildest imagination would our managers have
designed a four-day week. But it's endured, at the insistence
of our employees.[14]

What we learn from the ESI experiment differs slightly from
what Doug Strain learned. He discovered a way to downsize and
increase efficiency while keeping his workers happy and loyal. For
us, the important discovery is that the relation of time to productivity is more malleable than we usually assume, that our ideas about
what is a "normal" workday and a "normal" workforce can change
again, as they have many times in the past.[15]

Another kind of time innovation emerged from research at the
Xerox Company. Team director Lotte Bailyn studied a project team
of 350 Xerox engineers, designers, technicians, and administrative
support workers who regularly worked extralong hours. Nine out
of ten of them were prepared to work almost without limit on any
project; yet, despite an atmosphere of perpetual crisis, team deadlines
were chronically missed.[16] The question Bailyn asked was, "Why
can't workers get their work done during the day?" As she noted,

If someone finished his or her deliverables within a normal
time span, it was not assumed that they had been efficient and
creative—on the contrary—it was assumed that they had not
been given enough work to do.[17]

Workers "saved time" at home in order to devote it to work, but
once at work, Bailyn observed, they wasted time. This was because
at work, time felt "free"—as ideally we might hope it would feel at
home. With unlimited work time ahead, real work could often be
postponed. What also reduced the time available for real work,
Bailyn discovered, were constant managerial intrusions and the
meetings that followed:

Managers were always interrupting their engineers to discover whether they were on schedule, what problems they
might be encountering, and how they might deal with them.

These [problems and solutions] then were reviewed in meetings and incorporated into elaborately prepared reports that went up the managerial ladder, all of which contributed to long hours.[18]

In response to Bailyn's suggestion, Xerox set up midday interruption-free "library hours" and cut down on the number of meetings and reports required of these engineers. For the first time ever, the product development team regularly met its deadlines without working endless hours. Perhaps the explanation is that Bailyn's recommendations helped cut down on the aspect of work that had familial overtones—Daddy or Mommy bursting into one's room unexpectedly to check up on homework. Or perhaps time at work came to feel less like home life—less wasteable, less "free." Bailyn, her coworkers, and Xerox management learned that "library hours" helped workers do their work more efficiently and so increase productivity. What we learn is that the wholesale reversal of the time norms and habits of work and home—clearly bad for the home—is not necessarily good for work either.

A third kind of time innovation could be found right in Amerco's administration building, where workers processed credit accounts, pensions, mailings, payrolls, and health benefits. Work teams here, I discovered, managed their own time schedules. As I walked into the building in 1991, I noticed red, white, and blue bows strung over the walls. "Oh, that's the Decoration Committee's work for our boys back from Kuwait," explained James Flora, who managed the Administration Center's 130 workers. Along with a Furniture Committee and an Interior Design Committee, the Decoration Committee largely shaped the look of the place.

James oversaw the ten-person, self-managing, High Performance Teams that also staffed those committees. On average the workers on each of his teams were forty-two years old and had been with the company for seventeen years. Eighty percent of them were women, and a third were single parents. James explained how the teams designed their own schedules:

For example, a woman who worked the phones came back from maternity leave, and for a period of time she worked thirty hours a week. She decided she wanted to stay on thirty hours and work some of those hours from home. So she drew up a proposal to the team. The team said, "We need live phone coverage for customers eight to five. You go ahead and stay on thirty hours. Jane will pick up this part of your job. Mary will pick up that part. And Karen will pick up that other part, and we'll re-evaluate it at the end of the year." Each of the other team members figured, Someday that could be me.

The teams largely tailored such flextime schedules to their specific needs. The center, for example, had customers on the West Coast, which required it to stay open until 7 P.M. James described how one team rearranged its members' work hours:

One worker says, "What would really work for me is if I could come in at five-thirty in the morning and work until 2 P.M." Another says, "I can work 8 A.M. to 5 P.M." The third says, "I'm not a morning person, and if you need West Coast coverage, I'd just at soon work 10 A.M. to 7 P.M."

Such flexibility changed the unwritten rules about work time and disposed of the old norms about starting and stopping time. As James said,

The people who work here know what they have to do. They know they have to be out of here at a certain time to pick up their children. So they don't mess around. My secretary works nine to four-thirty during the summer so she can pick up her kids from summer camp, but summer months are usually slow anyway. If you have doctor's appointments, as long as the team is aware, just go. Billy telecommutes one day a week. I get messages from her all the time. Whether she's sitting down the hall or at home, what difference does it make? It saves her a two-hour commute. But mostly, the workers want to be back here. They're very career oriented.

In this experiment, the company learned that team governance can increase efficiency and worker morale. What we can deduce from this experiment is that workers can organize both their work lives and their home lives with an eye to efficiency and that they can do so without the intervention of a boss.

The time experiments at ESI, Xerox, and Amerco involve modest, practical adjustments whose true lesson is that our time bind is not an immutable given but something we could alter. To make such changes, however, we have to dare to want to change. Feeling that we are always late and low on time, trying to adapt as best we can to the confines of our time prisons—these are all symptoms of what has become a self-perpetuating national way of life. Even the simple act of trying to imagine other ways of living in time generates a certain amount of anxiety and fear. As a critic of the movement for the eight-hour day asked over one hundred years ago, what might people *do* with their new time? We must likewise ask, what will prisoners newly liberated from the time bind make of their freedom? What relationships will they build time-shelters for? How will they begin?

It will not be easy to face this anxiety and fear alone. In all three situations above, teams of people worked together in imagining other architectures of time. In each case, many eyes were focused on a common goal, and many hands worked together to make modest changes. One thing we can learn is that small groups of people can bring about changes in culture and habit that an individual would not dare to attempt alone.

Any successful movement for social change begins with a vision of life as it could be, with the notion that something potential could become real. So let's imagine Gwen Bell picking up her daughter Cassie at childcare twice a week at 3 P.M. instead of 6 P.M. and saving those fudge bars for late afternoon treats. Picture John Bell working a half-day Fridays and volunteering at Cassie's center. And what if Vicky King arranged with the eight male executives in her office for "coverage" and took Wednesdays off? Let's imagine PTA meetings to which a large majority of the parents come, libraries where working parents can afford to devote their spare time to reading or literacy programs, and community gardens in which they and their children have the leisure to grow fresh vegetables. Picture voting booths in which parents choose candidates who make flexible work time possible. Finally, let's imagine Janey King turning the music back on and finishing her dance.

But vision alone will not be enough. A time movement will not succeed without change in many of the underlying social conditions that make it necessary. The rising power of global capitalism, the relative decline of labor unions, and the erosion of civil society will all test the resolve of such a movement. Such trends tighten the time bind we live with, of course, but they also highlight the driving need for a way to gain release from it. Job scarcity can make people "work scared" (and thus work longer hours), but it can also force corporations and unions to look at ways to share more lower-hour jobs. Under the right political and social conditions, the growth of technology, which is extending the "anywhere, anytime" workplace into the home, might help people balance work and family even as it squeezes nonwork time even harder.

Finally, I believe that the rising number of working women—and their partners—are a growing constituency for a time movement. At all levels in the workforce, there are women and men whose potential selves are clamoring for more time at home. At a hypothetical future meeting of time activists, a unionized auto worker who wants to cut down on overtime in order to give hours back to laid-off comrades may yet join together with an upper-middle-class, working mom who wants to job share.

The two could find common cause in their children. In fact, the most ardent constituency for a solution to the time bind are those too young as yet to speak up. Fifteen years from now, ten-year-old Janet, home alone in the afternoons, and four-year-old Cassie, waiting to be picked up at the Spotted Deer Childcare Center, will have passed through a childhood of long waits for absent parents. They may say "enough" to the family equivalent of Charlie Chaplin's automatic feeding device. It is they who could form the core of a movement to reclaim private time. But if that would be a good thing in the future, why leave it as an angel of an idea now?

Appendix: Tables

	AMERCO	U.S.
Worker and Family Characteristics		
Of all workers, % who are women[a]	36%	45%
Of all working women, % who are married[b]	74%	55%
Of all working men, % who are married[b]	87%	Not available
Of all married women, % who are in two-job couples[c]	89%	87%
Of all married men, % who are in two-job couples[c]	69%	65%
Of working parents with children under age 13, % with no spouse at home[d]	84%	79%
Of children under age 13 of working mothers, % who are home alone some portion of the day or evening[e]	14%	8%

Average Number of Hours Worked Each Week

All full-time workers[f]	47 hours	43.5 hours
Full-time workers, with children under age 18	47 hours	Not available

Sources: In all cases, the data on Amerco workers come from a 1990 internal company survey.

[a]U.S. Bureau of the Census, *Statistical Abstracts 1994*, Table 616, "Employment Status of the Civilian Population: 1960 to 1993," p. 396 (based on Current Population Survey). These figures are from 1990, for comparison with Amerco figures. The 1993 figures are 46 percent women and 54 percent men.

[b]U.S. Bureau of the Census, *Statistical Abstracts 1994*, Table 625, "Marital Status of Women in the Civilian Labor Force: 1960 to 1993," p. 401. The table reflects 1990 figures, in order to compare with Amerco data. The 1993 figure for married women in the workforce is 55 percent.

[c]Galinsky et al., *The Changing Workforce* (1993), p. 42.

[d]Amerco figure includes 17 percent single working parents; the national figure includes 13 percent single working parents. National data from Galinsky et al., *The Changing Workforce* (1993), p. 43.

[e]U.S. Bureau of the Census, *Who's Minding the Kids?* (1987), p. 31. (Includes all marital status, children of employed mothers.)

[f]At Amerco single parents averaged 45 hours per week, "hourly" female single parents averaged 43 hours per week, "hourly" male single parents averaged 48 hours per week, "A-payroll" women with children in dual-earner marriages averaged 51 hours per week, and "A-payroll" men with children in dual-earner marriages averaged 53 hours per week.

Amerco work hours are close to those of other companies in the same industry. For all workplaces in the same industry as Amerco, the average weekly hours in 1990 was 41.7 plus 4.6 overtime, only slightly less than the Amerco average. National work hours are drawn from U.S. Bureau of Labor Statistics, Employment and Earnings (Washington, D.C.: January 1991, Table 34). This is data collected from households, so it includes a moonlighter's hours on second and third jobs.

TABLE B
PROPORTIONS OF ALL WORKERS USING VARIOUS SCHEDULES

SCHEDULE	AMERCO	U.S.
Regularly work overtime	70%	29.3%[a]
Regularly work weekends	49%	Not available
Regularly work flexible hours[b]	26%	15%
Regularly work part-time[c]	1%	17%
Work rotating shifts[d]	13%	3%
Work compressed workweek schedules	3%	Not available
Regularly work a "normal" shift[d]	81%	82%

[a]U.S. Bureau of Labor Statistics, Employment and Earnings, January 1991, Table 30.

[b]*Sources*: The data on Amerco workers come from a 1990 internal company survey.

[c]U.S. Bureau of the Census, *Statistical Abstracts 1994*, Table 634, "Workers on Flexible Schedules: 1985 and 1991," p. 405 (based on Current Population Survey).

[d]U.S. Bureau of the Census, *Statistical Abstracts 1994*, Table 632, "Employed and Unemployed Workers, by Work Schedules: 1990 to 1993," p. 404.

[e]U.S. Bureau of the Census, *Statistical Abstracts 1994*, Table 635, "Workers on Shift Schedules 1985 and 1991," p. 406.

TABLE C

WORKERS' NEEDS FOR FLEXIBLE OR SHORTER HOURS:
PROPORTIONS OF ALL WORKERS, WITH CHILDREN
UNDER 18, ADULT DEPENDENTS, OR
ELDER CARE RESPONSIBILITIES

RESPONSIBILITY	AMERCO	U.S.
With children under 18	51%	40%
Plan to have or adopt children in the next 3 to 4 years	8%	Not available
With disabled or elder care responsibilities[a]	12%	8%
Who expect elder care responsibilities in the next 3 to 4 years	25%	18%
With any dependent responsibilities	at least 51%	47%

Note: Percentages do not add to 100 percent because these categories are not mutually exclusive.

Sources: Figures for Amerco are from a 1990 internal study. U.S. data are from Galinsky et al., *The Changing Workforce* (1993), pp. 43, 59–61.

[a]Elder care/disabled care responsibilities can include direct personal care (bathing, dressing, feeding, etc.) and indirect care such as shopping for the person or staying in telephone contact (see Galinsky et al., *The Changing Workforce* [1993], p. 59).

TABLE D

FAMILY-FRIENDLY POLICIES OFFERED AND
USED IN FORTUNE 500 COMPANIES

The most comprehensive of four major studies on usage was conducted by the Families and Work Institute in New York, *The Corporate Reference Guide to Work-Family Programs* (Galinsky et al. 1991). It surveyed 188 manufacturing companies drawn from the largest 500 industrial and 500 service companies listed by *Fortune* magazine. Two hundred and ninety-eight companies were contacted; 63 percent replied. As Table D shows, many more companies offer policies such as part-time work, job sharing, flextime, and flexplace than report workers who take advantage of them.

POLICY	COMPANIES OFFERING BENEFIT INFORMALLY	COMPANIES OFFERING BENEFIT FORMALLY	WORKERS WHO USE FORMAL POLICY
Part-time jobs	88%	61%	3%–5%
Job sharing	48%	6%	1% or less
Flextime	77%	45%	10%
Flexplace	35%	3%	3%
Family leaves of absence	28% Mothers 22% Mothers and fathers	23%	Not Available

Source: Galinsky et al., *The Corporate Reference Guide to Work-Family Programs* (1991); drawn from pp. 84–90 and 312–429.

Other studies have reported a higher proportion of companies offering flexible schedules but have neglected to report on how many employees use them. For example, a 1992 study was conducted, by Buck Consultants, of 450 small and medium-size companies drawn from a list of their clients, among whom many were public sector and nonprofit organizations. Buck Consultants found that half the companies offered part time, 12 percent offered job sharing, and 32 percent offered flextime. Another 1992 study of 1,026 large industrial firms conducted by Hewitt Associates, also a benefits consulting firm, found that 35 percent of those companies offered part time, 18 percent offered job shares, and 42 percent offered flextime. Finally, a 1988 study of 521 companies conducted by The Conference Board found that 88 percent offered part time, 19 percent offered job sharing, and 45 percent offered flextime.

TABLE E
THE MALCOLM BALDRIGE AWARD WINNERS
AND FAMILY FRIENDLINESS

The Malcolm Baldrige National Quality Award is given out by the U.S. National Institute of Standards and Technology to American companies deemed to have the most outstanding business practices. Since the inception of this award in 1988, twenty-four companies have won this award. (Baldrige Awards are given to certain divisions in given locations within a larger company.) Are the winners also family friendly? That is, do companies that do well by Total Quality standards also do well by their employees?

I chose to include any Baldrige winner that was even *named* on a list of any of three major surveys of family friendliness. As Table E shows, only nine out of the twenty-four Baldrige winners (30 percent) were mentioned once or more as family friendly. Only two Baldrige Award–winning companies (8 percent) made it to all three lists—Corning and IBM Rochester.

BALDRIGE AWARD WINNERS[a]	WINNER MENTIONED IN MORGAN AND TUCKER?	WINNER MENTIONED IN LEVERING AND MOSKOWITZ?	WINNER MENTIONED IN *WORKING MOTHER?*
1. Corning Tele-communications Division (NC) Manufacturing 1995	Yes	Yes	Yes
2. IBM Rochester (MN) Manufac-turing division 1990	Yes	Yes	Yes
3. AT&T (NJ) Consumer services 1994	Yes	No	Yes
4. AT&T (NJ) Manufacturing division 1992	Yes	No	Yes

5. AT&T (FL) Service division 1992	Yes	No	Yes
6. Motorola, Inc. (IL) Manufacturing division 1988	No	Yes	Yes
7. Xerox Company (NY) Manufacturing division 1989	No	Yes	Yes
8. Armstrong Building Products (PA) Manufacturing 1995	No	Yes	No
9. Federal Express (TN) Service division 1990	No	Yes	No
10. Ames Rubber (NJ) Small business 1993	No	No	No
11. Cadillac (MI) Manufacturing division 1990	No	No	No
12. Eastman Chemical (TN) Manufacturing division 1993	No	No	No
13. Globe Metallur- gical (OH) Small business 1990	No	No	No
14. Granite Rock (CA) Small business 1992	No	No	No
15. GTE Direc- tories Corp. (TX) Service division 1994	No	No	No
16. Marlow Indus- tries (TX) Small business 1991	No	No	No
17. Milliken and Company (SC) Manufacturing division 1989	No	No	No

18. Ritz Carlton (GA) Service division 1992	No	No	No
19. Solectron Corporation (CA) Manufacturing division 1991	No	No	No
20. Texas Instruments (TX) Manufacturing 1992	No	No	No
21. Wainwright Industries (MO) Small business 1994	No	No	No
22. Wallace Company (out of business) Small business 1990	No	No	No
23. Westinghouse (PA) Manufacturing division 1988	No	No	No
24. Zytec Corporation (MN) Manufacturing division 1991	No	No	No
Totals	21% (5/24)	25% (6/24)	29% (7/24)

Sources: Malcolm Baldrige National Quality Award winners, National Institute of Standards and Technology, Gaithersburg, Md.; Morgan and Tucker, *Companies That Care* (1991); Levering and Moskowitz, *The 100 Best Companies to Work for in America* (1993); *Working Mother*, October 1995.
ªName of company (location of firm), type or division of business receiving award, and year of award.

TABLE F
INTERNATIONAL COMPARISONS OF WORK AND FAMILY LIFE

TIME	U.S.	GERMANY	SWEDEN	CANADA
Average hours worked, weekly (1988)[a]	41	40.1	38.4	38
Annual vacation time (in days)[b]	12	30	27	Not available
Proportion of workforce who are part-time workers, by gender[c]	Women 22.3% Men 7.7%	Women 30.0% Men 1.7%	Women 37.1% Men 6.0%	Women 26.2% Men 7.6%
QUALITY OF LIFE				
Life expectancy (years)[d]	75.3	75.8	77.3	77.1

[a]Note that the I.L.O. estimate of hours of work for U.S. workers in manufacturing differs from that made by the U.S. Bureau of Labor Statistics. International Labour Organization (1988), cited in Marianne Ferber and Brigid O'Farrell, eds., *Work and Family: Policy for a Changing Workforce* (Washington D.C.: National Academy Press, 1991), p. 174. Other sources report the following international weekly hours: U.S. workers average 40 hours per week; Germans, 38; Swedish workers, 40 (*World Labor Report*, vol. 5 [Geneva: International Labour Organization, 1992], p. 101). Another Canadian figure reported in "Working Time and the Distribution of Work: Report of the Advisory Group" (Ottawa: Human Resources Development, Bureau of Labor Information, Canada, 1994) is 37 hours per week. In another source, hours worked (as opposed to hours paid) reported by places of business (as opposed to workers' reports or time diaries) are as follows: U.S., 34.5 hours per week; Germany, 38.0; Sweden, 35.4; Switzerland 41.9; and Canada, 38.6 (*Yearbook of Labour Statistics* [Geneva: International Labour Organization, 1994]). Another source reports average hours worked per year: U.S., 1,904; Germany, 1,648; Sweden, 1,800; Switzerland, 1,873; France, 1,755; Britain, 769; and Japan, 2,143 (*World Labour Report*, vol. 5 [Geneva: International Labour Organization, 1992] p. 75).
[b]*New York Times*, 29 December 1993.
[c]Chris de Neuborg, "Part-Time Work: An International Quantitative Comparison," *International Labour Review* 24 (1985): 545–62.
[d]Source: Ferber and O'Farrell, *Work and Family*, 1991, p. 176.

ENDNOTES

Chapter 1: The Waving Window

1. See Arlie Hochschild with Anne Machung, *The Second Shift: Working Parents and the Revolution at Home* (New York: Viking Penguin, 1989).

2. For the 1950 figures, see *Historical Statistics of the United States, Colonial Times to 1970, Bicentennial Edition, Part 1,* "Series D63-74. Married Women (Husband Present) in the Labor Force, by Age and Presence of Children: 1948–1970" (Washington, D.C.: U.S. Bureau of the Census, 1975), p. 134. For the 1994 data, please see *Statistical Abstracts of the United States: 1995* (115th ed.), No. 638, "Employment Status of Women, by Marital Status and Presence and Age of Children: 1960 to 1994" (Washington, D.C.: U.S. Bureau of the Census, 1995), p. 406. Also see *Statistical Abstracts of the United States: 1995* (115th ed.), No. 639, "Labor Force Participation Rates for Wives, Husband Present, by Age of Own Youngest Child: 1975 to 1994" (Washington, D.C.: U.S. Bureau of the Census, 1995, p. 406).

3. Source: Bureau of Labor Statistics, cited in Schor, *The Overworked American* (1991), p. 32. On the key question of the rising number of work hours in the American workplace, scholars disagree. Based on a reanalysis of statistics gathered by the U.S. Department of Labor, Bureau of Labor Statistics, Schor believes there has been a "real" rise in hours over the last three decades. She found that in 1990 a quarter of all full-

time workers spent forty-nine or more hours per week on the job (Schor, *The Overworked American*, p. 30). Excluding part-year and part-time workers from her analysis, Schor argues that fully employed workers have become *more* fully employed.

Supporting the "rising hours thesis" are data gathered by the Bureau of Labor Statistics. In 1970 full-time workers averaged 42.7 hours per week; in 1988 this rose to 43.6 hours (*Handbook of Labor Statistics*, August 1989, Table 23, p. 121; see also Polly Callaghan and Heidi Hartmann, *Contingent Work: A Chartbook on Part-Time and Temporary Employment* [Washington, D.C.: Economic Policy Institute, 1991], p. 36). Also supporting the possibility of "rising hours" are results from Harris Polls, the National Opinion Research Center, and the General Social Survey. Louis Harris reports that "since 1973 the number of hours worked by Americans has increased by 20 percent while the amount of leisure people report has dropped 32 percent" (*Inside America* [New York: Vintage, 1987], p. 17).

Other scholars, however, argue that work hours have stayed the same (Mary Coleman and John Pencavel, "Changes in Work Hours of Male Employees, 1940–1988," *Industrial and Labor Relations Review* 46 [1993]: 262–83) or declined (F. Thomas Juster and Frank P. Stafford, "The Allocation of Time: Empirical Findings, Behavioral Models, and Problems of Measurement," *Journal of Economic Literature* 29 [1991]: 471–522; John Robinson, "The Time Squeeze," *American Demographics*, February 1990, pp. 30–33). Part of the "decline" in hours reported by Juster and Stafford may be due to workers' "porous" workdays. Juster and Stafford exclude as "work"—as Schor does not—any time a worker leaves the office to run an errand or takes a coffee break. Some research indicates that hours of work are rising, but only for certain categories of people: women aged twenty-five to fifty-four, better educated workers, men aged fifty-five to fifty-nine, black women aged fifty-five to sixty-four years (see Coleman and Pencavel, "Changes in Work Hours" [1993]; and Janice Neipert Hedges, "Work and Leisure," review of *The Overworked American*, by Juliet Schor, *Monthly Labor Review*, May 1992, pp. 53–54).

4. See "The Changing American Vacation," *Newsweek*, 28 August 1989, p. 8, cited in Sylvia Hewlett, *When the Bough Breaks: The Cost of Neglecting Our Children* (New York: Basic Books, 1991), p. 92.

5. Source: U.S. Bureau of the Census, 1960, and Current Population Survey, March 1986, cited in Victor Fuchs, *Women's Quest for Economic Equality* (Cambridge, Mass.: Harvard University Press, 1988), p. 111;

also in Victor Fuchs, "Are Americans Under-investing in Their Children?" *Society* 28, no. 6 (1991): 21.

6. In 1975, the proportion of women with children under three years old employed part time was 33.6 percent. By 1988 this had inched down to 31.7 percent. Twenty-six percent of employed single women with children under age three worked part time in 1975, and 23 percent in 1988 (Bureau of Labor Statistics, *Handbook of Labor Statistics* [1989], Table 56, "Employment Status of All Women and Single Women by Presence and Age of Children, 1975–1988," p. 241.) According to a recent Bureau of Labor Statistics report, 32 percent of all working women were part-timers in 1970, and 31 percent in 1993 (Bureau of Labor Statistics, Division of Labor Statistics, "Women in the Workforce: An Overview," Report 892, July 1995, p. 6). Since 1966 the proportion of mothers working full time year-round has increased from 38.6 to 49.6 percent. From 1968 to 1986, women aged twenty-five to thirty-four—those most likely to have young children—showed a steady decline in mobility in and out of the workforce throughout the year (Earl Mellor and William Parks, "A Year's Work: Labor Force Activity from a Different Perspective," *Monthly Labor Review*, September 1988, p. 15).

7. Men average 48.8 hours of work a week, including commuting time and overtime; women average 41.7. (Ellen Galinsky, James Bond, and Dana Friedman, *The Changing Workforce: Highlights of the National Study* [New York: Families and Work Institute, 1993], p. 9.)

8. See Ellen Galinsky, Dana Friedman, and Carol Hernandez, *The Corporate Reference Guide to Work Family Programs* (New York: Families and Work Institute, 1991); Robert Levering and Milton Moskowitz, *The 100 Best Companies to Work for in America* (New York: Penguin Books, 1993); and Hal Morgan and Kerry Tucker, *Companies That Care: The Most Family-Friendly Companies in America—What They Offer, and How They Got That Way* (New York: Simon and Schuster, 1991).

9. To deepen my understanding of "work–family balance" from as many perspectives as possible, I investigated work-family balance in companies top to bottom. As a consultant on a Ford Foundation project, I was able to follow the progress of three other research efforts on gender equity and work-family balance in corporations. In addition, in La Jolla, California, at a 1990 conference at the Institute for Research in the Behavioral Sciences for corporate leaders from across the country, I conducted a focus group of CEOs. Our discussions reflected the managerial perspective on the problems with—and benefits of—family-friendly policies for employees. In 1995, I co-designed a questionnaire sent

nationwide to over 1,200 parents whose children were placed in corporate childcare centers run by Bright Horizons, a company based in Boston.

10. In a national 1989 childcare study by the Urban Institute, the children of working mothers (whose youngest children were four or younger) averaged thirty-four hours a week in childcare (Sandra Hofferth, April Brayfield, Sharon Deich, and Pamela Holcomb, *National Child Care Survey, 1990*, A National Association for the Education of Young Children (NAEYC) Study, Urban Institute Report 91–5 [Washington, D.C.: Urban Institute Press, 1991], p. 105). In 1965, more preschoolers were cared for by relatives (33 percent) than by childcare centers (6 percent). By 1990, fewer (19 percent) were cared for by relatives, and more (28 percent) by centers, (p. 99).

11. Hewlett, *When the Bough Breaks* (1991), p. 81.

12. Gary Bauer, "Congress Gets the Child-Care Issue Wrong," *Wall Street Journal*, 10 October 1990, p. A18. Furthermore, in a recent Gallup poll, 41 percent of adult Americans said they had too little time to spend with their families (George Gallup, Jr., and Frank Newport, "Time at a Premium for Many Americans," *Gallup Poll Monthly*, November 1990, p. 45).

Chapter 2: Managed Values and Long Days

1. In 1983, the CEO issued a "mission statement" introducing a Total Quality Work System. Amerco allotted Total Quality a five-million-dollar budget and appointed four Total Quality executives for each of the company's four market sectors. Amerco also set up a Quality Institute, with faculty recruited from among respected midlevel managers. The first Total Quality class was offered in 1984. Over 26,000 employees have since taken the Total Quality course in any one of six languages in fifty-eight locations. The training took 3 percent of each employee's work time, about sixty-six hours per person in the first year of Total Quality.

2. See Gideon Kunda, *Engineering Culture: Control and Commitment in a High-Tech Corporation* (Philadelphia: Temple University Press, 1992). As a matter of fact, there is an entire academic subfield devoted to the study of "company culture."

3. See Catherine Casey, "Come Join Our Family: Discipline and Integration in the New Corporate Culture," paper presented at the American Sociological Association Conference, Los Angeles, 1994, p. 13; see also

Catherine Casey, *Work, Self, and Society: After Industrialization* (New York: Routledge, 1995).
4. See Table C, "Workers' Needs for Flexible or Shorter Hours," in the Appendix.

Chapter 3: An Angel of an Idea

1. These part-time jobs are not to be confused with jobs without benefits or job security, jobs in the so-called contingency labor force. The growth of "bad" part-time jobs may, indeed, be chilling the quest for "good" ones. See Vicki Smith, "Flexibility in Work and Employment: Impact on Women," *Research in the Sociology of Organizations* 11 (1993): 195–216.
2. See Table B in the Appendix. See also Galinsky et al., *The Corporate Reference Guide* (1991), pp. 85–87. Nationwide, a far higher proportion of firms claim to offer flexible schedules than report workers using them. In one study of flexible staffing and scheduling, of the twenty-nine firms offering the family-friendly benefit flexplace, for example, eighteen of the companies had five or fewer employees working from home (Kathleen Christensen, *Flexible Staffing and Scheduling in U.S. Corporations* [New York: The Conference Board, 1989], p. 18).

   What people *do* with the time freed up by flexible schedules is another story. One study of the use of flex benefits by workers in two federal agencies found no increase in working parents' time spent with children—although they did find an increase in women's time doing housework (Halcyone Bohen and Anamaria Viveros-Long, *Balancing Jobs and Family Life: Do Flexible Schedules Help?* [Philadelphia: Temple University Press, 1981]).

   A 1992 study conducted by Johnson & Johnson Company found that only 6 percent of employees used their "family-care leave" (unpaid leave for up to a year), and 18 percent used the "family-care absence" (time off with pay for short-term emergency care) Families and Work Institute, "An Evaluation of Johnson and Johnson's Work-Family Initiative," April 1993, p. 20. Despite the fact that in 1983, 37 percent of American companies made parental leave available to new fathers, one study of 384 companies found that only nine reported even one father taking a formal leave (Dana Friedman, *Linking Work–Family Issues to the Bottom Line* [New York: The Conference Board, 1991], p. 50).
3. Galinsky et al., *The Corporate Reference Guide* (1991), p. 123.
4. Arthur Emlen, "Employee Profiles: 1987 Dependent Care Survey,

Selected Companies" (Portland: Oregon Regional Research Institute for Human Services, Portland State University, 1987), reported in Friedman, *Linking Work–Family Issues to the Bottom Line* (1991), p. 13.

5. Hofferth et al., *National Child Care Survey 1990* (1991), p. 374. See also Bond and Galinksy, *Beyond the Parental Leave Debate* (1991), p. 74.

6. Families and Work Institute, *Women: The New Providers*, Whirlpool Foundation Study, Part 1, survey conducted by Louis Harris and Associates, Inc., May 1995, p. 12.

7. See Galinsky et al., *The Changing Workforce* (1993), p. 17.

8. For one thing, family-friendly part-time jobs come with full-time benefit packages, requiring the company to pay more money for less work. These benefits could be prorated, of course, but when companies have to give up something, they generally prefer to raise wages rather than lower hours. See Schor, *The Overworked American* (1991).

9. "The Workforce 2000," an influential 1987 Hudson Institute Report, predicted a shortage of skilled labor by the year 2000 due to the low U.S. birthrate in the 1970s. The report also noted that fewer white males and more of everyone else would be applying for jobs. To be sure, the layoffs of the 1980s put more skilled white men back on the market, but this has not significantly changed the long-term trend toward a more diversified workforce.

10. Friedman, *Linking Work–Family Issues to the Bottom Line* (1991), p. 12.

11. Barbara Presley Noble, "Making a Case for Family Programs," *New York Times*, 2 May 1993, p. 25.

12. Studies of Johnson & Johnson, the pharmaceutical giant, and of Fel Pro, a maker of automotive sealing products, found that family-friendly policies made workers more content and more likely to stay with their companies. See Friedman, *Linking Work–Family Issues to the Bottom Line* (1991), pp. 47–50.

13. Janet Norwood, "American Workers Want More: More Work, That Is," *Across the Board*, November 1987 (New York: The Conference Board). Based on a 1985 Bureau of Labor Statistics survey, Norwood notes that 28 percent of workers said they wanted a *longer* work week. Less than 10 percent wanted a cut in hours with reduced pay (p. 60).

In Europe, the findings are similar. Helmut Wiesenthal discovered in his research that European workers, too, exhibit no general preference for more time if more time means less money (see Helga Nowotny, *Time: The Modern and the Postmodern Experience* [Cambridge: Polity Press, 1994], p. 128).

14. Galinsky et al., *The Changing Workforce* (1993), p. 98.

15. According to Dana Friedman, "Perhaps the greatest obstacle to company activity is the absence of employee demand" (Dana Friedman, "Work vs. Family: War of the Worlds," *Personnel Administrator*, August 1987, p. 37).

16. Callaghan and Hartmann, *Contingent Work* (1991), Table 6, p. 38. Also see Deborah Swiss and Judith Walker, *Women and the Work/Family Dilemma: How Today's Professional Women Are Finding Solutions* (New York: Wiley, 1993), a study of 1,644 female Harvard alumnae and their travails taking parental leave.

Chapter 4: Family Values and Reversed Worlds

1. Christopher Lasch, *Haven in a Heartless World* (New York: Basic Books, 1977). To Lasch what matters about the family is its privacy, its capacity to protect the individual from the "cruel world of politics and work); this privacy has been invaded, he argues, by the cruel world it was set up to guard against.

2. Reed Larson, Maryse Richards, and Maureen Perry-Jenkins, "Divergent Worlds: The Daily Emotional Experience of Mothers and Fathers in the Domestic and Public Spheres," *Journal of Personality and Social Psychology* 67 (1994):1035.

3. Larson et al., "Divergent Worlds" (1994), pp. 1039, 1040.

4. Grace Baruch, Lois Biener, and Rosalind Barnett, "Women and Gender in Research on Work and Family Stress," *American Psychologist* 42 (1987):130–36; Glenna Spitze, "Women's Employment and Family Relations: A Review," *Journal of Marriage and the Family* 50 (1988):595–618. Even when researchers take into account the fact that the depressed or less mentally fit would be less likely to find or keep a job in the first place, working women come out slightly ahead in mental health (see Rena Repetti, Karen Matthews, and Ingrid Waldron, "Employment and Women's Health: Effects of Paid Employment on Women's Mental and Physical Health," *American Psychologist* 44 [1989]:1394–1401).

5. Families and Work Institute, *Women: The New Providers* (1995), p. 10.

6. Baruch et al., "Women and Gender in Research" (1987), p. 132.

7. Larson et al., "Divergent Worlds" (1994), p. 1041. See also Shelley MacDermid, Margaret Williams, Stephen Marks, and Gabriela Heilbrun, "Is Small Beautiful? Influence of Workplace Size on Work-Family Tension," *Family Relations* 43 (1994):159–67.

8. For supporting research about the importance of work to women, see

Baruch et al., "Women and Gender in Research" (1987), esp. p. 132. Also see Diane Burden and Bradley Googins, "Boston University Balancing Job and Homelife Study: Managing Work and Family Stress in Corporations" (Boston: Boston University School of Social Work, 1987). Researchers also find that simply being a mother doesn't raise satisfaction with life (E. Spreitzer, E. Snyder, and D. Larson, "Multiple Roles and Psychological Well-Being," *Sociological Focus* 12 [1979]: 141–48; and Ethel Roskies and Sylvie Carrier, "Marriage and Children for Professional Women: Asset or Liability?" paper presented at the APA convention "Stress in the 90s," Washington, D.C., 1992).

See also L. Verbrugge, "Role Burdens and Physical Health of Women and Men," in Faye Crosby, ed., *Spouse, Parent, Worker: On Gender and Multiple Roles* (New Haven, Conn.: Yale University Press, 1987). However, many factors come into play when we talk about working mothers' emotional well-being and mental health. For example, Kessler and McCrae found that a job improved mental health for women only if their husbands shared the load at home (R. Kessler and J. McCrae, "The Effect of Wives' Employment on the Mental Health of Men and Women," *American Sociological Review* 47 [1982]:216–27).

9. Andrew Scharlach and Esme Fuller-Thomson, "Coping Strategies Following the Death of an Elderly Parent," *Journal of Gerentological Social Work* 21 (1994): 90. In response to a mother's death, work was a more "helpful resource" than spouse or religion for women. For men, work was more helpful than family, friends, and religion.

10. Tamara K. Hareven, *Family Time and Industrial Time: The Relationship between Family and Work in a New England Industrial Community* (New York: Cambridge University Press, 1982). See Edward P. Thompson, "Time, Work-Discipline and Industrial Capitalism," *Past and Present* 38 (1967): 299–309. In this essay, Thompson describes a task-oriented way of noting time in peasant societies (p. 303). See also Michael O'Mally's *Keeping Watch: A History of American Time* (New York: Penguin, 1991).

11. Harry Braverman, *Labor and Monopoly Capital* (New York: Monthly Review Press, 1974), p. 106.

12. See Staffan Linder, *The Harried Leisure Class* (New York: Columbia University Press, 1974). Linder, an economist, argues that we assume that work time is money, and we apply this idea to leisure time. Thus a man on vacation may say to himself, "For every hour I'm on vacation, I could be earning thirty dollars!" Linden suggests that people continually substitute time with "high returns" for time with "low returns." In *The*

Management of Time (New York: Kend, 1987), Dale Timpe speaks of time as that which we must "audit" and offers this advice:

Many lawyers keep a log of how long the meter runs with each client. You can do the same by recording what transpired in a prior 15- or 30-minute period, or by taking a few minutes in the evening to record briefly the key events of the day and how much time was consumed by each. (p. 76)

See also Ross Webber, Time Is Money! The Key to Managerial Success (New York: Free Press, 1988). As Linder points out, in preindustrial societies, many business people with great entrepreneurial skills still didn't attach the idea of money to the idea of time.

Furthermore, the French sociologist Pierre Bourdieu has developed the concept of "cultural capital." Like economic capital, cultural capital helps the individual progress up the social class ladder. Beliefs about time and habitual ways of handling it can also be seen as a form of cultural capital (Pierre Bourdieu, Distinction [Cambridge, Mass.: Harvard University Press, 1984]).

Chapter 5: Giving at the Office

1. See also Helga Nowotny, "Time Structuring and Time Measurement: On the Interrelation between Timekeepers and Social Time," in J. Fraser et al., eds., The Study of Time II (Amherst: University of Massachusetts Press, 1975).
2. In his book, Hidden Rhythms, sociologist Eviatar Zerubavel describes another social world in which time was tightly scheduled and controlled—the medieval Benedictine monastery. Instructions about how to keep busy all day appeared in the Rule of Saint Benedict (Eviatar Zerubavel, Hidden Rhythms: Schedules and Calendars in Social Life [Chicago: University of Chicago Press, 1981], pp. 34, 35, 39). In the contemporary company, too, time is extremely ordered, regulated, rationalized. When executives at Amerco explained why they "loved" their work, they often mentioned the satisfaction of solving challenging problems, being part of the community of employees, and, of course, receiving money and prestige. But I wondered if some of that "love" didn't arise from the comforting regularity of their tasks.
3. See Table C in the Appendix, showing the proportion of workers

at Amerco and in the United States with various kinds of family responsibilities.

4. See Roma Hanks and Marvin B. Sussman, eds., "Where Does Family End and Corporation Begin: The Consequences of Rapid Transformation," in *Corporations, Businesses and Families* (New York: Haworth Press, 1990), p. 6.

Chapter 6: The Administrative Mother

1. Amerco offered full benefits to employees working thirty hours or more a week.

2. At Amerco, the highest-paid (A-payroll) mothers in dual-earner marriages averaged fifty hours at work and forty-five caring for children and home (for A-payroll men, the figures were fifty-three and twenty-five). Such women came in second in overall hours of work, after factory laborers who are single mothers. The third longest hours (ninety-four hours a week) are worked by mothers married to nonworking spouses. However, it's not simply the number of hours but the control one has over them that counts. See, for example, R. Karesek, "Lower Health Risk with Increased Job Control among White-Collar Workers," *Journal of Organizational Behavior* 11 (1990):171–85.

Chapter 7: "All My Friends Are Worker Bees"

1. See Felice Schwartz, "Management Women and the New Facts of Life," *Harvard Business Review*, January–February 1989, pp. 65–76. This controversial plan, first suggested in 1987 by Schwartz, sets a group of professional mothers on a permanently lower "non-career-dominant" track at work. The sociologist Lotte Bailyn envisions less static career trajectories, with "slow starters" achieving the same high levels of career accomplishment as do "burn outs" (people who start fast, rise quickly, and then level off in career achievement). See Lotte Bailyn, "The Slow-Burn Way to the Top: Some Thoughts on the Early Years of Organizational Careers," in C. B. Derr, ed., *Work and Family, and the Career* (New York: Praeger, 1980), pp. 94–105.

Chapter 8: "I'm Still Married"

1. Alan Dundes, ed., *The Evil Eye: A Folklore Casebook* (New York: Garland Press, 1981); for more on "the limited good," see p. 266.

Chapter 9: "Catching Up on the Soaps"

1. See Linda Haas, *Equal Parenthood and Social Policy: A Study of Parental Leave in Sweden* (Albany: State University of New York Press, 1992).
2. William Goode, "Why Men Resist," in Arlene Skolnick and Jerome Skolnick, eds., *Family in Transition*, 8th ed. (New York: HarperCollins, 1994), pp. 137–48.
3. All told, 39 percent of Amerco men thought that flexible hours for full-time workers was an idea of "great value"—47 percent of male lower managers, 54 percent of male administrative workers, and 59 percent of male technical workers. When male workers were asked about an absence policy covering illness of children, the same pattern showed up. Far fewer men favored job sharing, but those who did were not at the top (among the A- and B-payroll men, only 12 and 7 percent, respectively, supported it). They were the administrative and technical men (22 and 14 percent, respectively). Production workers weren't asked this question. In contrast, when women were asked about work–family policies for male employees a different pattern emerged, with women higher in the hierarchy favoring more flexible arrangements. Among women, 43 percent of A-payroll employees supported childcare leave for new fathers; this number dropped to 38 percent among B-payroll employees and to 27 percent among administrative and technical workers.

Chapter 10: What If the Boss Says No?

1. A 1990 Amerco survey showed that among mothers of children age thirteen and under, 12 percent of A-payroll women, 9 percent of B-payroll women, 23 percent of administrative women, 29 percent of technical women, and 50 percent of hourly women found it "very difficult" to schedule a medical appointment during work hours. Fewer fathers complained of this problem. Only 35 percent of fathers paid by the hour, for instance, said it would be "very difficult" to schedule medical appointments during work hours.

Chapter 11: "I Want Them to Grow Up to Be Good Single Moms"

1. " 'It's Too Much of a Good Thing,' GM Workers Say in Protesting Overtime," *New York Times*, 22 November 1994, p. A10.
2. Nationwide, 24 percent of children live in one-parent families at some point in their childhoods.

3. For discussions of contemporary childcare arrangements that working parents struggle with, see Lynne Casper, Mary Hawkins, and Martin O'Connell, "Who's Minding the Kids? Childcare Arrangements," Fall 1991, U.S. Bureau of the Census, Current Population Reports (Washington, D.C.: U.S. Government Printing Office, 1994); and Larry Bumpass, "What's Happening to the Family? Interactions between Demographic and Institutional Change," *Demography* 27, no. 4 (1990): 483–98.

4. For a discussion of these family issues, see Lynn White and Bruce Keith, "The Effect of Shiftwork on the Quality and Stability of Marital Relations," *Journal of Marriage and the Family* 52 (1990): 453–62. Rotating schedules and non–day-shift jobs—like those Becky and her friends so often had—seem to place a special strain on marriage and may also act as magnets for those seeking escape from relationships that were already problematic. In their study of 1,668 married men and women, White and Keith found that shift work increases the probability of divorce. The authors conclude:

> Shift work is associated with increased disagreements—but it cannot answer which came first. It is not improbable that those persons who wish to escape from their childcare responsibilities or who hope for sexual adventures may be more likely to choose shift work. To the extent that this is true, shift work is the first step in a process of disengagement that ultimately leads to divorce." (p. 461)

   See also Rosanna Hertz and Joy Charlton's thoughtful essay "Making Family under a Shift Work Schedule: Air Force Security Guards and Their Wives," *Social Problems* 36 (1989): 491–507; and Harriet Presser, "Shift Work and Childcare among Dual-Earner American Parents," *Journal of Marriage and the Family* 50 (1988): 133–48.

5. See Andrew Cherlin and Frank Furstenberg, *The New American Grandparents* (New York: Basic Books, 1986).

6. See Bumpass, "What's Happening with the Family?" (1990), p. 492; and Casper et al., "Who's Minding the Kids?" (1994), p. 7.

7. Casper et al., "Who's Minding the Kids?" (1994), p. 7.

8. See also Louise Lamphere, *Sunbelt Working Mothers: Reconciling Family and Factory* (Ithaca, N.Y.: Cornell University Press, 1993), for a discussion of how working-class mothers organize help and friendship with coworkers.

9. In her book *Worlds of Pain*, Lillian Rubin observes that working-class people live harder lives than middle-class people do. Their parents are more likely to be overtired, alcoholic, mentally ill, violent. Yet the adult children of working-class parents complain less about their parents than middle-class adults do (Lillian Rubin, *Worlds of Pain: Life in Working-Class Families* [New York: Basic Books, 1976]).

Chapter 12: The Overextended Family

1. Elizabeth Bott, *Family and Social Network: Roles, Norms, and External Relationships in Ordinary Urban Families* (New York: Free Press, 1967).
2. In a recent national survey, 1,502 women were asked, "If you had enough money to live as comfortably as you'd like, would you prefer to work full time, part time, do volunteer type work, or work at home caring for the family?" Over all, only 31 percent chose "work at home caring for the family." The more educated, the more interested in work. But even among women who never went to high school, two out of five opted for work (Families and Work Institute, *Women: The New Providers* [1995], p. 56.).

Chapter 13: Overtime Hounds

1. In 1990, two-thirds of hourly men at Amerco had working wives, and salaries for hourly workers at Amerco ranged between $25,000 and $49,999. In 1990, among hourly men at the company, 20 percent had a household income of $25,000 or less, 69 percent earned between $25,000 and $50,000, and 11 percent earned more. With their combined salary of $63,000, then, the Escallas were among the very top hourly earners. Among women—more of whom were single parents—household incomes were lower. A third earned less than $25,000, half had household incomes between $25,000 and $50,000, and 16 percent had higher incomes.
2. Harriet Presser, "Female Employment and the Division of Labor within the Home: A Longitudinal Perspective," paper presented at the Population Association of America, St. Louis, 1977.
3. For a portrait of nineteenth–century bonds of family and friendship at work, see Hareven, *Family Time and Industrial Time* (1982).
4. See Hertz and Charlton, "Making Family under a Shiftwork Schedule" (1989), 505.

Chapter 14: The Third Shift

1. Those whose time is not compensated by money—housewives, children, the elderly—are held in lower regard than those whose time is compensated by money, everything else held equal. (This holds true only for jobs that are not subject to moral censure; a prostitute is not more highly valued than a housewife because she has a paying job in public life.) For many paid workers themselves, the trade of time for money can take on very different cultural meanings depending on the societal context. (Thanks to Deborah Davis for clarification on the relation between work for money and time.) See Nowotny, *Time: The Modern and the Postmodern Experience* (1994); and Linder, *The Harried Leisure Class* (1974).

2. Founded in 1986, Bright Horizons was named the nation's leading work-site childcare organization in 1991 by the Child Care Information Exchange. The company offers a range of services: drop-in care, weekend programs, and programs for infants, toddlers, preschoolers, and school-age children. Bright Horizons pays its teachers 10 percent more than whatever the going rate may be at nearby childcare centers and has a rate of teacher turnover that averages only half of the industry-wide 40 to 50 percent a year.

3. Thirty-five percent of parents responded (9 percent were male and 90 percent female; 92 percent were married and 7 percent single). Percentages may not add up to 100 for some questions either because some respondents didn't answer that question or because the percentages that are reported were rounded to the nearest whole number.

4. Twenty percent of parents reported that their children were in childcare 41–45 hours a week; 13 percent, 46–50 hours; 2 percent, 51–60 hours. In the lowest income group in the study ($45,000 or less), 25 percent of parents had children in childcare 41 hours a week or longer. In the highest income group ($140,000 or higher), 39 percent did.

5. Parents were asked how many hours they spent doing work they brought home from the office "on a typical weekday." Eighteen percent didn't answer. Of those remaining, half said they did bring work home. The largest proportion—19 percent—brought home "between six and ten hours of work [per week]." They estimated even longer hours for their partners.

6. Burden and Googins, "Boston University Balancing Job and Homelife Study" (1987), p. 30.

7. Yet friends may not be a working parent's main source of social support.

When asked which were the "three most important sources of support in your life," nine out of ten men and women mentioned their spouses or partners. Second came their mothers, and third "other relatives." So people turned for support to kin first. Among *friendships*, however, those at work proved more significant than those around home. As sources of emotional support, 10 percent of the respondents also mentioned "books and magazines," the same percentage as mentioned "church or temple"; only 5 percent mentioned neighbors. Thirteen percent turned for support first to friends at work—as many as turned to their own fathers.

8. Jim Spring, "Seven Days of Play," *American Demography* 15 (March 1993): 50–54. According to another study, in the average American home, a television is on for almost half of all waking hours. Teenagers watch approximately twenty-two hours of television each week (Anne Walling, "Teenagers and Television," *American Family Physician* 42 [1990]: 638–41), and children watch an average of two to three hours each day (Althea Huston, John Wright, Mabel Rice, and Dennis Kerkman, "Developmental Perspective of Television Viewing Patterns," *Developmental Psychology* 26 [1990]: 409–21).

9. William Julius Wilson, *When Work Disappears: The World of the New Urban Poor* (New York: Knopf, 1996).

10. W. Edwards Deming, "Improvement of Quality and Productivity through Action by Management," *National Productivity Review*, Winter 1981–82, pp. 2–12. See Mary Walton, *The Deming Management Method* (New York: Dodd, Mead & Co., 1986); Frederick Taylor, *The Principles of Scientific Management* (New York: Harper, 1911). While the Total Quality movement has come to many corporations, the influence of Frederick Taylor is hardly dead. Many low-skill workers are vulnerable to Taylorization of their jobs. In her book *The Electronic Sweatshop* (New York: Simon and Schuster, 1988), Barbara Garson describes a McDonald's hamburger cook whose every motion is simplified, preset, and monitored.

11. Hugh Mulligan, "Employers Foster Friendly Workplaces [Associated Press release]," *Louisville Courier Journal*, 1991. In some companies, such as Hudson Food Inc.'s processing plant in Noel, Missouri, the company hires chaplains as company counselors. As Barnaby Feder describes in his *New York Times* article,

As the workers chop and package the birds' carcasses, others talk about their battles with drinking or drugs, marital tensions, sick parents, runaway children and housing crises. Such chats (with the chaplain) frequently lead to private counseling sessions, hospital visits and other forms of pastoral ministry.

Companies hiring chaplains are, in a sense, offering themselves as sources of the spiritual help that workers need to cope with problems at home (Barnaby J. Feder, "Ministers Who Work around the Flock," *New York Times*, 3 October 1996).

12. The Myers-Briggs Type Indicator (MBTI) is a "self-report question-naire designed to make Carl Jung's theory of psychological types under-standable and useful in everyday life." An Amerco manual states that, among many uses, understanding your type on the MBTI "enhances cooperation and productivity." Types are based on various dimensions of personality—extroversion, introversion, sensing, intuition, thinking, feeling, judging, and perceiving. Each type is assumed to make a dif-ferent kind of contribution to a work team and to need a different kind of support. See Isabel Myers-Briggs, *Introduction to "Type": A Guide to Understanding Your Results on the Myers-Briggs Type Indicator* (Palo Alto, Calif.: Consulting Psychologists Press, 1993), p. 1.

13. Just as Total Quality *expands* workers' authority at work, the declining size of the family and, for men, pressure to share the second shift at home *diminish* their authority at home. On the other hand, women who already have a low degree of authority in marriages with traditional men sometimes relish jobs where they can at last speak up and be heard. For very different reasons, then, both men and women can feel that their authority is curtailed at home and enhanced at work.

14. As Ella Taylor observes, over the years many television situation come-dies have centered on "fun" family-like relationships between coworkers at a workplace. *The Mary Tyler Moore Show* featured a work-family that ran a television news operation; *M*A*S*H* depicted a work-family that operated an army medical unit during the Korean War; and the "familial" coworkers in *Taxi* worked at a cab company. See Ella Taylor, *Prime-Time Families: Television Culture in Postwar America* (Berkeley: University of California Press, 1989); see also Gerard Jones, *Honey, I'm Home! Sitcoms: Selling the American Dream* (New York: St. Martin's Press, 1992).

15. Andrew J. Cherlin, ed., *The Changing American Family and Public Policy* (Washington, D.C.: Urban Institute Press). See Judith Wallerstein and Sandra Blakeslee, *Second Chances: Men, Women, and Children a Decade*

after Divorce (New York: Tichnor and Fields, 1989). The authors, unfor-
tunately, do not compare the children from divorced families with those
from intact marriages, so we do not know to what degree the children
of intact families have comparable experiences. See also P. Bohannon,
*Divorce and After: An Analysis of the Emotional and Social Problems of
Divorce* (New York: Anchor Books, 1971); and William Goode, *World
Revolution and Divorce* (New York: Free Press, 1956).

16. One partial sign of the devaluation of home life is the low status of the
homemaker. A national 1981 Harris poll asked, "If you had to place a
dollar value on the job of a homemaker, what do you feel fair wages for
a year's work would be?" Men said $12,700, women $13,800. Those
women who did *paid* work gave homemaking a higher dollar value
($24,000) than homemakers themselves ($13,400), and feminists gave it
a higher value ($21,500) than traditionalist women ($19,600). In particular, the value of caring for children seems to have declined. A Harris
poll asked adults and teenagers whether they agreed that "parents today
don't seem as willing to sacrifice for their children as parents did in the
past." Two-thirds of men and women forty years old and over agreed, as
did half of those aged eighteen to thirty-nine (Louis Harris and Associates, *The General Mills American Family Report 1980–81*, conducted by
Louis Harris and Associates Inc., Minneapolis, 1981).

17. Wendy Tanaka, "90s Trends Bite into Business Lunch," *San Francisco
Examiner*, 9 October 1994, p. A4.

18. Gary Cross, "If Not the Gift of Time, At Least Toys," *New York Times*,
3 December 1995.

Chapter 15: Evading the Time Bind

1. In the *Second Shift*, I call this emotional asceticism a "strategy of needs
reduction." Also see my "Politics of Culture: Traditional, Postmodern,
Cold Modern and Warm Modern Ideals of Care," *Social Politics* 2
(1995).

2. Clair Vickery, "The Time-Poor: A New Look at Poverty," *Journal of
Human Resources* 12 (1977): 27–48.

3. Surprised and concerned by these findings, the Human Resources Division at Amerco proposed to senior management to institute a "Hobby
Club" for older children after school, which management agreed to
fund. Many parents and children can now choose to participate, but
work hours have, of course, stayed the same.

4. In 1976, the U.S. Department of Commerce estimated that 1.6 million,

or 13 percent, of the nation's children between the ages of seven and thirteen were without adult supervision before or after school. A 1982 Department of Labor report estimated that 7 million children under age ten cared for themselves when not in school (both cited in Bryan Robinson, Bobbie Rowland, and Mick Coleman, *Latchkey Kids: Unlocking Doors for Children and Their Families* [Lexington, Mass: Lexington Books, 1986]). A recent article suggests that there may be between 3 and 12 million children in "self-care" (Charlene Marmer Soloman, "Special Report: Latchkey Kids," *Parents*, March 1994, pp. 43–45). See also Mary Lou Padilla and Gary Landreth, "Latchkey Children: A Review of the Literature," *Child Welfare* 68 (1989): 445–54.

5. Jean Richardson, Kathleen Dwyer, Kimberly McGuigan, William Hansen, Clyde Dent, C. Anderson Johnson, Steven Sussman, Bonnie Brannon, and Brian Flay, "Substance Use among Eighth-Grade Students Who Take Care of Themselves after School," *Pediatrics* 84 (1989): 556–66. See also D. G. Vandell and M. A. Corsaniti, "The Relation between Third-Graders' After-School Care and Social, Academic, and Emotional Function," *Child Development* 59 (1988): 868–75.

6. T. J. Long and L. Long, "Latchkey Children: The Child's View of Self Care," ERIC No. ED 211 229 (Arlington, Va.: Educational Resources Information Center Documents Reproduction Service, 1982). See also Nicholas Zill, *American Children: Happy, Healthy, and Insecure* (New York: Doubleday Anchor, 1983).

7. Earl A. Grollman and Gerry L. Sweder, *Teaching Your Child to Be Home Alone* (New York: Macmillan, 1983), p. 14.

8. Grollman and Sweder, *Teaching Your Child* (1983), p. 4. The authors do acknowledge some problems: "Through our interviews and surveys, we have found that children age twelve and younger who were regularly left home alone for two hours or more scored significantly lower on tests measuring self-esteem than did their peers who were home alone only one hour or less. These children reported having problems in their ability to communicate with their parents, a lower degree of self-confidence, and poor school performance. Teachers, principals, and guidance counselors agree with this assessment and speak of a gradual increase in the number of children in their classrooms who are needy of nurturance" (p. 26).

9. Grollman and Sweder, *Teaching Your Child* (1983), pp. 59, 96.

10. *I Can Take Care of Myself: The Family Handbook on Children in Self-Care* (Boston: Work–Family Directions, 1989), p. 10.

11. Barbara Dales and Jim Dales, *The Working Woman Book* (New York:

Andrews, McMeel, and Parker, 1985). *New Yorker* cartoons and Hallmark cards described in Hewlett, *When the Bough Breaks* (1991), p. 110.

12. Barbara Ehrenreich and Deirdre English, *For Her Own Good: 150 Years of Experts' Advice to Women* (New York: Doubleday, 1978).
13. Christopher Lasch, *The Culture of Narcissism: American Life in an Age of Diminishing Expectations* (New York: Norton, 1978).
14. Lynne Dumas, "At Your Service," *Working Mother*, August 1995, pp. 60–66.
15. Jacqueline Z. Salmon "For Hire: Helpers for Harried Parenting," *Washington Post*, 17 September 1995.
16. *Working Mother*, August 1995, p. 72. A parallel "frontier" of commodification can be seen in the celebration of Christmas. Once, many family members made the gifts they exchanged. Making a gift was a part of the ritual of Christmas, something meaningful in and of itself. Then shopping for the gift became the meaningful activity, because it saved the time it takes to make a gift. Now, increasingly, people check catalogs and order gifts by mail to save the time it takes to shop.
17. On another frontier of disappearing family time, many families are also outsourcing their volunteer activities. Instead of actually getting involved with a local environmental group, for example, they simply contribute money. See Eric Oliver, "Buying Time: City Affluence and Organizational Activity," Chapter 5, unpublished Ph.D. dissertation, University of California, Berkeley, 1996.
18. Salmon, "For Hire" (1995).
19. John Gillis, "Making Time for Family: The Invention of Family Time(s) and the Reinvention of Family History," *Journal of Family History* 21 (1996): 4–21, on 13.

Chapter 16: Making Time

1. See Michael Ventura, "The Age of Interruption," *Networker*, January–February 1995, pp. 19–31.
2. Robert D. Putnam, "Bowling Alone: America's Declining Social Capital," *Journal of Democracy* 6 (January 1995): 65–78, esp. 68. Putnam faults television, not longer hours at work, for the decline in civic participation. For a critique of this thesis, see Theda Skocpol, "Unraveling from Above," *American Prospect*, March/April 1996, p. 23.
3. Amy Saltzman, *Downshifting: Reinventing Success on a Slower Track* (New York: HarperCollins, 1991). In *Working Ourselves to Death* (San Francisco: Harper & Row, 1990), Diane Fassel sees workaholism as a disease

like alcoholism. She presents it as an uncontrollable urge inside oneself, which one can only battle privately through the work equivalent of abstinence. Obviously, however, most people can not just "abstain" from work the way they can from drink. See also Nina Tassi, *Urgency Addiction* (New York: Signet, 1991).

4. Joe Dominguez and Vicki Robin, *Your Money or Your Life: Transforming Your Relationship with Money and Achieving Financial Independence* (New York: Viking, 1992). See also Duane Elgin's *Voluntary Simplicity* (New York: Morrow, 1993); and M. Saint James, *Simplify Your Life* (New York: Hyperion, 1994).

5. Carey Goldberg, "The Simple Life Lures Refugees from Stress," *New York Times*, 21 September 1995. On the movement back to the land, see Keith Schneider, "Fleeing America's Relentless Pace, Some Adopt an Amish Life," *New York Times*, 1 March 1995.

6. Paul Avrich, *The Haymarket Tragedy* (Princeton, N.J.: Princeton University Press, 1984).

7. See Robert Levering, *A Great Place to Work: What Makes Some Employers So Good (and Most So Bad)* (New York: Random House, 1988).

8. A new time movement could call for "family impact statements" showing the effect of economic trends on the family. This is the brain child of the work–family specialist Kathleen Christensen. If environmental impact statements can help protect the spotted owl from deforestation, family impact statements can help protect another endangered species, the American family, against a workplace speedup. Environmental impact statements assess the effect of a particular industrial emission on, say, the quality of the air or water. A family impact statement could assess the effect of required overtime on, say, the time parents spend with children.

9. See "Eight Hours," in *Public Opinion: A Comprehensive Summary of the Press throughout the World on All Important Current Topics*, vol. 1 (Washington, D.C.: Public Opinion Co. Publishers, April–October 1886), p. 50. See also Benjamin Kline Hunnicutt, *Work without End: Abandoning Shorter Hours for the Right to Work* (Philadelphia: Temple University Press, 1988); Carmen Sirianni's superb article, "The Self-Management of Time in Post–Industrial Society," in Karl Hinrichs, William Roche, and Carmen Sirianni, eds., *Working Time in Transition* (Philadelphia: Temple University Press, 1991); and Cynthia Negrey, *Gender, Time, and Reduced Work* (Albany: SUNY Press, 1993).

10. *Public Opinion* (1886), p. 51.

11. Henry David, *The History of the Haymarket Affair* (New York: Collier Books, 1963), p. 173.

12. See Ellen Galinsky, *The Implementation of Flexible Time and Leave Policies: Observations from European Employers*, (New York: Families and Work Institute, 1989). Japanese workers, of course, average much longer hours. But Japan is undergoing a gradual "perestroika" against long hours, according to New York economist San Nakagama (see Hobart Rowen, "Taking It Easier in Japan," *Herald Tribune*, 13 June 1991). Japan suffers 10,000 *karoshi* deaths a year—men who *die* of overwork.

13. Haas, *Equal Parenthood and Social Policy* (1992), pp. 18, 29, 36. See also Phyllis Moen, *Working Parents: Transformations in Gender Roles and Public Policies in Sweden* (Madison: University of Wisconsin Press, 1989).

14. Proponents of a national reduced workweek argue that it would decrease unemployment and reduce the government's need to support the unemployed as well as combat technologically induced unemployment and relieve stress on the job. With more people employed, they also point out, income tax revenue and consumer demand would rise.

    Opponents think work time reduction will increase labor costs and lead to a decline in productivity if unqualified people fill the extra jobs created. It will, they say, be "inflationary" because increased labor costs will lead to higher prices (as companies pass increased costs on to the consumer). Also employers might try to offset higher labor costs with more mechanization, which will put more people out of work. See Negrey, *Gender, Time, and Reduced Work* (1993), pp. 119–20; see also Ronald G. Ehrenberg and Paul L. Schumann, *Longer Hours or More Jobs?: An Investigation of Amending Hours Legislation to Create Employment* (Ithaca, N.Y.: Cornell University Press, 1982); Sar A. Levitan and Richard S. Belous, *Shorter Hours, Shorter Weeks: Spreading the Work to Reduce Unemployment* (Baltimore: Johns Hopkins University Press, 1977); Paul Blyton, *Changes in Working Time: An International Review* (London: Croom Helm, 1985).

15. Outside the United States, Germany already has work sharing, and Sweden is considering a pilot project that has shown Swedish workers can be more productive with a six-hour day because of reduced sick leave, work injuries, and job turnover (Haas, *Equal Parenthood and Social Policy* [1992], p. 34).

16. Bailyn, a sociologist at MIT's Sloan School of Management, led a team of researchers in "action-research," research designed to bring about direct change. See Lotte Bailyn, "The Impact of Corporate Culture on Work–Family Integration," talk given at Fifth International Stein Conference, Drexel University, November 1994.

17. Bailyn, "The Impact of Corporate Culture" (1994), p. 3.
18. Bailyn, "The Impact of Corporate Culture" (1994), p. 4. Bailyn found that "rather than satisfied workers being more productive, productive workers are more satisfied. . . . If workers are empowered to manage the boundaries—including the work family boundary—that influences their productivity, morale increases along with productivity." After Xerox switched to team governance, absenteeism declined 30 percent, and workers were better able to meet the customer's needs.

BIBLIOGRAPHY

Acker, Joan. 1990. "Hierarchies, Jobs, Bodies: A Theory of Gendered Organizations." *Gender and Society* 4: 139–58.

Adam, Barbara. 1995. *Time Watch: The Social Analysis of Time.* Cambridge: Polity.

Adler, Jerry. 1994. "Kids Growing Up Scared." *Newsweek,* 10 January.

Adolf, Barbara. 1992. "Work and Family Benefits Come of Age: An Overview of Public- and Private-Sector Programs." *Government Finance Review* 8, no. 5.

Agassi, Judith, and Stephen Heycock, eds. 1989. *The Redesign of Working Time: Promise or Threat?* Berlin: Edition Sigma.

Ahrons, Constance, and Roy Rodgers. 1987. *Divorced Families: A Multidisciplinary Developmental View.* New York: Norton.

Allen, Joseph P. 1988. "European Infant Care Leaves: Foreign Perspectives on the Integration of Work and Family Roles." In Edward F. Zigler and Meryl Frank, eds., *The Parental Leave Crisis: Toward a National Policy.* New Haven, Conn.: Yale University Press.

Alvesson, Mats, and Per Olof Berg. 1992. *Corporate Culture and Organizational Symbolism: An Overview.* Berlin: de Gruyter.

Andrews, Amy, and Lotte Bailyn. 1993. "Segmentation and Synergy: Two Models of Linking Work and Family." In Jane C. Hood, ed., *Men, Work, and Family.* New York: Sage.

Avrich, Paul. 1984. *The Haymarket Tragedy.* Princeton, N.J.: Princeton University Press.

Axel, Helen. 1985. *Corporations and Families: Changing Practices and Perspectives.* New York: The Conference Board.

Bailyn, Lotte. 1980. "The Slow-Burn Way to the Top: Some Thoughts on the Early Years of Organizational Careers." In C. B. Derr, ed., *Work and Family, and the Career.* New York: Praeger.

———. 1993. *Breaking the Mold: Women, Men and Time in the New Corporate World.* New York: Macmillan.

———. 1994. "The Impact of Corporate Culture on Work–Family Integration." Talk given at Fifth International Stein Conference, Drexel University, Philadelphia, November.

Barnett, Rosalind C., Lois Beiner, and Grace K. Baruch. 1987. *Gender and Stress.* New York: Free Press.

Baruch, Grace, Rosalind Barnett, and Caryl Rivers. 1985. *Lifeprints: New Patterns of Love and Work for Today's Women.* New York: Signet.

Baruch, Grace, Lois Biener, and Rosalind C. Barnett. 1987. "Women and Gender in Research on Work and Family Stress." *American Psychologist* 42: 130–36.

Bauer, Gary. 1990. "Congress Gets the Child-Care Issue Wrong." *Wall Street Journal,* 10 October, p. A18.

Beechey, Veronica, and Tessa Perkins. 1987. *A Matter of Hours: Women, Part-Time Work and the Labour Market.* Minneapolis: University of Minnesota Press.

Berg, Barbara. 1978. *The Remembered Gate: Origins of American Feminism: The Woman and the City, 1800–1860.* New York: Oxford University Press.

Besharov, Douglas J., and Michelle M. Dally. 1986. "How Much Are Working Mothers Working?" *Public Opinion,* November/December, pp. 48–51.

Best, Fred. 1988. *Reducing Workweeks to Prevent Layoffs: The Economic and Social Impacts of Unemployment Insurance-Supported Work Sharing.* Philadelphia: Temple University Press.

Blau, Melinda. 1993. "Bridging the Generation Gap: How to Keep Kids and Grandparents Close." *Child,* September, pp. 54–58.

Blyton, Paul. 1985. *Changes in Working Time: An International Review.* New York: St. Martin's Press.

Bohannan, P. 1971. *Divorce and After: An Analysis of the Emotional and Social Problems of Divorce.* New York: Anchor.

Bohen, Halcyone, and Viveros-Long, Anamaria. 1981. *Balancing Jobs and*

Family Life: Do Flexible Schedules Help? Philadelphia: Temple University Press.

Bond, James T., and Ellen Galinsky. 1991. *Beyond the Parental Leave Debate.* New York: Families and Work Institute.

Bott, Elizabeth, 1957. *Family and Social Network: Roles, Norms, and External Relationships in Ordinary Urban Families.* New York: Free Press.

Bowen, Gary L., and Dennis K. Orthner. 1991. "Effects of Organizational Culture on Fatherhood." In F. W. Bozett and S. M. H. Hanson, eds., *Fatherhood and Families in Cultural Context.* New York: Springer.

Braverman, Harry. 1974. *Labor and Monopoly Capital.* New York: Monthly Review Press.

Buck Consultants, Inc. 1990. *Parental Leave: An Employer View.* New York: Buck Consultants, Inc.

———. 1992. *Work and Family: A Survey of Employer Practices.* New York: Buck Consultants, Inc.

Bumpass, Larry L. 1990. "What's Happening to the Family? Interactions between Demographic and Institutional Change." *Demography* 27, no. 4: 483–98.

Burden, Diane S., and Bradley K. Googins. 1987. "Boston University Balancing Job and Homelife Study: Managing Work and Family Stress in Corporations." Boston: Boston University School of Social Work.

Bureau of National Affairs. 1989. "Sick Child Care: Employers' Prescriptions for the 1990s." BNA Special Report Series on Work & Family, no. 14. Washington, D.C.: Bureau of National Affairs, Inc.

———. 1990. "Flexible Scheduling for Managers and Professionals: New Work Arrangements for the 1990s." BNA Special Report Series on Work & Family, no. 27. Washington, D.C.: Bureau of National Affairs, Inc.

Burris, Beverly H. 1991. "Employed Mothers: The Impact of Class and Marital Status on the Prioritizing of Family and Work." *Social Science Quarterly* 72: 50–66.

Callaghan, Polly, and Heidi Hartmann. 1991. *Contingent Work: A Chartbook on Part-Time and Temporary Employment.* Washington, D.C.: Economic Policy Institute, Institute for Women's Policy Research.

Casey, Catherine. 1994. "Come Join Our Family: Discipline and Integration in the New Corporate Culture." Paper presented at the American Sociological Association annual meetings, Los Angeles, August.

———. 1995. *Work, Self, and Society: After Industrialization.* New York: Routledge.

Catalyst. 1990. *Flexible Work Arrangements: Establishing Options for Managers and Professionals.* New York: Catalyst.

Champoux, Joseph. 1978. "Perceptions of Work and Nonwork: A Re-examination of the Compensatory and Spillover Models." *Sociology of Work and Occupations* 5, no. 4: 402–22.

Cherlin, Andrew, ed. 1988. *The Changing American Family and Public Policy.* Washington, D.C.: Urban Institute Press.

———. 1992. *Marriage, Divorce, Remarriage.* Cambridge, Mass.: Harvard University Press.

Cherlin, Andrew, and Frank Furstenberg, Jr. 1986. *The New American Grandparents.* New York: Basic Books.

Chira, Susan. 1993. "Obstacles for Men Who Want Family Time." *New York Times,* 21 October.

Christensen, Kathleen E. 1989. *Flexible Staffing and Scheduling.* New York: The Conference Board.

———. 1988. *Women and Home-Based Work: The Unspoken Contract.* New York: Henry Holt and Company.

———, ed. 1988. *The New Era of Home-Based Work: Directions and Policies.* Boulder: Westview Press.

Clark, P., and Helga Nowotny. 1978. "Temporal Inventories and Time Structuring in Large Organizations." In J. T. Fraser, N. Lawrence, and D. Park, eds., *The Study of Time III.* Amherst: University of Massachusetts Press.

Coleman, Mary T., and John Pencavel. 1993. "Changes in Work Hours of Male Employees, 1940–1988." *Industrial and Labor Relations Review* 46: 262–83.

———. 1993. "Trends in Market Work Behavior of Women Since 1940." *Industrial and Labor Relations Review* 46: 653–76.

Coolsen, Peter. 1989. *I Can Take Care of Myself: The Family Handbook on Children in Self-Care.* Boston: Work/Family Directions, Inc.

Coolsen, P., M. Seligson, and J. Garbino. 1986. *When School's Out and Nobody's Home.* Chicago: National Committee for the Prevention of Child Abuse.

Coontz, Stephanie. 1992. *They Way We Never Were: American Families and the Nostalgia Trap.* New York: HarperCollins.

Cross, Gary. 1988. *Worktime and Industrialization: An International History.* Philadelphia: Temple University Press.

Csikszentmihalyi, Mihaly, and Judith LeFevre. 1989. "Optimal Experience in Work and Leisure." *Journal of Personality and Social Psychology* 56: 815–22.

Cuvillier, Rolande. 1984. *The Reduction of Working Time: Scope and Implications in Industrialized Market Economies.* Geneva: International Labour Office.

Dales, Barbara, and Jim Dales. 1985. *The Working Woman Book.* New York: Andrews, McMeel, and Parker.

David, Henry. 1963. *The History of the Haymarket Affair.* New York: Collier.

Delavigne, Kenneth, and J. Daniel Robertson. 1994. *Deming's Profound Changes: When Will the Sleeping Giant Awaken?* Englewood Cliffs, N.J.: PTR Prentice Hall.

Deming, W. Edwards. 1981–1982. "Improvement of Quality and Productivity Through Action Management." *National Productivity Review,* Winter, pp. 2–12.

de Neubourg, Chris. 1985. "Part-Time Work: An International Quantitative Comparison." *International Labour Review* 124: 5455–5562.

Dennehy, Katherine, and Jeylan T. Mortimer. 1993. "Work and Family Orientations of Contemporary Adolescent Boys and Girls." In Jane C. Hood, ed., *Men, Work, and Family.* New York: Sage.

Dizard, Jan, and Howard Gadlin. 1990. *The Minimal Family.* Amherst: University of Massachusetts Press.

Dominguez, Joseph, and Vicki Robin. 1992. *Your Money or Your Life: Transforming Your Relationship with Money and Achieving Financial Independence.* New York: Viking.

Dubinskas, Frank A., ed. 1988. *Making Time: Ethnographies of High Tech Organizations.* Philadelphia: Temple University Press.

Duffy, Ann, and Norene Pupo. 1992. *Part-time Paradox: Connecting Gender, Work and Family.* Toronto: McClelland and Stewart.

Dumas, Lynne. 1995. "At Your Service." *Working Mother,* August, pp. 60–66.

Dundes, Alan, ed. 1981. *The Evil-Eye: A Folklore Casebook.* New York: Garland.

Ehrenberg, Ronald G., and Paul Schumann. 1982. *Longer Hours or More Jobs? An Investigation of Amending Hours Legislation to Create Employment.* Ithaca, N.Y.: Cornell University Press.

Elgin, Duane. 1993. *Voluntary Simplicity.* New York: William Morrow.

Emlen, Arthur, and Paul Koren. 1984. *Hard to Find and Difficult to Manage: The Effects of Child Care on the Workplace.* Portland, Oreg.: Regional Research Institute for Human Services, Portland State University.

Emlen, Arthur, Paul Koren, and Dianne Louise. 1987. "Dependent Care Survey: Sisters of Providence." Final report. Portland, Oreg.: Regional Research Institute for Human Services, Portland State University.

Ehrenreich, Barbara, and Deirdre English. 1978. *For Her Own Good: 150 Years of Experts' Advice to Women*. New York: Doubleday.

Evans, Paul, and Fernando Bartolome. 1986. "The Dynamics of Work–Family Relationship in Managerial Lives." *International Review of Applied Psychology* 35: 371–95.

Families and Work Institute. 1993. "An Evaluation of Johnson and Johnson's Balancing Work and Family Program" (Executive summary). New York: Families and Work Institute.

———. 1995. *Women: The New Providers*. Whirlpool Foundation Study, Part One. Survey conducted by Louis Harris and Associates, Inc., May.

Fassel, Diane. 1990. *Working Ourselves to Death: The High Cost of Work Addiction and the Rewards of Recovery*. San Francisco: Harper & Row.

Feder, Barnaby J. 1996. "Ministers Who Work Around the Flock." *New York Times*, 3 October.

Ferber, Marianne A., and Brigid O'Farrell, eds. 1991. *Work and Family: Policies for a Changing Workforce*. Washington, D.C.: National Academy Press.

Fisher, Anne B. 1992. "Welcome to the Age of Overwork." *Fortune*, 30 November.

Friedan, Betty. 1993. *The Fountain of Age*. New York: Simon and Schuster.

Friedman, Dana E. 1987. "Work vs. Family: War of the Worlds." *Personnel Administrator*, August, pp. 36–38.

———. 1990. "Work and Family: The New Strategic Plan." *Human Resource Planning* 13, no. 2: 79–90.

———. 1991. *Linking Work–Family Issues to the Bottom Line*. New York: The Conference Board.

Friedman, Dana E., and Theresa Brothers. 1993. *Work–Family Needs: Leading Corporations Respond*. Conference Board Report no. 1017. New York: The Conference Board.

Friedman, Dana E., and Ellen Galinsky. 1992. "Work and Family Issues: A Legitimate Business Concern." In Sheldon Zedeck, ed., *Work, Families and Organizations*. San Francisco: Jossey-Bass.

Friedman, Dana E., Ellen Galinsky, and Veronica Plowden. n.d. *Parental Leave and Productivity: Current Research*. New York: Families and Work Institute.

Fuchs, Victor. 1988. *Women's Quest for Economic Equality*. Cambridge, Mass.: Harvard University Press.

———. 1991. "Are Americans Underinvesting in Their Children?" *Society* 28, no. 6: 14–25.

Galinsky, Ellen. 1989. *The Implementation of Flexible Time and Leave Policies:*

Observations from European Employers. New York: Families and Work Institute.

Galinsky, Ellen, James T. Bond, and Dana E. Friedman. 1993. *The Changing Workforce: Highlights of the National Study*. New York: Families and Work Institute.

Galinsky, Ellen, Dana E. Friedman, and Carol A. Hernandez. 1991. *The Corporate Reference Guide to Work Family Programs*. New York: Families and Work Institute.

Gallup, George, and Frank Newport. 1990. "Time at a Premium for Many Americans." *Gallup Poll Monthly*, November, pp. 43–56.

Gardner, Saundra. 1991. "Exploring the Family Album: Social Class Differences in Images of Family Life." *Sociological Inquiry* 61: 242–51.

Garson, Barbara. 1988. *The Electronic Sweatshop: How Computers Are Transforming the Office of the Future into the Factory of the Past*. New York: Simon and Schuster.

Gillis, John. 1996. "Making Time for Family: The Invention of Family Time(s) and the Re-Invention of Family History." *Journal of Family History* 21: 4–21.

———. 1996. *A World of Their Own Making: Myth, Ritual, and the Quest for Family Values*. New York: Basic Books.

Glass, Jennifer. 1994. "Employment, Job Conditions, and Depression among Mothers Postpartum." Unpublished paper, University of Iowa.

Glass, Jennifer, and Tetsushi Fujimoto. 1994. "Employer Characteristics and the Provision of Family Benefits." Unpublished paper, University of Iowa.

Glass, Jennifer, and Lisa Riley. 1994. "Family Friendly Policies and Employee Retention following Childbirth." Unpublished paper, University of Iowa.

Glenn, Norval D., and Charles N. Weaver. 1988. "The Changing Relationship of Marital Status to Reported Happiness." *Journal of Marriage and the Family* 50: 317–24.

Goldberg, Carey. 1995. "The Simple Life Lures Refugees from Stress." *New York Times*, 21 September.

Goldsmith, Elizabeth B., ed. 1989. *Work and Family: Theory, Research, and Applications*. Newbury Park, Calif.: Sage.

Goode, William, Jr. 1963. *World Revolution and Family Patterns*. New York: Free Press.

Goode, William. 1994. "Why Men Resist." In Arlene Skolnick and Jerome Skolnick, eds., *Family in Transition*, 8th ed. New York: HarperCollins.

Gordon, David. 1996. *Fat and Mean: The Corporate Squeeze of Working Ameri-*

cans and the Myth of Managerial Downsizing. New York: Martin Kessler Books.

Grollman, Earl A., and Gerry Sweder. 1989. *Teaching Your Child to Be Home Alone.* New York: Macmillan.

Haas, Linda. 1992. *Equal Parenthood and Social Policy: A Study of Parental Leave in Sweden.* Albany: State University of New York Press.

Hackstaff, Karla. 1994. "Divorce Culture: A Breach in Gender Relations." Unpublished dissertation, University of California, Berkeley.

Hall, Edward. 1983. *The Dance of Life: The Other Dimension of Time.* Garden City, N.Y.: Anchor/Doubleday.

Hamilton, Richard. 1991. "Work and Leisure: On the Reporting of Poll Results." *Public Opinion Quarterly* 55: 347–56.

Hanan, Mack, and Tim Haigh. 1989. *Outperformers: Super Achievers, Breakthrough Strategies, and High-Profit Results.* New York: AMACOM.

Hanks, Roma S., and Marvin B. Sussman, eds. 1990. *Corporations, Businesses, and Families.* New York: Haworth.

Hareven, Tamara. 1978. *Amoskeag: Life and Work in an American Factory-City.* New York: Pantheon.

———. 1982. *Family Time and Industrial Time: The Relationship between Family and Work in a New England Industrial Community.* New York: Cambridge University Press.

Harris, Louis. 1987. *Inside America.* New York: Vintage.

Harris, Louis, and Associates. 1981. *The General Mills Family Report 1980–1981.* General Mills, Inc.

Hedges, Janice Neipert. 1992. "Work and Leisure: A Book Review of *The Overworked American.*" *Monthly Labor Review,* May, pp. 53–54.

Hertz, Rosanna, and Joy Charlton. 1989. "Making Family under a Shiftwork Schedule: Air Force Security Guards and Their Wives." *Social Problems* 36: 491–507.

Hewitt Associates. 1990. *Work and Family Benefits Provided by Major U.S. Employers in 1990.* Lincolnshire, Ill.: Hewitt Associates.

Hewitt, Patricia. 1993. *About Time: The Revolution in Work and Family Life.* London: Institute for Public Policy Research, United Kingdom Rivers Oram Press.

Hewlett, Sylvia Ann. 1991. *When the Bough Breaks: The Cost of Neglecting Our Children.* New York: Basic Books.

Hibbard, Janet, and Robert Candrum. 1987. *The Management of Time.* New York: Kend.

Hobart, Charles. 1987. "Parent–Child Relations in Remarried Families." *Journal of Family Issues* 8, no. 3: 259–77.

Hochschild, Arlie. 1983. *The Managed Heart: Commercialization of Human Feeling.* Berkeley: University of California Press.

———. 1989. *The Second Shift.* New York: Avon.

———. 1995. "The Politics of Culture: Traditional, Cold Modern, and Warm Modern Ideals of Care." *Social Politics: International Studies in Gender, State, and Society* 2, no. 2: 331–46.

Hofferth, Sandra, April Brayfield, Sharon Deich, and Pamela Holcomb. 1991. *National Child Care Survey 1990.* Sponsored by NAEYC, ACYF, and the U.S. Department of Health and Human Services. Washington, D.C.: Urban Institute.

Hogg, Christine, and Lisa Harker. 1992. *The Family-Friendly Employer: Examples from Europe.* New York: Daycare Trust, in association with Families and Work Institute.

Hood, Jane C., ed. 1993. *Men, Work and Family.* Newbury Park, Calif.: Sage.

Hood, Jane, and Susan Golden. 1984. "Beating Time/Making Time: The Impact of Work Scheduling on Men's Family Roles." In Patricia Voydanoff, ed., *Work and Family: Changing Roles of Men and Women.* Palo Alto, Calif.: Mayfield.

Hughes, Diane, and Ellen Galinsky. 1988. *Balancing Work and Family Life: Research and Corporate Application.* New York: Bank Street College of Education.

Hunnicutt, Benjamin Kline. 1988. *Work without End: Abandoning Shorter Hours for the Right to Work.* Philadelphia: Temple University Press.

Hyde, Janet Shibley, Marilyn J. Essex, and Francine Horton. 1993. "Fathers and Parental Leave: Attitudes and Experiences." *Journal of Family Issues* 14: 616–38.

" 'It's Too Much of a Good Thing,' GM Workers Say in Protesting Overtime." 1994. *New York Times,* 22 November, p. A10.

Jankowski, Jon, Marnell Holtgraves, and Lawrence Gerstein. 1988. "A Systemic Perspective on Work and Family Units." In Elizabeth Goldsmith, ed., *Work and Family: Theory, Research and Applications.* London: Sage.

Johnson, Colleen Leahy. 1988. *Ex Familia: Grandparents, Parents, and Children Adjust to Divorce.* London: Rutgers University Press.

Jones, Gerard. 1992. *Honey, I'm Home! Sitcoms: Selling the American Dream.* New York: St. Martin's Press.

Juster, F. Thomas, and Frank P. Stafford. 1991. "The Allocation of Time: Empirical Findings, Behavioral Models, and Problems of Measurement." *Journal of Economic Literature* 29: 471–522.

Kamarck, Elaine C., and William A. Galston. 1990. *Putting Children First: A*

Progressive Family Policy for the 1990s. Washington, D.C.: Progressive
   Policy Institute, 27 September.
Kamerman, Sheila B., and Cheryl D. Hayes, eds. 1982. *Families That Work:
   Children in a Changing World.* Washington D.C.: National Academy
   Press.
Kamerman, Sheila B., and Alfred J. Kahn. 1987. *The Responsive Workplace:
   Employers and a Changing Labor Force.* New York: Columbia University
   Press.
————. 1991. *Child Care, Parental Leave, and the Under 3's: Policy Innovation
   in Europe.* New York: Auburn House.
Kamin, Dan. 1984. *Charlie Chaplin's One-Man Show.* London: Scarecrow
   Press.
Kanter, Rosabeth Moss. 1977. *Work and Family in the United States: A Critical
   Review and Agenda for Research and Policy.* New York: Russell Sage Foun-
   dation.
Karasek, R. 1990. "Lower Health Risk with Increased Job Control among
   White-Collar Workers." *Journal of Organizational Behavior* 11: 171–85.
Kessler, R., and J. McRae. 1982. "The Effect of Wives' Employment on the
   Mental Health of Men and Women." *American Sociological Review* 47:
   216–27.
Kingston, Paul. 1988. "Studying the Work–Family Connection: Atheoreti-
   cal Progress, Ideological Bias, and Shaky Foundations for Policy." In
   Elizabeth Goldsmith, ed., *Work and Family: Theory, Research and Applica-
   tions.* London: Sage.
Kingston, Paul Williams, and Steven L. Nock. 1987. "Time Together
   among Dual Income Couples." *American Sociological Review* 52: 391–400.
Kunda, Gideon. 1992. *Engineering Culture: Control and Commitment in a High-
   Tech Corporation.* Philadelphia: Temple University Press.
Lamphere, Louise. 1985. "Bringing the Family to Work: Women's Culture
   on the Shop Floor." *Feminist Studies* 11: 519–40.
————. 1993. *Sunbelt Working Mothers: Reconciling Family and Factory.* Ithaca,
   N.Y.: Cornell University Press.
Larson, Reed, and Maryse Richards. 1994. *Divergent Realities: The Emotional
   Lives of Mothers, Fathers, and Adolescents.* New York: Basic Books.
Larson, Reed, Maryse H. Richards, and Maureen Perry-Jenkins. 1994.
   "Divergent Worlds: The Daily Emotional Experience of Mothers and
   Fathers in the Domestic and Public Spheres." *Journal of Personality and
   Social Psychology* 67: 1034–46.
Lasch, Christopher. 1977. *Haven in a Heartless World.* New York: Basic
   Books.

————. 1978. *The Culture of Narcissism: American Life in an Age of Diminishing Expectations*. New York: Norton.

Levering, Robert. 1988. *A Great Place to Work: What Makes Some Employers So Good (and Most So Bad)*. New York: Random House.

Levering, Robert, and Milton Moskowitz. 1993. *The 100 Best Companies to Work for in America*. New York: Penguin.

Levitan, Sar A., and Richard S. Belous. 1977. *Shorter Hours, Shorter Weeks: Spreading the Work to Reduce Unemployment*. Baltimore: Johns Hopkins University Press.

Lewis, C. S. 1950. *The Chronicles of Narnia*. New York: MacMillan.

Linder, Staffan. 1974. *The Harried Leisure Class*. New York: Columbia University Press.

Long, T. J., and L. Long. 1982. "Latchkey Children: The Child's View of Self Care." ERIC no. ED 211 229. Arlington, Va.: Educational Resources Information Center Documents Reproduction Service.

Lynd, Robert, and Helen Lynd. 1929. *Middletown: A Study in Contemporary American Culture*. New York: Harcourt, Brace.

MacDermid, Shelley, Margaret Williams, Stephen Marles, and Gabriela Heilbrun. 1994. "Is Small Beautiful? Influence of Workplace Size on Work-Family Tension." *Family Relations* 43: 159–67.

Martin, Joanne. 1992. *Cultures in Organizations: Three Perspectives*. New York: Oxford University Press.

Mattox, William R., Jr. 1991. "The Parent Trap: So Many Bills, So Little Time." *Policy Review*, no. 55: 6–13.

McDonald, Gerald, Michael Conway, and Mark Ricci. 1965. *The Films of Charlie Chaplin*. New York: Citadel.

McEnroe, Jennifer. 1991. "Split-Shift Parenting." *American Demographics*, February, pp. 50–52.

McNeely, R. L., and Barbe A. Fogarty. 1988. "Balancing Parenthood and Employment: Factors Affecting Company Receptiveness of Family–Related Innovations in the Workplace." *Family Relations* 37: 189–95.

Mellor, Earl F., and William Parks. 1988. "A Year's Work: Labor Force Activity from a Different Perspective." *Monthly Labor Review*, September, pp. 13–18.

Meyer, John W., W. Richard Scott, Brian Rowan, and Terrance E. Deal. 1983. *Organization Environments: Ritual and Rationality*. Beverly Hills, Calif.: Sage.

Mintz, Steven, and Susan Kellogg. 1988. *Domestic Revolutions: A Social History of American Family Life*. New York: Free Press.

Moen, Phyllis. 1989. *Working Parents: Transformation in Gender Roles and Public Policies in Sweden.* Madison: University of Wisconsin Press.

————. 1992. *Women's Two Roles: A Contemporary Dilemma.* New York: Auburn House.

Moen, Phyllis, and Donna Dempster McClain. 1987. "Employed Parents: Role Strain, Work Time, and Preferences for Working Less." *Journal of Marriage and the Family* 49: 579–90.

Morgan, Hal, and Kerry Tucker. 1991. *Companies That Care: The Most Family-Friendly Companies in America—What They Offer and How They Got That Way.* New York: Simon and Schuster.

Myers-Briggs, Isabel. 1993. *Introduction to "Type": A Guide to Understanding Your Results on the Myers Briggs Type Indicator.* Palo Alto, Calif.: Consulting Psychologists Press, Inc.

Negrey, Cynthia. 1993. *Gender, Time, and Reduced Work.* Albany: SUNY Press.

New York Times. 1996. *The Downsizing of America.* New York: Times Books/Random House.

Nippert-Eng, Christene. 1996. *Home and Work: Negotiating Boundaries through Everyday Life.* Chicago: University of Chicago Press.

Norwood, Janet. 1987. "American Workers Want More: More Work, That Is." *Across the Board* (The Conference Board), November, pp. 60–62.

Nowotny, Helga. 1975. "Time Structuring and Time Measurement: On the Interrelation between Timekeepers and Social Time." In J. T. Fraser, N. Lawrence, and D. Park, eds., *The Study of Time II.* Amherst: University of Massachusetts Press.

————. 1994. *Time: The Modern and the Post-Modern Experience.* Cambridge: Polity.

Oliver, Eric. 1996. "Buying Time: City Affluence and Organizational Activity," chapter 5. Unpublished Ph.D. dissertation, University of California, Berkeley.

Olmsted, Barney, and Suzanne Smith. 1989. *Creating a Flexible Workplace: How to Select and Manage Alternative Work Options.* New York: American Management Association.

O'Malley, Michael. 1991. *Keeping Watch: A History of American Time.* New York: Penguin.

O'Neill, John. 1994. *The Missing Child in Liberal Theory: Towards a Covenant Theory of Family, Community, Welfare, and the Civic State.* Buffalo, N.Y.: University of Toronto Press.

Ortiz, Steve. 1993. "When Happiness Ends and Strength Begins: The Private Pains of the Professional Athlete's Wife." Unpublished Ph.D. dissertation, University of California, Berkeley.

Owen, John. 1989. *Reduced Working Hours: Cure for Unemployment or Economic Burden?* Baltimore: Johns Hopkins University Press.

Padilla, Mary Lou, and Garry L. Landreth. 1989. "Latchkey Children: A Review of the Literature." *Child Welfare* 68: 445–54.

Panikkar, R., and L. Rowell. 1978. "Time and Sacrifice: The Sacrifice of Time and the Ritual of Modernity." In J. T. Fraser, N. Lawrence, and D. Park, eds., *The Study of Time III.* Amherst: University of Massachusetts Press.

Piotrkowski, Chaya S. 1979. *Work and the Family System: A Naturalistic Study of Working-Class and Lower Middle-Class Families.* New York: Free Press.

Piotrkowski, Chaya S., Diane Hughes, Joseph Pleck, Susan Kessler-Sklar, and Graham L. Staines. 1993. "The Experience of Childbearing Women in the Workplace: The Impact of Family-Friendly Policies and Practices." Prepared by the National Council of Jewish Women. Washington, D.C.: U.S. Department of Labor, Women's Bureau.

Pleck, Joseph. 1994. *Family-Supportive Employer Policies and Men: A Perspective.* Working Paper Series, no. 274. Wellesley, Mass.: Wellesley College Center for Research on Women.

Presser, Harriet. 1977. "Female Employment and the Division of Labor within the Home: A Longitudinal Perspective." Paper presented at the Population Association of America meetings, St. Louis.

———. 1988. "Shift Work and Child Care among Young Dual Earner American Parents." *Journal of Marriage and the Family* 50: 133–148.

———. 1989. "Can We Make Time for Children? The Economy, Work Schedules and Child Care." *Demography* 26: 523–43.

Public Opinion Co. 1886. *Public Opinion: A Comprehensive Summary of the Press Throughout the World on All Important Current Topics,* vol. 1. Washington, D.C., April–October.

Putnam, Robert D. 1995. "Bowling Alone: America's Declining Social Capital." *Journal of Democracy* 6: 65–78.

Rapoport, Rhona, and Robert N. Rapoport. 1980. "Balancing Work, Family, and Leisure: A Triple Helix Model." In C. Brooklyn Derr, ed., *Work, Family and the Career.* New York: Praeger.

———. 1980. *Dual Career Families.* London: Penguin.

Repetti, Rena L., Karen A. Matthews, and Ingrid Waldron. 1989. "Employment and Women's Health: Effects of Paid Employment on Women's Mental and Physical Health." *American Psychologist* 44: 1394–1401.

Richardson, Jean L., Kathleen Dwyer, Kimberly McGuigan, William Hansen, Clyde Dent, C. Anderson Johnson, Steven Sussman, Bonnie Brannon, and Brian Flay. 1989. "Substance Use among Eighth-Grade Students Who Take Care of Themselves after School." *Pediatrics* 84: 556–66.

Rifkin, Jeremy. 1995. *The End of Work: The Decline of the Global Labor Force and the Dawn of the Post–Market Era.* New York: G. P. Putnam's Sons.

Robinson, Bryan, Bobbie Rowland, and Mick Coleman. 1986. *Latchkey Kids: Unlocking Doors for Children and Their Families.* Lexington, Mass.: Lexington Books.

Robinson, John. 1977. *How Americans Use Time: A Social-Psychological Analysis.* New York: Praeger.

———. 1989. "Time's Up: Do We Have More Free Time?" *American Demographics*, July, pp. 32–35.

———. 1990. "The Time Squeeze." *American Demographics*, February, pp. 30–33.

Roskies, Ethel, and Sylvie Carrier. 1992. "Marriage and Children for Professional Women: Asset or Liability?" Paper presented at American Psychological Association conference "Stress in the 90's," Washington, D.C.

Rowen, Hobert. 1991. "Taking It Easier in Japan." *Herald Tribune*, 13 June.

Rubin, Lillian. 1976. *Worlds of Pain: Life in Working-Class Family.* New York: Basic Books.

Rubin, Sylvia. 1994. "Court Says Grandma Is Better Than Day Care." *San Francisco Chronicle*, August 17.

Salmon, Jacqueline. 1995. "For Hire: Helpers for Harried Parenting." *Washington Post*, 17 September.

Saltzman, Amy. 1991. *Downshifting: Reinventing Success on a Slower Tract.* New York: HarperCollins.

Saint James, M. 1994. *Simplify Your Life.* New York: Hyperion.

Scharlach, Andrew E., and E. Fuller-Thomson. 1994. "Coping Strategies following the Death of an Elder Parent." *Journal of Gerontological Social Work* 21: 85–101.

Scharlach, Andrew E., Beverly F. Lowe, and Edward L. Schneider. 1991. *Elder Care and the Workforce: Blueprint for Action.* Lexington, Mass.: Lexington Books.

Schneider, Keith. 1995. "Fleeing America's Relentless Pace, Some Adopt an Amish Life." *New York Times*, 1 March.

Schor, Juliet B. 1992. *The Overworked American: The Unexpected Decline of Leisure.* New York: Basic Books.

Schwartz, Felice N. 1989. "Management Women and the New Facts of Life." *Harvard Business Review*, January–February, pp. 65–76.

———. 1992. *Breaking with Tradition: Women and Work, The New Facts of Life.* New York: Warner.

Sirianni, Carmen. 1991. "The Self-Management of Time in Post-Industrial Society." In Karl Hinrichs, William Roche, and Carmen Sirianni, eds., *Working Time in Transition*. Philadelphia: Temple University Press.

Sirianni, Carmen, and Cynthia Negrey. 1986. "Working Time as Gendered Time." Princeton, N.J.: Institute for Advanced Study.

Skocpol, Theda. 1996. "Unraveling from Above." *American Prospect* No. 25, March/April, pp. 20–26.

Smith, Vicki. 1993. "Flexibility in Work and Employment: Impact on Women." *Research in the Sociology of Organizations* 2: 195–216.

Solomon, Charlene Marmer. 1994. "Special Report: Latchkey Kids." *Parents*, March, pp. 42–46.

Spitze, Glenna. 1988. "Women's Employment and Family Relations: A Review." *Journal of Marriage and the Family* 50: 595–618.

Spreitzer, E., E. Snyder, and D. Larson. 1979. "Multiple Roles and Psychological Well-Being." *Sociological Focus* 12: 141–48.

Stafford, Frank P. 1991. "Time and Consumption—A Book Review." *Journal of Economic Literature* 29: 1198–99.

———. 1992. "The Overworked American—A Book Review." *Journal of Economic Literature* 30: 1528–29.

Staines, Graham L. 1980. "Spillover versus Compensation: A Review of the Literature on the Relationship between Work and Nonwork." *Human Relations* 33: 111–29.

Staines, Graham L., and Joseph H. Pleck. 1983. *The Impact of Work Schedules on the Family*. Ann Arbor: Institute for Social Research, University of Michigan, Survey Research Center.

Stalk, George, and Thomas Hout. 1990. *Competing Against Time: How Time-Based Competition Is Reshaping Global Markets*. New York: Free Press.

Swiss, Deborah, and Judith Walker. 1933. *Women and the Work/Family Dilemma: How Today's Professional Women Are Finding Solutions*. New York: Wiley.

Tassi, Nina. 1991. *Urgency Addiction: How to Slow Down without Sacrificing Success*. New York: Signet.

Taylor, Ella. 1989. *Prime-Time Families: Television Culture in Postwar America*. Berkeley: University of California Press.

Taylor, Frederick. 1911. *The Principles of Scientific Management*. New York: Harper.

Thompson, E. P. 1963. *The Making of the English Working Class*. New York: Vintage.

————. 1992. "Time, Work-Discipline and Industrial Capitalism." In Anthony Giddens and David Held, eds., *Classes, Power and Conflict: Classical and Contemporary Debates*. Berkeley: University of California Press.

Till, Charles, and Edward Shorter. 1974. *Strikes in France, 1830–1968*. New York: Cambridge University Press.

Timpe, A. Dale, ed. 1987. *The Management of Time: The Art and Science of Business Management*. New York: Kend.

Tocqueville, Alexis de. 1969. *Democracy in America*. J. P. Mayer, ed., and George Lawrence, trans. Garden City, N.Y.: Anchor/Doubleday.

Tolstoy, Leo. 1942. *War and Peace*. Louise and Aylmer Maude, trans. New York: Simon and Schuster.

United States Bureau of the Census. 1991. "Childcare Arrangements: Population Profile of the United States 1991." Current Population Series P-23, no. 173. Washington, D.C.: Government Printing Office.

————. 1995. *Statistical Abstracts of the United States*, 115th ed. Washington, D.C.: Government Printing Office.

————. 1989. *Historical Statistics of the United States, Colonial Times to 1970*. Bicentennial Edition, part 1. Washington, D.C.: Government Printing Office.

U.S. Bureau of Labor Statistics. 1989. *Handbook of Labor Statistics*. Washington, D.C.: U.S. Bureau of Labor Statistics.

Vandell, Deborah Lowe, and Mary Anne Corsaniti. 1988. "The Relation between Third Graders' after School Care and Social, Academic, and Emotional Function." *Child Development* 59: 868–75.

Ventura, Michael. 1991. "Someone Is Stealing Your Life." *Utne Reader*, July/August, pp. 78–81.

————. 1995. "The Age of Interruption." *Networker*, January/February, pp. 19–31.

Verbrugge, L. 1987. "Role Burdens and Physical Health of Women and Men." In Faye Crosby, ed., *Spouse, Parent, Worker: On Gender and Multiple Roles*. New Haven, Conn.: Yale University Press.

Veurier, Henri. 1983. *Charles Chaplin*. Paris: Tarak Makhlouf.

Vickery, Clair. 1977. "The Time-Poor: A New Look at Poverty." *Journal of Human Resources* 12: 27–48.

Waerness, Kari. 1978. "Invisible Welfare State: Women's Work at Home." *Acta Sociologica Supplement* 21: 193–207.

Wallerstein, Judith, and Sandra Blakeslee. 1989. *Second Chances: Men,*

Women, and Children a Decade after Divorce. New York: Tichnor and Fields.

Walton, Mary. 1986. *The Deming Management Method.* New York: Dodd, Mead.

Webber, Ross. 1988. *Time Is Money! The Key to Managerial Success.* New York: Free Press.

Weber, Max. 1976 [1904]. *The Protestant Ethic and the Spirit of Capitalism.* New York: Charles Scribner's Sons.

White, Lynn, and Bruce Keith. 1990. "The Effect of Shift Work on the Quality and Stability of Marital Relations." *Journal of Marriage and the Family* 52: 453–62.

Zedeck, Sheldon. 1992. "Introduction: Exploring the Domain of Work and Family Concerns." In Sheldon Zedeck, ed., *Work, Families and Organizations.* San Francisco: Jossey-Bass.

Zedeck, Sheldon, Christina Maslach, Kathleen Mosier, and Linda Skitka. 1988. "Affective Response to Work and Quality of Family Life: Employee and Spouse Perspectives." In Elizabeth Goldsmith, ed., *Work and Family: Theory, Research and Applications.* London: Sage.

Zerubavel, Eviatar. 1981. *Hidden Rhythms: Schedules, and Calendars in Social Life.* Chicago: University of Chicago Press.

Zill, Nicholas. 1983. *American Children: Healthy, Happy, and Insecure.* New York: Anchor/Doubleday.

INDEX